KU-761-651

SIMON SHAW

SIMON SHAW

WITH CHRIS JONES

EDINBURGH AND LONDON

To my wife Jane and my children
Samantha, Tyler and Beau

First published in Great Britain in 2009 by
MAINSTREAM PUBLISHING COMPANY
(EDINBURGH) LTD
7 Albany Street
Edinburgh EH1 3UG

ISBN 9781845965112

This book is a work of non-fiction based on the life, experiences and recollections of the author. In some cases, names of people, places, dates, sequences or the detail of events have been changed to protect the privacy of others. The author has stated to the publishers that, except in such respects, not affecting the substantial accuracy of the work, the contents of this book are true

All photographs in picture section courtesy of the author
unless otherwise stated

A catalogue record for this book is available
from the British Library

Typeset in Caslon and London

Printed in Great Britain by
Clays Ltd, St Ives plc

CONTENTS

FOREWORD

Simon Shaw will go down in English rugby history as one of the all-time greats, and to achieve that standing in the same era as Martin Johnson has been no small feat.

There isn't a second-row forward playing in European rugby who is held in more esteem and his selection for the 2009 Lions tour to South Africa was testament to this fact. Simon was the only survivor from the 1997 test series-winning squad, a remarkable achievement given the amount of rugby he has played in those intervening 12 years, but the Lions needed big-game players and they don't come any better than my London Wasps team-mate.

His record with England and London Wasps speaks for itself and the longevity of his career has been amazing. He was well ahead of his time in terms of fulfilling all the criteria you need in the game and has always been the prop's best friend. As a prop forward, you wanted him packing down behind you because there was never any chance of the opposition prop moving you backwards. Simon's athleticism marked him out as a special forward, a man with real physical power, but also someone who had good hands and real footballing ability – no doubt he will mention in this book the drop goal he kicked against Bath. If you look at all the finals Wasps have played in, he has always produced the goods. When you want your big names to stand up and be counted, they don't come much taller than this guy. His all-round game is phenomenal and there is no one better at defending the front of the lineout – we call him the 'padlock', because he wraps up the ball carrier so completely. You don't have to commit many players into that situation because he has it all under control – single-handedly.

Obviously, playing at the same time as Johnno has been a factor in his career, although any player who collects 50 test caps can feel very satisfied. The one time when Simon should have been assured of starting for England came in 2004 when Johnno had retired, but the selectors turned to a whole list of alternatives, none of whom proved to be the answer.

I first came across Simon when I was playing for the London Colts in the Divisional Championship and we were told there was a new player arriving from Surrey. No one had any prior knowledge of him: then this giant appeared and we all had smiles from ear to ear because we knew the opposition wouldn't have a guy as big as our new second row. Even those of us who were big for our ages were dwarfed. With this huge asset, we won the Divisional Championship before they realised he was too young to play Colts rugby and Simon headed off to the Under-18s where his size would have come as an even bigger shock.

At Bristol, Simon suffered that horrendous ankle break and did remarkably well to come back from such a terrible injury. I suffered the same fate on the 2005 Lions tour to New Zealand: my plate and screws are in a glass jar at home; Simon, on the other hand, still carries his around in his leg more than a decade later. His entire career at London Wasps has covered the professional era – nearly 13 years – and he has been a key part of our entire journey, winning every possible trophy in club rugby and establishing the record for most Guinness Premiership games played and minutes on the pitch. Having helped the Lions win the test series against South Africa in 1997, he was called up as replacement for England's 2003 Rugby World Cup triumph. I know that Simon doesn't believe he actually contributed much because he didn't play during the tournament, but he richly deserved to be involved in that success.

On our pre-World Cup trip to New Zealand, Simon played so well against the Maoris the locals all wanted to know who this Shaw guy was, because they knew we had Martin Johnson but here was this other second row who did untold damage to the formidable Maoris. He was the best player on the pitch that night. In 2007, Simon was a huge part of our World Cup challenge that took us into the final against South Africa. It was the first time he had been given a real run of matches at international level – which was something that should have happened far more frequently in this special rugby player's career.

Having finally been given the chance to pull on the coveted Lions test jersey for the second test against South Africa in Pretoria, he produced one of the greatest individual performances ever witnessed by a Lions forward, moving Stephen Jones, the renowned *Sunday Times* rugby correspondent to give him 10 out of 10. It was an unprecedented mark from one of the game's most respected writers and an assessment I wholeheartedly agreed with.

Lawrence Dallaglio OBE

INTRODUCTION

My mobile rang in the morning as I was driving the hired removal van to the new home I was desperate to furnish before abandoning Jane and our three week-old daughter Samantha and head to Australia for the 2003 Rugby World Cup. Expecting Jane to be on the phone, I didn't register the name or number that came up, and the first indication that my day was about to go rapidly downhill was the sound of a familiar voice: 'Hello . . . hello . . . Simon, this is Clive Woodward. Sorry, but you haven't made the World Cup squad.' To be fair he had called me twice already and this time I managed to pick it up. Among the England squad it was a standing joke that if you didn't want to be dropped, you should never put your mobile phone on. However, as I said, he had at least made an effort to call me until he got hold of me.

I respected Clive's ability to put together a system that allowed England to become the best team in the world, but when it came to the personal touch he didn't hang about in giving you bad news. With so much to do before the tournament started, I needed to ensure my young family was OK, so I was in the van working when I had to hear the bad news. As it turned out, I had plenty of time to get the house straight before being called up as a replacement for the injured Danny Grewcock and going on to collect a World Cup-winners' medal – despite never playing a single minute of the tournament. Even when I took part in the amazing open-top bus tour of central London to celebrate the win, I made a point of never touching the World Cup trophy. Why should I? I had done absolutely nothing to bring it back to England and that is why the 2007 World Cup final loss to South Africa hurt so badly. If we had beaten the Springboks in Paris I would have hugged the Cup all night because I really had been part of a winning team, not the 31st man who would always be the answer to the pub-quiz question: which England rugby player received a 2003 World Cup-winners' medal and never played a minute of the tournament?

Walking around the Stade de France four years later, I wanted the ground to open and swallow me up, to take me away from the desperate feelings of disappointment that flooded over my body as I thanked our amazing fans for their support during the final. The Rugby World Cup has been a constant mental and physical obstacle throughout my career. If I haven't been ruled out of the tournament by serious injury, it was decided I was surplus to requirements and it wasn't until Brian Ashton put together the 2007 campaign that I was truly able to embrace a tournament that has transformed a sport I deeply love.

I had no idea that having won a place on the 2009 Lions tour to South Africa, I would experience such contrasting emotions. Twelve years after having failed to win a test place on my first Lions tour, I earned the right to wear the famous red jersey in a test match for first time at 35 years of age, and then endured the heartbreaking loss to the Springboks in Pretoria which meant we lost the series 2–0.

The emotional devastation after losing to a last gasp penalty was eerily similar to the way I felt two years earlier in Paris after the World Cup defeat by the same team. What have I ever done to make South African rugby players want to ruin my biggest days on a regular basis? I was named man of the match but would have gladly played poorly and been substituted if it meant we had kept the series alive. We did win the third test at Ellis Park and while the record books will show South Africa as the series winners, it will not tell the full story. I was part of a squad that ensured the Lions name was honoured and, I believe, enhanced in the way we played and handled everything that was thrown at us.

Whenever injury or the vagaries of selection invaded my rugby life, I have been able to draw strength and inspiration from my family and my team-mates, first at Bristol and then, since 1997, at London Wasps, the club I joined to win trophies and with whom I subsequently collected every possible club honour. While my 2003 and 2007 World Cup experiences suggest I am, by nature, a grumpy old sod with a deep scowl on my face and anger seeping from every pore, I hope that what follows proves just how much I love rugby and cherish every honour that has come my way. The social side of the sport is what initially attracted me to rugby and having a beer with mates and opponents is something I never take for granted. I always believed rugby was going to turn professional, even though my teachers tried to convince me that cruising through the education system, clinging to the false hope of earning a crust from the sport, was pure folly. I never accepted their argument. I was going to be a professional rugby player and nothing else mattered. What else was a 6 ft 9 in., 19 st. guy going to do anyway?

CHAPTER 1

MACHETES AND BLUE-FACED BABIES: WELCOME TO KENYA

My father Charles has taken great delight in embarrassing me throughout my life and I love him for it. He is also 6 ft 9 in., which answers the question: why are you so tall, Simon? I have always known that my father was involved in an incident with some machete-wielding robbers in Kenya, but the full story of why he carries scars on his arms and back only came to light when I asked him, for the first time, to recall the whole incident. What unfolded made me realise just how close the Shaw family had come to disaster when I was a couple of weeks away from being born in Nairobi in 1973.

My heavily pregnant mother was happy to stay at home while my father, grandfather and 18-month-old sister Sarah headed off to the local polo grounds with our dogs. During a break in the match, they took the dogs into a nearby wooded area for a run and were set upon by six machete-wielding locals who wanted their watches and wallets. My father recognised that this could turn into a very gory situation and launched himself at the nearest robber; the rest of the gang panicked and started hitting him with their machetes. At this point, while the attackers were concentrating on my father, my grandfather grabbed my sister to protect her. He then ran up behind the guy my father was battling and kicked him square between the legs; this grounded him immediately. It allowed my father to snatch the attacker's machete, lash out and, he believes, almost slice the guy's head off. With one of their gang screaming in agony, they all panicked and scattered – including the guy with half a neck – into the woods.

Five of the attackers were arrested shortly afterwards by the Nairobi police, but no one ever found the one with the deep neck wound. The police were not concerned that my father may have killed one of the attackers and assumed the others had buried him in the wooded area. My grandfather (my mum's father) had only set foot in Nairobi the day before and had never been to the polo or the main hospital in Nairobi where they took my father to be stitched up. Somehow, my grandfather found his way back to our house, without getting lost, and turned up holding my sister and covered in blood. He then had to explain to my understandably concerned, and heavily pregnant, mother, exactly whose blood it was. My sister was too young to have any recollection of the incident and it had always been one of those stories that existed without anyone filling in the details. One of the most surprising facts that emerged was that the attackers were neither down-and-outs nor particularly poor; they were professional men – airline stewards and bankers. It made their actions all the more bizarre and bemusing.

There was another incident involving my father, his brother (James Shaw) and my grandfather on my father's side (Robert Shaw) when they were all travelling in the same car and were stopped at traffic lights at a busy junction in Nairobi, which you weren't supposed to do in those days. Some youths stepped out in front of the vehicle and made it clear they were going to attempt a violent car-jacking. I assume my father, given the machete incident, was fed up with this kind of situation and, along with his brother and father, piled out of the car in a show of defiance.

My granddad is 6 ft 3 in., while my father and uncle are both 6 ft 9 in., which must have come as a huge shock to the locals, who ran off pursued by three huge white men. Those tales portray Kenya as an intensely violent country and certainly not the place to bring up two young English children, but nothing could be further from the truth. We had a wonderful life in Nairobi and the happy memories remain with me to this day.

I was born in the Misericordiae Hospital in Nairobi weighing in at what I now consider to be a very impressive 11 lb 12 oz. My mother, who is 5 ft 8 in., gave birth to me naturally, much to the amazement of the nurses, medical staff and other new mothers at that time. Everyone appears to have made a beeline for my incubator to catch a glimpse of this enormous baby. I was so big, my arms and legs dangled over the side of the inadequate equipment, much to the delight and astonishment of the throng. At that time there were three major hospitals in the city: one, The Nairobi National, which mainly catered for Europeans and ex-pats; another one was called the Aga Khan, which was aimed at the rich; and then there was the third, the one I was born in. It appears it was the hospital of choice for vagrants and my mother said I was the only white baby in there. The staff used to look at this newborn child, who was so much bigger than anything they had ever seen, and wanted to know who the mother was, and if she was still alive! Part of the fascination was probably due to the fact I was born blue because of a lack of oxygen.

My father has always had wanderlust. He was born in Assam, in India, where his father ran a tea plantation and travelling has been a huge part of his life, even when he was married. He would be away a lot, particularly when we were in Africa, and I don't think it surprised my mother that he missed my birth. Then again, I was, by all accounts, a happy accident. It meant my mother dealt with the birth alone and it was my uncle James who was the first visitor after the birth. Because I was so enormous, and given my uncle's height, the hospital immediately assumed he was the father.

Uncle James was in Kenya with the Royal Corps of Signals and eventually became a Major General although, at this time, he was just starting out with the regiment. Given my father's absence, he had to fill the void as the male half of family Shaw at the hospital. Because I was born blue, I had breathing problems throughout my infancy and it wasn't clear exactly what treatment I needed or what the cause of it was. Doctors tried to identify the reason for my constant ear, nose and throat problems and the only thing they were certain about was the problem didn't appear to be asthmatic fits, although I did cause alarm on a couple of occasions when I knocked myself out, stopping breathing. No one, however, was really sure why. I have a distinct memory of once waking up in hospital with other children who also had respiratory problems and who had been given a tracheotomy, and being completely freaked out. Finding yourself surrounded by kids with holes in their throats does not make for a good night's sleep when you are a young lad and I thought I had been sent to another planet where aliens were performing awful experiments on children. Thankfully, I never needed that kind of intervention and, being the sort of character I am, the ability to induce self-inflicted fainting became a party trick, and one I started to use to my advantage.

Whenever I got into trouble, I had this ability to hold my breath, turn blue and pass out. Adults used to be sent into a state of understandable panic, which often meant I got sympathy and avoided whatever sanction had been planned for the naughty Shaw boy. I still hold my breath now to stop myself arguing back, but I don't think I carried on using it as a get-out-of-jail card for too long, which came as a blessing for the rest of the family and the maids who helped look after us in Nairobi.

My father showed up again a month or so after my birth. My parents and elder sister had moved to Kenya in the year I was born and my father was, at that time, working in the tea business for Marshalls Engineering and Agricultural Machinery. Marshalls was a large company at the time with their major manufacturing depot in Lincolnshire. That is where my mother was born and where my parents met. He was put on an apprenticeship at Marshalls in Gainsborough after ending up in Lincolnshire following an eventful schooling. My father had received a middle- to upper-class upbringing and used to go to boarding school at Ludgrove, the prep school of choice for some of the Royal Family. This was possible because my grandfather's brother owned Ludgrove and it is still in the hands of the other side of the family. My father was an unruly child who got into trouble a fair bit and who was always being suspended. Exasperated, my grandfather then sent him to Shrewsbury, where he was eventually thrown out for drinking. My grandfather's final effort to keep him on the straight and narrow was to contact a friend who worked at Marshalls and they offered him an apprenticeship. My grandfather told my father this was his last chance and that he wasn't going to help him any more.

Because of my father's background – he flew back and forth to India a lot during his formative years – life was quite nomadic for the Shaw family. My father was always going off somewhere and when I was a child we never really stood still for too long, even if it was only within the country we were living in. We were always here, there and everywhere. My early life in Nairobi was this mix of memories of my father turning up followed by long periods of his not being part of our family. It fell to my mother to provide the stability for the two young children and, patently, there wasn't a credit crunch affecting business travel during the 1970s.

With my father away so much, my mother had to show great strength of character to live in a country that is not renowned for its safety. She was a very understanding wife. We had an American lodger living with us as well. Basically, it was two ladies living on their own and a few incidents occurred that would have had most people running out of Nairobi and jumping on the next plane home. My mother, however, stuck it out for nine years even on one occasion when a burglar broke into the house while my father was away. Mum heard the noises and decided to confront the intruder. She armed herself with one of my father's golf clubs and our lodger picked up a tennis racket – it was clear, even in times of crisis, that we were a sporting family! They slowly moved towards the sounds emanating from the living room and confronted the burglar armed with their weapons of choice. They also added a few loud screams to the mix and the burglar, who must have been either high on drugs or drunk, was so frightened by their sudden appearance and formidable arsenal, that he disappeared out of the window he had entered by and was never seen again. The incident became the subject of a cartoon in the local paper with my father, allegedly, having a go at my mother for using his favourite seven-iron. This particular golf club would feature again in a very dangerous incident that my father and I were caught up in during my teenage years back in Britain.

My sister and I had a very multicultural upbringing, mixing with Kenyans and Asians, and this is where my love of curry first started. I am still in touch with my school-friend Jeremy Pickis from those early days in Kenya and we were the only white kids in my class. My parents always used to comment that it didn't matter how many kids were in my class, I always seemed to befriend the smallest. Jeremy was minute and so we did look a bit odd. While in Nairobi, we used to go on trips to Tanzania and Uganda as well as making sporadic returns to my mother's family home in Gainsborough in Lincolnshire. When we did make those visits, England didn't feel like home at all to me. It seemed a strange place and, apart from seeing snow on the peak of Kilimanjaro, I didn't really know what it was. It came as a huge shock to suffer one of the worst winters on record during one of our trips back to England, and I remember thinking what a hellish place this is.

In spite of the weather, though, I loved spending time with my grandparents and the thing that really used to stand out when I came to the UK from Kenya was the huge choice on TV compared to Nairobi. I would also look forward to spending time at my grandparents because of my grandmother's exceedingly good cakes. For years I used to think that this Mr Kipling guy was just my granny in disguise. I have always had a particularly sweet tooth. In Kenya we didn't even seem to have jam to spread on our toast and our only substitute was tomato ketchup. This made me yearn for apple crumble even more

I wasn't really connected with any sport in Kenya. My father played for Harlequins rugby club in Nairobi and had been very, very sporty during his unruly schooldays, captaining pretty much every team going at Ludgrove. At Shrewsbury he played first XV rugby, football, cricket and fives, although his involvement in team sports could not outweigh the other problems he was causing, hence the need to leave those learning establishments. In Kenya, I didn't play much sport; mainly it would be a playground game, involving kicking a tin can around like a football, because the school didn't do a lot of organised games, through a basic lack of equipment.

My main sporting interest at this time was swimming, as everybody seemed to have a pool. All our holidays would be beach holidays or at lakes, which meant we were always swimming or diving and I remember its being a very, very happy time. I wasn't particularly clever at school, although my sister was. If the teachers said anything involving a report to my parents, I would just go and stand in the corner and hold my breath. At this stage I wasn't blacking out, but it usually got the teachers quite concerned. They initially questioned my parents, suggesting they might have been abusing me because I used to run and stand in the corner with my head down. The school wondered whether I was getting beaten at home. This was understandable given the fact I had a bearded 6 ft 9 in. father who looked a bit like Grizzly Adams. He had a beard most of the time, but did remove it once and seeing him clean-shaven was even more fearsome. The maximum punishment we got at school was the ruler across the knuckles or the back of the legs, which left a stinging sensation, but it wasn't really a deterrent and I was able to establish a lifelong ability to do just enough in the classroom and no more.

We lived in a middle-class area of Nairobi with an absolutely enormous garden that, by the end of our stay, resembled a zoo. We had various rabbits, dogs, tortoises, birds and different types of snakes who took up residence without our agreement. We had a chameleon in a tree at the bottom of the garden that never seemed to go anywhere, probably aware of the snakes looking for food. My mother found two tortoises mating when she was out one day and I don't know whether she had enjoyed a drink or two, but she decided it was very unfair on the lady tortoise. So, she picked up the female one and brought her home. Suddenly, our garden featured a giant tortoise as a pet, which obviously caused some stir in the local community and considerable confusion. One day we discovered someone had thrown another giant tortoise over our fence in the misguided view that we were running some kind of sanctuary for the animals.

For me, Kenya will always be summed up by a photograph of my sister and me sitting in our pyjamas at a safari park with Kilimanjaro in the background and a herd of elephants no more than 100 metres away. What shines through from that photograph are the wonderful open spaces and the fantastic wildlife. There are plenty of other memories of family trips we took when my father was back in Nairobi. We would go to Mombasa, enduring a pretty horrendous journey from Nairobi because the roads were appalling. There were potholes everywhere and we used to get stuck three or four times on each trip. For us children in the back of the car, it seemed to take an entire week to get there; we would stay for a week and then need another week to get back. Besides the dreadful road, the trip to Mombasa would offer the chance to see giraffes, the occasional lion and other wild animals. We had a couple of scares with lions, although coming into contact with potentially dangerous animals was just a part of everyday life. On one occasion, I remember a friend of my father was packing a case on top of a roof rack when we were preparing to come back from Mombasa and a green mamba fell out of a tree, landing on his shoulder. Everyone else was screaming and running in all directions, leaving the poor man and the venomous snake to sort themselves out.

CHAPTER 2

BYE, BYE KENYA, HOLA SPAIN

After nine years of life in Nairobi, my father returned one day and announced we were leaving Kenya. I immediately burst into tears. My parents humoured me and, as was to happen so many times, we just packed up and got on with the next move. Years later, I desperately wanted to return to Kenya for my honeymoon, but it would have been the worst time of year to go out there. I still very much want to take my family to see the sights that formed such a big part of my childhood and I have made it a goal to run a charity event of some kind in the country. I have spoken to Serge Betson, my team-mate at London Wasps who does charity work in Cameroon, and have discussed how to use rugby to help a charitable organisation, probably to aid life in a township in Nairobi.

Looking back, it felt like we moved home about every six months (this was a misconception induced by my tender years), which meant my sister and I were sent to new schools on a regular basis. We would stick together like mates and were always pretty close during those awkward times when you have to find new friends and deal with the fact you are the new kids on the block. We went back to the UK briefly and stayed in Gainsborough for a while, living in a two-bedroomed council house in a not very pleasant part of the town. We had no heating during another dreadful winter and I thought: 'This is the worst place in the world.' I really didn't want to be there. I ran away from the comprehensive school I was attending a couple of times and, after the life we had enjoyed in Kenya, I was convinced it was the end of the world. Gainsborough was just a stop-gap for my father while he found a new job, which then took us to Huntingdon in Cambridgeshire. We were there for just a year – and then we were off to Spain. I think we went to Spain because my father got itchy feet again and felt like a new challenge. Needless to say, when he broke the news to us, I burst into tears again.

I would have been about ten years old when we went to Madrid and, with the aid of hindsight, I now realise any tears I shed were wasted ones, because Spain turned out to be a wonderful experience, one that even stopped me thinking about how I could get back to Kenya. We were enrolled in a private school and lived in an apartment for about a year. The apartment had a very nice pool, which satisfied my continuing passion for swimming. Shortly after that we moved to where the wealthier Madrid folk resided and I started a new school – Kings College, Madrid. My sister and I tried desperately to make friends, but first we needed to learn Spanish. Thanks to the international school we attended, I managed to pick up the language pretty quickly and was quite fluent before the age of 11. It is a language I can still use, which is particularly useful as my parents are now living, once again, in Spain. I have retained only a couple of words of Swahili from my time in Kenya, although this may be due to the lack of opportunities to actually use it in London apart from the odd bit of drunken banter with unlicensed cab drivers.

It was at Kings, where sporting teams were organised and equipment was plentiful, that sport became more of a passion for the first time in my life. I swam for my school and, with Spain being football mad, I started to get into that, too. Because I was tall, they put me in the centre of defence and I also played Sunday league football at a club organised by some ex-pats. I wasn't watching any rugby at the time and my first memory of the game comes from the short period family Shaw spent in Huntingdon. We used to live next door to a Welsh family and my father and Carl, who was the Welsh rugby fan over the fence, used to watch the first half of Five Nations Championship matches and then open the doors to the respective houses and swear at each other for about ten minutes, before going back inside and watching the second half. I didn't really know what was going on, although they were actually good friends and this was just part of some nonsensical ritual I was aware of when rugby was on the television.

My father was around a lot more in Spain, which meant the family unit became rather normal for a change. One of the great aspects of life in Spain is the siesta: it meant my father was at home more than ever and that was great. It also gave him more time to try and get me involved in various sports and I was conscious that he wanted me to follow in his footsteps. However, the big difference between my father and me was our schooling. He had enjoyed a very privileged education from a sporting perspective whereas, up until that point, I hadn't played an awful lot of organised sport and this was also a natural point when a father tends to get more involved in his kid's sporting activities. I know it is different for a lot of people, particularly when it involves mini rugby, but I don't think you can tell whether a child is going to be really good or bad at that stage. In my view, when you get to ten there are going to be some signs of natural talent. My father used to take me to the Sunday football and tried to encourage me at every sport. As a family we became involved with a running club called the 'Hash House' Harriers which meant we spent most Sundays running for about 10 kilometres around the Spanish countryside following a trail of flour. The adults would then drink copious amounts of beer and wine, eat and sing a lot. I soon wised up to there apparent madness. The running merely provided all these middle-aged parents the chance to over indulge, guilt free. They were in the great rugby tradition, earning their piss! I have very strong memories of watching the 1982 football World Cup with my father. The tournament was held in Spain and we went to all the England games. It was just one of the many highlights of our five years in the country.

Having been so upset at leaving Kenya, the time in Spain was well worth the heartache and also erased the memories of those bloody awful British winters, but now, having reached the age of 15, I was about to be uprooted again.

CHAPTER 3

HOW DID I GET SO TALL?

It was at this time that the growing pains in my body started to become a real issue. I shot up to 6 ft 9 in. at 15, which meant I now had to deal with being the biggest boy at whatever school I attended and stood out in any sporting team photograph. For a very brief period when we were in Huntingdon, I played rugby for the first time in my life and, because of my size, was put into the second row. It was to be a recurring theme whenever I opted to play rugby, proving that size, rather than all-round ability, dictates, to a great extent, where teachers think you should play. Still, given my rugby career, the teachers appear to have made the right call at a very early stage! I only played a couple of games and really didn't have a clue what was going on.

We then moved south to Guildford and school sports revolved around football. My favourite team was Tottenham, because when I first came back from Kenya they were in an FA Cup final and that was good enough to make me a lifelong Spurs fan. I was determined to avoid choosing Wolverhampton Wanderers, my father's team, and it was a bonus that this decision really wound him up. Like so many early forays into sport, football was an interest but not a passion, and that remained the case until I switched schools, yet again, to complete my sixth-form studies at Godalming College. I didn't realise it at the time, but my life was about to undergo a dramatic change. It became abundantly clear that, having already discovered girls, the way to meet these delightful creatures on a more regular basis was to become a member of the rugby team, because the school's entire social life appeared to revolve around those players and their matches.

Godalming College was the first school I attended where rugby was the number one sport and the way the establishment was run meant it was more of a preparation for life at university. You had periods, as opposed to lessons, in hour-long blocks, and were given an awful lot of free time. For some students, this doesn't serve them very well, but if you were into sports and the extra-curricular stuff, it was a pretty cool education. It made you feel like an adult and a free spirit who could come and go as you pleased. It suited me down to the ground. There were various other things going on, like freshers' week, and you were encouraged to join various clubs.

Despite recognising the benefits of being in the rugby club, I opted for football because I had more experience playing the game, but others had noticed this 6 ft 9 in. lump wandering around with a smile on his face. As well as boasting an enthusiastic rugby coach, the college also featured a New Zealander who taught economics, and together, they actively encouraged me to give up football and start playing rugby. I made it clear I had only played a couple of times and didn't really know what I should be doing, but this proved a pretty feeble defence, particularly in the eyes of the Kiwi, and they won me over by pointing out that the basic principle of rugby is to get the ball and put it over the try-line. It seemed pretty simple to me! I had a trial where I played at number 8 because there weren't any second rows tall enough to bind alongside me and when we tried to make it work, it totally unbalanced the scrum. The only answer was to put me at number 8 and following the basic instruction to 'just put the ball over the line', I started scoring at will. I imagine the biggest opponent I came across at that time would have been 6 ft 2 in. and not very heavy, probably about 14 st. I was 15 going on 16 and my weight at this point was already 19 st. I was quite heavy set and it wasn't puppy fat. It created an unsolved mystery for my team-mates and coaches who could not fathom how I had ended up like that without having lifted any weights at all. I wasn't fat and I wasn't thin. I could carry the weight because I was 6 ft 9 in., although I did start to stoop when I walked because I was so much taller than anyone else at the school.

With rugby now opening new doors for me, in term of friendships and attention from girls, I suddenly realised the sport had serious benefits for a young guy. Having been living in Spain up to that point, the whole dating scene and 'growing up' tended to be a few years behind the UK. At Godalming, it was all quite intimidating. I had never really had a girlfriend or been on a date, all of which made my new life with the rugby lads a real eye opener. It was a bit daunting because the rugby team attracted a number of females. Up until that point, I had never been terribly proud of my height and tried to hide it as best as I could by using a slight stoop.

Rugby also helped me come out of my shell. I remember amazing myself and my mother on a Red Nose Day when I voluntarily got up on stage in front of the whole school and sang. I had never sung before and, as the performance did not attract any rotting fruit or howls of derision, I assume it was a success of sorts. Building on this new talent, I agreed to take part in a fashion show and, basically, stripped down to my boxer shorts and a bow tie for the event. Given that Godalming was a mixed college, it really was a massive step forward in terms of putting myself in the public eye. The singing and boxer-short exhibitionism gave me a lot more confidence and, looking back, it was due to the college's style of education. It allowed me a feeling of real freedom and meant I was able to become more of an adult rather than a teenager in a very tall man's body.

I have to point out that my schooling didn't solely comprise sunny days, opportunities to strip off and games of rugby after returning to the UK. Bullying did rear its ugly head, particularly during the short spells in Gainsborough and Huntingdon. I went to schools that weren't particularly nice, featuring pupils who didn't do too much schoolwork and who spent most of their time smoking and hanging around the school gates waiting for a bit of trouble. There were a couple of occasions when things flared up, but although I never instigated anything, I would always defend myself. There was a group of skinheads who stole my bag as I was walking through the school courtyard and I just stood my ground and asked for it back. I didn't throw any punches and they just ended up giving me the bag. It gave me an indication that my size could be intimidating enough on its own, without my actually having to back it up with violence.

Turning the other cheek was another option I took and it came in useful when I was playing football with some friends and booted the ball, by accident, straight at a couple of school bullies. They turned around and the ball hit one of them smack in the face. They came up and punched me in the face, but I didn't flinch. At this stage I wasn't terribly confident in my ability as a pugilist. I just took the punch and they walked away, apparently satisfied the score had been evened up. I wasn't hurt or really bothered to have been thumped. I don't think I was looked upon by school-mates as a gentle giant, but if quizzed, I am sure they would have described me as a quiet person.

Playing rugby at Godalming gave me the confidence that permeated throughout my schooling, although I was never a real worker and, more often than not, did the subjects that came easily to me. When I took my GCSEs it was mostly languages because, having lived in Madrid, I could speak Spanish and had learned Latin at an early age, which meant French and German came relatively easy to me. I was particularly good at art, mainly pencil drawings: figures and faces. It is something that has remained a great interest in my life and I have kept a portfolio from those formative years because my original intention when thinking about university was to go to art school. It was a choice born out of knowing I found it easy rather than one fuelled by a passion to make it my career in later life. I did reasonably well at Mathematics and English, but I didn't really commit myself, which led to the inevitable school reports that always said 'could have tried harder'. I had the intelligence, but was never really bothered; I think it was because I wasn't really passionate about anything – until, that is, rugby entered my life.

Having earned the right to be part of the school rugby social scene, my next problem was dressing to fit in. I have clear recollections from an early age of being very concerned that my hair was cut just right because it always stuck out at the front. When I was just four years old, I cut a big chunk out of my hair and ended up having to have a crew cut, which is confirmed by some delightful pictures taken after the shearing. I used to hate whatever my mother dressed me in, as she was a very colourful lady who liked bright colours and I wasn't particularly a big fan. As a result, I used to adapt my clothing after my mother had decided it was just right for me. As my father was the same height, the other option was to raid his wardrobe and I consider this to be one of my more illogical teenage choices. The end result was that I would go out in 1970s' suits nicked from my father that featured ludicrous flares. I would have fitted in perfectly if the retro look had been in at the time but, sadly, it wasn't. I must have looked an absolute shocker at sixth-form college as everyone else was wearing normal stuff and there I was appearing in three-piece suits. Despite being 6 ft 9 in., I refused to go to specialist shops, like High & Mighty, for my clothing. Traditionally, it is an older man's shop and my answer to this problem was to buy the longest pair of jeans I could find in a 'normal' shop, cut down the sides and then get my mother to stick inserts on the bottom so that they were long enough. With shirts, I used to nick my dad's stuff – avoiding the ones with the desperate patterns and frilly cuffs. By far the biggest issue, however, was finding shoes that fitted, because I quickly became a size 14 and this caused serious problems, particularly when we were in Spain. The locals there are historically a short and petite race of males and certainly didn't require size-14 shoes. As a result, the only shoes I could wear were Doc Martins that I hated and Dunlop Green Flash trainers that, of course, came back into fashion, but about ten years too late for me.

I have a distinct memory of the embarrassment I felt in Spain when everyone went to PE in their trendy trainers and I had to wear my size-14 Green Flash. I got the piss ripped out of me quite often and things weren't much better when it came to casual shoes. I wore something like a policeman's shoe and even my mother had to agree they were quite horrendous, because it was a style that made your foot look 12 times bigger than it was, even though it was already a size 14. Originally, the only manufacturer of rugby boots in my size was Magnus from Northampton. You had to send off a print of your feet and they would come up with something like those functional police-style shoes. When I first started playing, I would always make the excuse that one of my heroes was Dean Richards and he wore his socks rolled down, but it was mainly to half cover the horrendous boots I was wearing underneath. It was to remain a problem until I got the chance to travel to New Zealand when I was 17. Down Under, I found a couple of pairs of Asics that looked very flash and, most importantly of all, that fitted. I think there were only a couple of pairs of size 14s in the entire Australia/New Zealand region, so I grabbed them with both hands and tried to make the boots last as long as possible. Fortunately, Nike and Puma Kings started to make bigger boots to ease my pain.

At college, virtually the whole team I played with joined Cranleigh Rugby Club, but that was a bit far to travel and my father decided it was probably a good idea for me to have a trial for Guildford & Godalming. I was completely against this as all my mates were at Cranleigh where I knew the social life would be outstanding. I also played a couple of times for Rosslyn Park and Harlequins junior teams. I never gave the Quins shirt back and also did something that became a hobby of sorts – I nicked one of the corner flags that featured the Quins multi-colours. Why?

Well, I had this grand idea to make a big towel out of corner flags I stole from all the teams I played against. I took corner flags from all the clubs in the Surrey area, but the Quins one was extra special. It was made out of silk (it wouldn't be today) and it had all the Harlequins colours. I can't really remember how I actually nicked the corner flags, but sometimes part of your post-match duties was to clear everything up, just grab the drinks bottles and corner flags and head back, laden down and covered in mud to the dressing-room where it was all dumped on the floor. I would leave the pole and just take the flag. I was going to sew them all together, but I really don't know where they ended up although, from enquiries I made, the evidence of my criminal past has been disposed of. I had a much shorter criminal career as a turf thief. On one visit to Twickenham, I joined lots of other kids who charged onto the pitch at the end of an international and I pulled up some turf and started growing it in my back garden. Patently, rugby was affecting me in very strange ways. I joined to meet women and ended up a thief!

To be honest, one of the other major motivations for wanting to join as many rugby teams as possible was the opportunity to drink large quantities of alcohol under age. When I played in the Colts games I would always go out and have a beer, even though I was only 16 and a couple of years younger than most of my team-mates. Playing for Guildford & Godalming allowed me to be selected for various age-group teams at county level and then I was asked to take part in an England Colts session. They didn't realise I was still a schoolboy, a fact that only came to light after I made it all the way through to the England Colts final selection. Before I could take part in the match, I got a telephone call saying: 'You can't play in that as you are too young. You're going to have to go with the England Schools.' The England Under-18 Schools lads didn't greet the decision with universal delight. The team had already been selected and so I had to break into that side from a standing start and without knowing anyone. It was pretty serious stuff and a turn-off for me because I was the only comprehensive schoolboy in the ranks. That set me apart from the rest of the squad, who didn't like me much anyway because I was trying to oust one of their mates from the team. It was a very different culture, one that I didn't particularly enjoy, and the fact they were so unwelcoming only added to my discomfort. Most of those guys competed against one another at private school and even though Godalming College had gone unbeaten for two years, we never played private schools. The England Under-18's squad included several players who would go on to win senior honours, such as Will Green, who became one of my best friends at London Wasps, Tony Diprose (Saracens), Matt Dawson (Northampton) and Tim Stimpson (Leicester). At my college we played Charterhouse, but that was at football not rugby, and I found the whole England Schools thing a bit snobby. I took the place of a guy called Charlie Simpson in the second row and the animosity that resulted was all very alien to me. I was used to being with my mates and had never felt this kind of reaction, even when I started playing senior rugby for Godalming at the age of 16. I also appeared in the Surrey Cup final at that age and no one really seemed bothered that there was a schoolboy in the second row because my height and weight made it appear I was much older. Something the bar staff also seemed to believe.

It was at Guildford & Godalming that I first came across the concept of the ringer: the good player drafted in by an ambitious club when they needed extra help in a big league or cup match. The club used to bring in people from nowhere for one-off games because we wanted to be top of the league. Even at that tender age, I didn't feel it was right and it certainly didn't help engender any team spirit. There were a lot of really good players at the club already, but no one stuck around after the games for a pint with a very large underage drinker. It was purely a case of turning up for games, playing rugby and heading off home. I would get a lift from my parents as soon as the game had finished and I had showered. My father did try to encourage me to have a beer, but all I could think about was getting out of the club and heading off to meet up with my mates who were playing for Cranleigh.

The following year, I made the decision to leave G&G and link up with the lads at Cranleigh, even though the standard of rugby was worse. The effect was immediate. I really started to get excited about my rugby because the atmosphere was great. Cranleigh didn't have as much money and the facilities may have been inferior, but that didn't matter to me. It was an inevitable move: the previous season I had played for G&G against the Cranleigh lads and actually opted to go to their end-of-season drinks rather than the one at G&G. It really was a no brainer, particularly after that last night of the season, which saw me having to eat a Cadbury's cream egg with some hot chillies in it and various horrible concoctions of drink: Guinness with Baileys – all sorts of stuff. I was in a terrible state and managed to throw up in the back of my girlfriend's Citroen. For some reason, she dumped me very shortly after.

It was only a temporary setback on the girlfriend front, however, because lots of the college girls were regular supporters of Cranleigh RFC, which made the after-match drinking sessions even more of a social occasion. While it probably appears as if Cranleigh RFC was just an extension of our school social set-up, we did train hard and I knew the England Schools selectors would not be impressed if they found out their lock forward was having more fun off the pitch than on it. I was doing just enough to deal with the training sessions at the RFU's Castlecroft centre, where they gave the players all kinds of tests and information. I remember sitting opposite Richard Hill, who would play such a key role in England's 2003 Rugby World Cup win, and noticing that he had put on a few pounds since our last England Schools session. The coaches noticed as well and he got an almighty rollicking in front of the rest of the players and was sharply reminded about his nutrition and drinking. Hilly was one of the quieter guys in the group and I sat there thinking about following the strictures they had laid down. The thought lasted for about a second. It pretty much went in one ear and out the other: rugby, at that time, was one long Happy Hour.

I was 16 years old when I joined Cranleigh. During my time at G&G, because the standard of rugby had been higher, and the referees better, the opposition had largely avoided trying to thump me into submission. How things changed: at Cranleigh I met opposition players who were prepared to give me a whack because I was so big. To work my way into the first team I played a couple of second-team games that featured players either on their way down, but who wanted to prove they could still hack it, or guys coming back up the ladder who were ready to thump their weight, particularly against some 6 ft 9 in. upstart. It was a price worth paying in my book. I had managed to turn playing for Cranleigh into a three-day weekend that started with me jumping on my bike with my kit on my back and heading off to one of my mate's homes. I told my parents I was making the extra effort because we were training on the eve of the match when, in fact, we all got totally pissed on a Friday night, before cycling back from the pub to my mate's house where I would stay for the night and then play for various teams over the weekend. I played a first-team game, a Colts game and representative fixtures – sometimes all in the one weekend, without England knowing. The selectors would have gone ballistic and, while I knew the risks, I was having so much fun I didn't even think about what would happen if I got injured. I was just enjoying all the fruits of rugby life and meeting girls, before cycling home with a kitbag on my back on a Sunday evening completely shattered. My parents thought they must have been hard games because I fell asleep early. They considered my early departure to bed as a sign that I wanted to be ready for school – how wrong they were.

At this stage, all I could think about was getting the next week's schooling out of the way before the rugby weekend. Of course, I took punishment from opponents who didn't like the idea of this schoolboy winning ball off them at the lineout. When it comes to remembering opponents intent on hammering me all match, the one who really stands out is Bill Cuthbertson, the Scotland lock, who was playing for a second team we came up against. He was on the way down after having played international rugby and for Harlequins and he made it abundantly clear from the outset that I was going to have my lights punched out from the first whistle to the last. He clobbered me a couple of times and I just had to accept it as part of my rugby education.

When I played for the first team, there was a chap I packed down with in the second row who was about the same height as me, and who looked like Herman Munster. You could tell he had been around a bit and that he knew how to handle the rough stuff, but down in the seconds it was a case of me having to take my medicine. Why didn't I throw a few punches myself? Well, taking into account how old Cuthbertson was and the fact I was a schoolboy and had no chance of beating him up, my only option was to try and outwit him on the pitch. I did, scoring a couple of tries during the game. I didn't even give him any verbals back after scoring those tries as I, wisely, realised that would only make him even angrier. So, I just got on with the game and was able to talk everyone through those tries in the bar after the match.

That season saw Cranleigh head to Wales on tour and we played against Llandudno and Abertillery. I think Wayne, one of our coaches at Cranleigh was a Welsh guy and he wanted to take us back to his old rugby club and we enthusiastically agreed to head over the border. Again, my parents packed me off and assumed that I was getting a good rugby education, but I spent virtually the entire five days plastered and playing rugby in between. Abertillery were the Welsh Colts champions at the time and their pitch is set in a wonderful park area with a big old wooden stand that wouldn't pass any safety rules today. The locals adopted the attitude that they were playing a bunch of Surrey softies and one or two got stuck into us. There were a couple of brawls during the game and I wondered what would happen when both teams met up in the clubhouse bar area after the match. It wasn't long before I realised that giving and taking a few hits was part of the game in Wales. We had a few beers with the Abertillery boys after the game and it was all forgotten. I realised then that in rugby you could whack opponents during the match and then share a civilised drink with them afterwards. What a great game!

My first representative game for England Under-18s saw me playing alongside Charlie Simpson, the guy whom I had replaced after being sent to the Schools squad from the Colts. It was Ireland, away in Limerick, and also in the team were Matt Dawson, Will Greenwood and Will Green. We won all our games until we played Wales at Colwyn Bay and Matt – as I have often reminded him – had a bit of a shocker. He was playing scrum-half and we ended up losing the match when we were on for the Grand Slam. Everyone had predicted a Slam for the team and we did play some very impressive rugby, only to fall at the last hurdle. We were all given the infamous purple England tracksuits, which would have gone well with those 1970s' suits I used to nick from my father. The tracksuit constituted the first bit of 'stash' I collected at England level, although I hasten to add that I was no longer stealing corner flags. As the largest ever England school boy, I was asked to do a photo-call for one of the 'red tabs', standing next to a lamppost – how original! I was asked about joining Harlequins (they obviously hadn't fingered me for nicking that silk touch flag), but turned down their overtures to ensure my rugby weekends remained centred on Cranleigh RFC. I didn't need to play for a higher-ranked club because I was already in the England Schools Under-18 team and had also played for London and Surrey Colts.

Despite my love of cider and lager shandy – OK, that's not exactly heavy-duty stuff – I never really got into any trouble with the police and so my drinking habits never attracted the attention of my parents. Despite all my rugby commitments, injuries were something I never thought about: the only problem I had dealt with so far was a broken nose. I broke it for the first time while playing football in Spain, crashing into a goalpost while playing goalkeeper – perhaps the first sign I wasn't going to make football my professional sporting career. The first rugby injury was a cauliflower ear – a painful inflammation that eventually leaves you with a lughole that looks like, well obviously, a cauliflower.

Unfortunately, my first ugly ear flared up when we were having a Children in Need charity week at college and that meant I spent the entire time with a bandage round my head and looking like Pudsey Bear. It was all very embarrassing. I think somebody's elbow had connected with the side of my head and the ear blew up straightaway. It was enormous and, because I was very concerned about my appearance at that stage, I can remember thinking it was the end of the world. A large bandage on a 6 ft 9 in. schoolboy is quite noticeable and, although I was supposed to keep pressure on the ear for a week, I managed about three days. I just couldn't be bothered. I hated taping my ears up as I seemed to get the tape in my hair and it stayed stuck there until the following week. My answer to this problem was to tie a sock (the colour that we were playing in) around my head Rambo-style. For some reason, despite wearing a sock around my head, I never got the piss ripped out of me. If somebody turned up to a match like that today, I would laugh my head off. To stop its coming off in the scrums, you have to tie it incredibly tight and I used to, virtually, burst a blood vessel in my head with all the pressure. I carried on doing that until I went to New Zealand when I was 17. I am the first to admit that my strange appearance on the rugby pitch was all down to vanity. Looking back, I find myself asking the question: 'What the hell were you thinking, you muppet!' A 6 ft 9 in. rugby player with socks rolled down over his boots to hide the maker's name and another sock tied tightly around his brow to avoid some sticky tape in his hair. Ludicrous. However, when I started to pick up battle scars on my face, the cauliflower ear didn't seem very important and so the sock went back into the drawer to join the other one.

CHAPTER 4

FENCING WITH GOLF CLUBS AND POOL CUES

While my teenage rugby life was, thankfully, free from too many violent incidents, away from the game I was caught up in a couple of situations that were both frightening and dangerous. The first came when I lived in Ash, near Aldershot, for a brief period before I went to Godalming College. As I have mentioned, even at 15 years of age I was already 6 ft 9 in., and one afternoon I went to the cinema with a neighbour's daughter. On the way back home from Ash Station, we took a short cut that led directly to my house. A group of guys had got off at the same station and were walking a short distance behind us – they were clearly either drunk or on something. I just sensed they were going to cause trouble and this was confirmed when they also used the short cut. As we walked along, I said to the girl: 'Listen, when I say three, just run.' There were about six of them, so it was pointless getting into anything. On the count of three we both sprinted. As we ran, I realised that if I stopped and she carried on, she wouldn't get hurt. If I did, then that wasn't going be so much of a problem. She carried on running and I stopped when one of the guys was about to reach me. I had seen a couple of martial arts films and thought I would try and replicate one of the moves. With my back toward the first would-be attacker, I elbowed the guy while I was running and then swing round and punched him square on the nose and knocked him out almost straightaway. It gave me a bit of confidence. I then carried on running, but was never going to be able to stay ahead of them. By this stage, the second guy arrived and I wrestled with him before swinging him round and throwing him against a tree and he slumped on the floor. I thought, 'I'm doing rather well,' but then a third guy arrived and I had a bit of a wrestle and scuffle with him before managing to wriggle free and run off. I got home with a bit of blood on my face and, as I walked through the front door, my mum burst into tears and my father got all aggressive. I told them what had happened and he rang the neighbour to find out if his daughter had arrived back safely. She hadn't. There was a bit of a panic and my father and I went back out in the car to try and find her. In doing so, we drove past the local pub, which wasn't a particularly nice hostelry, and the same six guys were causing havoc outside this pub, throwing bottles. At this point, my father, much to my surprise, got out of the car, went to the boot and emerged with his favourite seven-iron – the very same one my mother had chosen to ward off the intruder in Nairobi. Why is a seven-iron such a weapon of choice in these situations?

My father was using it as a cane as he walked over to the troublemakers. He announced: 'Right chaps, I have rung the police and you will all remain here until they arrive.' I was watching, thinking: 'What in the hell does he think he is doing?' At this point all six of them jumped him. One of the guys managed to pull the golf club out of his hand and started banging my father on the head with it, which wasn't a very pleasant thing to see. I went to the boot and picked another iron out of the bag and joined in, creating a surreal moment in all this mayhem when I stood there battling with this attacker. I can clearly remember fencing with two golf clubs while all the people standing around in the pub car park did absolutely nothing. They just watched while I was screaming: 'Someone ring the bloody police.' Then one of the troublemakers' girlfriends got into their car and tried to run me over, at which point I jumped in front of a nearby lamppost, moved before the car arrived and she crashed straight into it, making a huge noise. Meanwhile, the guy I was fencing with had made the most of this distraction and wrapped the seven-iron around my neck. In the mayhem, the gang of six ran off leaving me with a golf club wound cartoon style around my neck and my father covered in blood on the road. He had some pretty bad cuts to his forehead, which he had collected when being attacked with his own golf club on the floor. As he went down, he had managed to hold on to two of the gang, who evidently were also being hit with the club. Not surprisingly, the golf clubs were ruined; giving my father an excuse to buy some new ones, although that particular seven-iron will always have a special place in our family. The police arrived about an hour later, but nothing really happened, despite a fencing match with golf clubs and a car being rammed into a lamppost.

My father and his golf clubs did not feature in the other incident, although it did involve sport. I was 16 and in a bar in Godalming where I was playing pool with a few mates. If you wanted a game you stuck money on the side and the winner stayed on and, after an hour or so, we decided to move on. We played the last game and I won it, put the cue back and was about to leave when one of the guys who had put a coin down to play said: 'I've got to play you.' 'No, you're all right, play your mates, it's fine, I'm off,' I replied. He wasn't impressed and kept on saying: 'The winner stays on.' I replied: 'Seriously, I've got to go somewhere.' He continued to be a little bit aggressive, so I played and did my best to lose. Remarkably, I won and I thought: 'Oh Christ, here we go.' I won the next few games as well and he still wouldn't let me leave. I announced again that I had to go and, at this point, he said: 'You're taking the mickey out of me,' so I said: 'No, I'm going, I've won very flukily if that makes you feel any better, I'm off.' It didn't go down well: 'Now you really are taking the piss,' he said before attacking me with a pool cue.

So, once again, I was involved in a sword fight, but this time the weapons were pool cues instead of golf clubs. I must have developed some fencing skills, because I managed to escape and left my irate opponent to take out his wrath on the pub staff. He was taken to court and I had to appear as a witness for the prosecution.

Those incidents were potentially very dangerous and only occurred because I was a big guy who had become a target. I couldn't understand the logic of trying to hit a teenager just because he was much taller than you and it all seemed pretty stupid. Those incidents didn't put me off golf or pool, though, and my father still swings his clubs as often as possible – on the course. And fencing? Well, I retired from that the moment I left the pub.

Although I confess to being a pupil who always took the easy option, I did end up with 9 GCSEs and an O-level. I took Latin early, due to my time spent in Spain when it was part of the syllabus. Doing it a year early would have marked me out as a bit of swot and so I kept it pretty quiet. When it came to GCSEs , I opted to study Art, Craft and Design Technology because, as I have mentioned, I was artistic and had always loved to draw. It wasn't necessarily a passion – nothing really was in my teenage years except rugby and drinking – but I used to draw all the time: other children, teachers and my mates seemed to think my pictures were worth looking at. What also appealed to my lazy side was the fact that I could produce a drawing or painting in next to no time and still get a good grade, whereas all the other kids in my class used to take ten hours over one painting. So, even when it came to exam time and the teacher announced with due reverence that 'You've got ten hours,' I used to spend an hour on my work, hand it in and then head off. Understandably, all my school reports said: 'Has all the potential if he worked harder,' but, in my defence, I would like to point out that I passed those GCSE examinations.

When it came to picking A-levels, I really didn't have a clue. I didn't have a definite career path to follow, although I had toyed with the idea of being a chef, which probably stemmed from my creative side. It didn't happen, though, and in the end I chose Spanish, art and, for some bizarre reason, economics – just to have a range of subjects and something that might help me in the future. As it turned out, I was bloody awful at economics because I could never understand all the theories behind it; they just didn't seem to marry up with everyday life and I could never get my head around it. My economics teacher came to the understandable conclusion that I was wasting my time in his class, but I still showed willing and took the exam, which I failed. While playing rugby in New Zealand a year later, I retook the economics exam and somehow managed to pass.

I got an A and a B in the other subjects, which I found easier to deal with, and whenever classes became a little bit too much of a chore, I claimed I had to leave to train for an upcoming England Schools international. This was a get-out-of-jail card I used on numerous occasions. I remember being quite distracted by girls at this point and all the good-looking ones used to go to the same pubs as the rugby team. Even at school we used to go to the pub at lunchtime, which mirrored a university-type culture, and during this rather bohemian period, I was asked to do a mural for a local town project at the police station. I designed the mural, got three or four of my mates to come and help me with it, on the basis that we would be required to hang around for half an hour in the police station painting and then head to the pub, where we could spend most of the afternoon indulging in formation underage drinking – something that would, no doubt, have interested the police officers. I would like to be able to talk about my police-station mural in terms of having left an artistic legacy but, sadly, they knocked the place down and my masterpiece was lost for ever.

CHAPTER 5

GAY BARS AND LIFE AS A KIWI RUGBY PLAYER

Despite being a dreadful economics student, those teaching the subject kept taking a close interest in my progress for other reasons. I remember playing in a Surrey Cup tie and another economics teacher (not mine) was helping with the coaching of the team. He could see that I had all the raw elements, although I lacked the basic techniques of the game, because my size allowed me to get away with just knocking opponents out of the way. His brother-in-law had arrived in England on holiday and was a second row for Dunedin Pirates. He spotted me in that Surrey Cup match when I was 16 going on 17 and said: 'He seems pretty good, I'm retiring, does he fancy a season over in New Zealand?' This idea was put to me shortly after that match and in a nano-second I said 'Yes.' As I was already spending extended weekends away from home, the idea of turning my rugby into an even longer period away seemed just too good to turn down. Not surprisingly, my father immediately said 'yes'; my mother, on the other hand, was very distraught at the prospect of her little boy being 12,000 miles away and doing who knows what. The thought going through my father's head was 'let him go, at least we won't have to feed the lump for a while, that should halve our grocery bills!' My sister wasn't jealous because, at this stage, we had gone to separate schools for the first time. We had been extremely close and then, all of a sudden, we hated each other: one of the reasons was probably my insistence that I was going to the right school and that she had made a dreadful mistake. Consequently, she was more than happy for this irritating person to be out of her hair.

It only took a weekend to sort out all the details and, as soon as school finished, I was packed and heading to the airport for a rugby trip to New Zealand. Dunedin Pirates paid for all my travel expenses and, while I didn't turn left on entering the plane and settle into one of the larger seats, I did manage to get an emergency exit place. The club even arranged for me to stop off in Sydney for a short holiday, which allowed me to catch up with some friends who were in their twenties. I was arriving as a 17 year old, totally unaware of what lay in wait and I immediately started making the kind of basic errors associated with 'new boys' in Oz, turning bright red after excessive sunbathing on Bondi Beach. I spent the entire afternoon trying to surf and the locals accused me of stealing their waves. I have to admit to causing widespread havoc in the surf because I didn't know what the hell I was doing. The same could be said of my love life and I was about to be given a few lessons by an experienced local lady. I have a distinct memory of Australia having very friendly ladies and, while I wasn't a virgin when I went out there, I only had a hazy idea of what I was supposed to be doing. There had been girlfriends, for a month here and there, but they had been as naïve as I was.

Now, this is going to sound like one of those ludicrously crass tales of sex, drink and gay bars that 17 year olds recount about their first night in Sydney, but it is all true. I was standing at a bar called Jacksons on George Street when a young woman approached me. I was completely baffled because, normally, I was the one to make the first move, but I was discovering that different rules apply in this part of the world. She asked me if I wanted a drink. I thought: 'Yes, absolutely fine, nothing wrong with that.' We sat for a while and then she said: 'Do you want to go somewhere else?' Being a friendly sort of guy, I rapidly agreed. I then found myself in Kings Cross in a gay bar. As I walked in there I was struck by the images burning themselves into my corneas: there were blokes in extraordinary outfits or wearing next to nothing and I wondered what the hell I had let myself in for. The young woman said she would order a drink (hey, if she was happy to pay, why cause a scene!) and so I went off to the toilets. Men in leather straps were littered up and down the urinal area, so I concentrated on my own bodily function while looking straight down. I had no intention of making eye contact with anyone. However, I was hugely unnerved to discover the bottom of the communal urinal was mirrored. The reason for this became blindingly obvious: I couldn't wait to finish, zip up and get my very young and innocent arse out of there. I very ungallantly demanded to know why she had brought me to this bar and her answer was: 'Well, I never get chatted up here and I thought we could spend some time, just the two of us.' It was an explanation that started to calm me down, but at this point, a 6 ft 4 in. black guy with studded straps pinched me on the arse. We left a few seconds later – I wasn't going to be anyone's fresh meat. We ended up in her apartment and I went from knowing next to nothing about sex to being taught everything. It prepared me well for New Zealand.

Dunedin is a great university city and comes alive when tens of thousands of students are present in term time. When I arrived, the scenery and the beaches blew me away, which gave me a rather rose-tinted view of the most southerly of New Zealand's main cities. The Pirates Rugby Club, where I played, has a fantastic position, with sand dunes acting as a fence between the pitch and one of the longest beaches you will ever see. It was an incredible setting and I couldn't help thinking I had arrived in rugby heaven. This, of course, was New Zealand's short summer and, in a couple of months, it would become a lot clearer what I had let myself in for.

I immediately had a trial game and got straight into their first XV, which sounds dramatic, but highlighted the dearth of big second-row forwards playing local club rugby. I noticed straightaway that they had so many backs and back-rowers it was untrue. The one area where they didn't have endless options was in the front-five forwards and most of their props were a lot smaller than the guys I had been playing with. It was clear that hookers tended to be back-rowers who weren't going to make it in that position, which explains why their forwards were so happy with the ball in hand. Because of my height and size, I was the perfect asset for Pirates, as there wasn't any lifting in the lineout in those days and that gave me an obvious advantage.

I had been lucky enough to travel to Dunedin with Rowan Westside, who also played at Guildford & Godalming. He was playing in that Surrey Cup game, had been offered the same package as I had and although I didn't know him terribly well, that would change very quickly. We were given a share of a house near the famous home of Otago rugby at Carisbrook and moved in with what they call in Auckland, 'Westies', chavvy girls, who had moved down south to Dunedin. It was a shock to us and a shock to them to all be living under the same roof. Rowan, who was a big, burly back-rower, became particularly raucous after a few drinks and we used to go out midweek as well as at weekends, something that set us apart from the rest of the local rugby community that works and trains all week and then gets totally trolleyed at weekends. It was a completely different culture and while we enjoyed our midweek sessions and had a laugh and repeated the effort at weekends, the locals just went paralytic on a Saturday night. Very quickly, Rowan decided to go 'native', but with a twist. He got paralytic at weekends with our team-mates and also in the middle of the week, to the obvious concern of our two house-mates. After about two months they ended up moving out, having decided they could no longer tolerate Rowan and his japes, which included pouring bottles of vodka and whiskey into their fish tank. There were also the enormous phone bills to add to the extremely high irritation level.

Suddenly, the two young lads from England had their own pad.

The system for looking after players who were in town to help the Pirates was quite simple and involved the club secretary turning up at our house in his open-backed pick-up truck. We jumped in the back and he proceeded to drive us around the city to meet local rugby legends. This guy knew everyone. We then headed to the outskirts of Dunedin and, whenever we stopped, a club member would present us with crates of vegetables or a side of lamb. We also picked up milk and cheese and by the end of this trip the truck was full of food. The main problem with this wonderfully generous system was that neither of us had ever lived away from home and had no idea of what to do with lamb or eggs. We ended up sticking whole sides of lamb in the oven, turning it on, just poking it now and again and hoping for the best.

The main idea was that the rest of the club didn't know we were on a 'freebie' and to create a smokescreen, jobs were found for us to do each day. My first part-time job was to clear about two acres of gorse with a pair of secateurs and that lasted for about two days. I was torn to shreds and asked for something different. The club secretary sold caravans and I became what seemed like an extra on *Home and Away*, because I was tasked with cleaning the caravan park and also had to wash the individual caravans. That job only lasted a week. Then I tried building work and landscape gardening, again without finding my true vocation, but we were earning enough to fund those nights on the drink and that kept us happy.

At that time, the All Blacks players used to turn out for their clubs every week to earn selection for provincial rugby. That meant that, aged 17, I was playing against test stars such as John Timu, Jamie Joseph, Mark Ellis, Stu Forster and the Bachop and Cooper brothers. I was playing a great standard of rugby and I remember the Dunedin University third team had Josh Kronfeld in their back row, a player who would very soon become an All Blacks legend. I was amazed by the level of fitness required for club rugby in Dunedin and, having come straight from our season, I thought I was pretty fit.

However, my rugby world was about to be turned upside down, because on the first day of training we ran the length of a golf course and I was just left for dead. We then did a couple of sand-dune sessions and both Rowan and I were completely whacked. It was patently obvious to everyone that these two Poms were way off the levels needed to be a member of the Pirates first XV. Even at that point, in terms of hours, the Pirates players were putting in the same amount of training you now associate with professional rugby in England. That's how far ahead they were in terms of physical conditioning and it was obvious to me then that in New Zealand you don't just do sports for a laugh, it is part of life.

When Pirates players were not training at the club they would do extra sessions of running, swimming and rowing. The Pirates hooker had rowed for New Zealand, while the first-team coach was also a highly rated swimming coach, who would spend his evenings driving around the city. If he didn't see you out running when he was out on that drive, you didn't get picked for the next game. In one of our more sober moments, it dawned on the two of us that we really had to move up a gear.

When I played in the UK, even in senior rugby, it was a lot slower and more forward-oriented. I was very comfortable mauling and doing all those sorts of jobs and my tackle count was consistently high. I used to tackle a lot and if I wanted to get the ball back the easiest thing to do was wrap up an opponent and slam him down on our side of the ruck. I would do this week in and week out in the UK, we would turn over the ball every time and I would receive lots of pats on the back from team-mates and coaches. I was to learn very quickly that the only thing I would get on my back doing that kind of trick in New Zealand was the rounded metal of eight pairs of rugby studs. Rucking wasn't an art form in English rugby, but it was the way New Zealanders produced quick ball. In the first week my shirt was ripped off my back, it was shredded and, not surprisingly, I thought twice about doing it again. However, being young and headstrong, I kept dumping guys on our side of the ruck and the punishment I was receiving felt like a price worth paying because my team-mates were hugely impressed with my work and said so. No doubt, they were also thinking that I had to be a little dense to upset the opposition willingly and then lie down while they kicked seven bells out of me at every ruck. I thought, in my naïvety, that if I was getting 'rucked', I must have been doing something right, so I just carried on.

One of the biggest differences in the type of rugby being played in New Zealand involved the backs, who spent a ridiculous amount of time running into each other at 100 mph. There was a ferocity in everything they did, which came as a real shock and I couldn't understand how they were able to bounce back up after being wiped out by a massive hit. There were guys in our first XV who would have been good enough to play international rugby for England but who didn't even make the provincial side in Otago. One wing, in particular, seemed to score two or three tries every time he played, bouncing off would-be tacklers and causing mayhem in the opposition ranks. I was convinced he was a certainty for test honours, but he never got higher than club level and, obviously, someone else was seeing different aspects to his game. It only convinced me I didn't really have an understanding of rugby at all. However, playing in New Zealand fast-tracked me in the game, and spending that time away from English rugby was hugely important in my development. I started playing rugby because it was pure enjoyment, but now I had been shown a different side to the sport and had mentally and physically grown up during my time at Pirates.

Dunedin was great when the university was open, but when it was closed down between terms, there was absolutely nothing happening, because the city thrives on the students and their enthusiasm. I had to stay there when the students had all gone home and, with the onset of winter, it all became a bit of slog. I had hoped to experience more of the country, but opportunities to take sightseeing trips were limited because I had to operate as a professional rugby player at just 17 years of age. However,

I decided to break out of Dunedin and headed to Queenstown to see the amazing snow-capped peaks and stunning scenery and, on arrival, agreed to do a bungee jump. After surviving that experience, I received a telephone call from the coach demanding to know where I was. 'You should be back training this evening.' It was that intense and, for the first time, I started to think: 'Oh Christ, is this how it's going to be?' They were looking after me on and off the pitch and so I just had to knuckle down. To be honest, it got a bit boring at the end and I just wanted to head back home and see my friends at the rugby club. I had travelled out in the February and, in September, came back to start university and although they tried to convince me to stay in New Zealand, it really was time to leave.

CHAPTER 6

BRISTOL: HOW TO MESS UP YOUR UNIVERSITY STUDIES AND HAVE A GREAT TIME

When I came back home from New Zealand, my thoughts were rugby, rugby, rugby, but I had pressure from my parents to go to university. By this time, they had moved back to Spain and were living in Barcelona, but we still had the house in Surrey and I temporarily moved back in with my sister, which really pleased her! I was too late to apply in the normal way for a university place and had no option but to dig out a card one of the England Schools committee guys had given me. He had made it very clear that if I was having any trouble getting into university I should give him a call. There were family links with Cambridge and Oxford, but I wasn't capable of getting there and so I gave this chap a ring. He said: 'How do you fancy Bristol?' I thought that sounded great and while I did take a look at a couple of other options, it was my first choice. Ludicrously, I went to Preston because I thought I could play for Preston Grasshoppers, the club that had launched the career of England lock Wade Dooley, but I didn't really have a clue. I went to Manchester because a good mate lived there and the art college had a good reputation, but I was always going to opt for Bristol and it was a choice that would shape my entire rugby career. The university had a good art college and the chap sorting out my place had links with Bristol RFC. Initially, I was going to art school, until I found out I had to do a foundation year before I even started my degree. Because rugby was my main priority, I didn't want to spend too long studying and, looking back, I didn't really know what I was going to do with my life except become a professional player. The slight drawback at the time was the fact that the game was still amateur and didn't appear to be about to go professional at all. Because I had paid my way through rugby in New Zealand, I just assumed that my future was mapped out and even at school, my economics master would say: 'Shaw, you can't just keep playing rugby, because it is not a professional sport.' I was this blind fool going: 'No, no, it will become professional.' He was saying: 'No, no, it's an amateur sport and has been for hundreds of years and will remain so.'

For some outlandish reason I hatched an idea of playing professional rugby in America, assuming – wrongly – that they had established that kind of system. I don't know what I was thinking, but I was clearly ahead of my time. I eventually plumped for the Spanish Business Studies option at university on the basis I already spoke Spanish and that the business bit would be a useful back-up position in the highly unlikely event that Mystic Meg Shaw wasn't going to be right about rugby becoming professional.

Although I was supposed to be concentrating on the first year of my studies, all my energy went into rugby training. Having been shown a new way of preparing for matches in Dunedin, I was determined to maintain that standard of fitness and skills work. The guys at Bristol must have thought I was crackers, as I arrived and immediately started to spend every spare minute training with whichever team or squad turned up that evening. However, there was a reason to the training madness: my grant had not arrived in the bank, so I was in desperate need of feeding at someone else's expense. I knew if I trained at the club I would get fed at the end of each session and so it would be the Under-21s one night, then the Colts and finally the senior squad. In my mind, I was maintaining a professional attitude, while eating platefuls of stodge, and it must have impressed someone because I was given a place in the first team. The guy who made way for me was one of the great legends of Bristol rugby – Phil 'Grizzly' Adams. Having just arrived at the club, I didn't know his fearsome reputation and in an effort to make an impression during a tackle-bag drill, I decided to really wallop the bag he was holding. I knocked him flying and all his mates who had been around him for years were saying: 'Come on, Phil, what are you going to do about that?' Thankfully, Grizz just looked at them with cold eyes and growled: 'Nothing, he's only a kid.' I got on with Phil almost straight away, so dumping him on his backside wasn't an issue. Bristol had a really good pack at the time and I seemed to be viewed as a worthwhile asset: a tall kid with a bit of talent and a seemingly insatiable appetite for training!

Guys like Peter Stiff, Derek Eves, Alan Sharpe and Mark (Ronnie) Regan were in the squad and ten-man rugby was Bristol's forte, with Mark Tainton kicking everything at outside-half, while Ralph Knibbs got the tries when we bothered to give the ball to him at centre. My cause was helped by the fact I had played the running/passing rugby in New Zealand after starting my career learning the traditional forward-oriented English stuff. Early press reports noted that I gave the pack an extra back-row forward and enjoyed getting my hands on the ball. As a result of this success, my university coursework was coming a distant second to my blossoming rugby career and, looking back, I regret not focusing more on that first year in university. That is when you really have a great laugh and I wrongly assumed that, having been to a sixth-form college with a relaxed attitude, there was nothing new to experience.

I was also so wrapped up in training and playing that I became serious beyond my years and missed out on what the university had to offer. At this point, I was sharing a house under the arches on Gloucester Road with fellow students, but only occasionally joined them for a night out, which only pushed me closer to the rugby lads at Bristol. I was playing against some of the most famous rugby clubs in Wales on wet and windy Wednesday nights and loving every minute of the experience. Not having made the trips before, I was eager to experience Llanelli at their famous Stradey Park pitch and Pontypool on their park pitch with the huge grass bank populated by locals baying for our blood. For old hands like Peter Stiff, the sight of teeming rain drew a very different response as we crossed into Wales. 'Oh shit,' was the usual refrain. There was a lot of animosity towards the English teams and the Welsh sides were incredibly dominant. Their squads seemed to be so much stronger than ours, even though we would take a virtual first team to places like Llanelli. In my first game at Stradey I scored our only try and we got beaten by 50 points. The Llanelli players would spend the game telling us how crap we were and that we were soft English bastards. Even so, I quite enjoyed it.

That sort of sledging had been part of the club rugby scene in New Zealand and I was working on the basis that whatever the Welsh threw at me it wouldn't be as frightening as facing Green Island in the Dunedin league. When I had arrived in New Zealand, I was told they were going to put me down as being 19 years old, not 17, in the local paper. Their argument was that as a 17 year old you would get torn apart and picked on and I had already had enough of that back in England. Green Island were almost entirely made up of Maoris and matches against them were always a ferocious battle. The first time I played Green Island I was told just before kick-off that this was going to be the hardest game we were playing all season and that I should expect to get punched a few times. To hear a team-mate warning you about impending doom prior to a match was quite intimidating for a 17 year old. If you get punched during a game then you accept it, but if you are waiting for it, that's a very different story. Sure enough, the punch duly arrived and boy did it hurt! I didn't get injured in that match and managed to avoid any real problems, even though you did take a few cheap, high shots. In Dunedin, if you hurt someone in a tackle, they would be gunning for payback and it came mainly in a legal way, although the ferocity of the tackles meant that if you went into contact with your ribs exposed then a shoulder would quickly arrive and crack a few bones. In contrast, in Wales, there was far more gouging and 'handbag grabbing' – the twisting of your scrotum by an uninvited male hand.

As the youngster of the Bristol pack, I was largely oblivious to the potential dangers of making a positive contribution because, at that stage of your career, you aren't scared of anything. As a result, you stick your head in places you shouldn't and are completely blind to the potential physical damage lurking in dark areas of the game. I split my head a number of times, but again it didn't really bother me at all. Up until that point I had never really suffered a major injury. Life was sweet and got even better when I was selected for the England Under-21 tour of Australia, the country that had opened my eyes to what life could offer a testosterone-fuelled teenager. It was an England squad that contained a number of the players who would return to that country in 2003 and win the Rugby World Cup. The back row was made up of Lawrence Dallaglio, Richard Hill and Tony Diprose, with Darren Crompton and Ronnie Regan in the front row and Will Greenwood, Austin Healey and Tim Stimpson among the backs. The outstanding player in the opposition was George Gregan, who would be the Aussie captain in that World Cup final, although my first sighting of him came in the tour match against ACT Brumbies U-21s and he had a 'mare. I was convinced that Gregan would fail to make the test side after that shocker, but the selectors knew him better and he would be a real pain at number 9 for Australia in the test match at the end of what is still my favourite ever rugby tour.

I had first come across Lawrence when I was selected to play for England Colts and by the Under-21 tour it was patently obvious that he was going to be a star – on and off the pitch. Although I did keep an eye out for her, the young lady who had made my first trip to Sydney such a delight didn't appear at any of our matches.

There were, however, plenty of other female distractions. We operated the traditional yellow T-shirt for the tour leader, the player who was sleeping with the most ladies – and it was hotly contested between Austin and me. Modesty, however, prevents me from revealing who brought it home. It was a monumental tour in every possible respect and, looking back, we played a standard of rugby not expected of an Under-21 side.

There were guys with special talents and, despite being a major pain almost every minute of every day, Austin was a guy who could change a game with a moment of individual brilliance. We didn't rely on the usual strengths of England representative teams: scoring tries with rolling mauls and grinding out wins through forward dominance. This was a squad equipped to score wonderful tries. The skills that would make so many of them World Cup winners were already in evidence and the fact that a number of the players involved were also real characters only increased the enjoyment level as we took care of every opponent and cut a swathe through the local female population.

John Elliott was the team manager, and the whole tour was very professionally run. It was the first trip where I thought: 'I am wearing an England jersey and this really means something special.' At schools level, we had stayed in shitty hotels, especially when I was playing at the RFU centre in Castlecroft, and as an English student representative you would stay at Bisham Abbey, miles from the nearest bright light. The Australian tour accommodation was five-star hotels and with a daily allowance thrown in: it really didn't get better than that. Well, in fact it did, because after one game in Brisbane we were joined by a load of high school girls and, even though this was a good-time tour, this was a night that stood out from the rest. The girls went to extraordinary lengths to meet up with us again during the tour and I remember playing a match in Sydney and recognising some of them from a couple of nights earlier in Brisbane. They had travelled down to have another party. It was quite unnerving: most of the guys had seen films about 'bunny boilers' and when you waved goodbye to a 'special lady' in Brisbane, it was on the understanding that she would not jump on a plane, or train, and travel thousands of miles for another kiss and a cuddle. Still, this kind of commitment had to be rewarded.

Besides an outstanding social life, the tour also gave me a feeling of being comfortable in an England representative squad, something I had not experienced before because of the dominance of guys from public schools. In this squad, there was a real mix of players from different backgrounds: some had been products of their local clubs, others had been through the schools system, like Ampleforth-educated Lawrence and Campion boy Diprose, but we all bonded quickly and strongly under manager Elliot and this underpinned our rugby performances. The feeling of alienation that surfaced when I first came into contact with the England Schools players was erased from my memory, even though many of those players, like Dawson and Green, were still in the mix. I received a significant amount of publicity from the tour, although thankfully it revolved around my playing ability rather than any success I may have enjoyed in the bars and clubs of various Australian cities and towns. Any plaudits we received, individually or as a squad, were down to the outstanding coaching and management, which never left the players feeling institutionalised. No doubt the parents of those lovely young ladies would have liked us put away!

The tone for the tour was set on the first night in Australia when the management encouraged us to go out and have a few drinks. We weren't going to be treated like schoolboys and we repaid this trust with our performances on the pitch and success in the test against the Wallabies. The same attitude to the players existed on the Lions tour to South Africa in 1997, another trip that was huge fun and, for me, this mutual trust is the major reason I enjoyed both tours.

The Under-21s wanted to finish the tour on a massive high and that meant beating the Australians at Concord Oval in Sydney, a stadium that is some way out of the city on a road that is populated by used-car outlets. New South Wales played Queensland in the fiercely contested State of Origin senior game and then we took to the pitch, which meant a good-sized crowd was still in the stadium. We were having such a good time and playing with real success that facing Australia in the test wasn't a big problem. Our attitude was: 'This is great, let's go and have a good time.' And we did.

Having achieved something significant, the only way to celebrate was to try and beat David Boon's drinking record on the flight back to London. Boon, the great Aussie cricketer, had consumed 52 cans during a flight and it is a standard few have ever managed to match. Our entrants were my London Wasps team-mate Darren Molloy and Mark Mapletoft, the outside-half, who is now coach to the England Under-20s. Mapletoft got himself into a right state and by the time we got to Singapore was definitely the worse for wear, and had endured having half his hair shaved off. The flight attendants were encouraging him not to get off the flight, because they feared the local officials wouldn't let him get back on board. The response of his caring team-mates was to hack even more hair off his head with shavers.

CHAPTER 7

WHY AM I HEAD-BUTTING THE ROAD?

On my return to Bristol, I made a promise to myself to start taking university life more seriously and to spend time getting to know my fellow students, but I hadn't bargained on Ronnie Regan becoming such a large part of my life. I'd also say he was a legendary guy to tour with (as you'll read) but also I wouldn't be the player I am today without his support and humour. Ronnie had made the biggest impact on me during the Australian tour and we just seemed to hit it off from the start, even though we came from very different backgrounds. One thing we did have in common, however, was our commitment to play for Bristol RFC.

When we first met I was struggling to pay for food, while Ronnie was getting paid rather well by his dad to work at his maintenance business: Regan Cranes. He drove around in a Peugeot 205 GTI, which was his pride and joy, though for my height and size, it was a tight fit. I used to get a lift with him to Castlecroft for the students or Under-21s get-togethers and he used to charge me petrol money, even though he would get his expenses from the RFU. During this period, Ronnie started referring to me as the

'Welded Wallet'. In fact, it was Ronnie who had the welded wallet and he remains one of the stingiest guys in the world.

When we were in the car he talked mostly about himself, a subject he finds absolutely fascinating but, as I have discovered, if you let Ronnie talk long enough he will come up with some outstanding gems that have helped form the basis of the legend that is Ronnie Regan. Like many of us back then in our younger days, he was headstrong with a lot of aggression to get out of himself – usually on the park. I have to say, though, he is now a well-respected figure in Bristol – after all, he did win a world cup! Ronnie is ultra-competitive and takes an instant dislike to anyone who is also selected for any team in his position. On the tour, we had three hookers – Ronnie, Gareth Adams from Bath and Northampton's Chris Johnson – and they were all eyeing each other suspiciously from the first training session. For some reason, Ronnie took an immediate, and certifiable, dislike to Adams, with the fact he played for Bath providing him with an extra incentive to put one over him at every opportunity.

Ronnie is a lovable guy who'd do anything for you, and he has for me many times. But his humour failed him throughout the tour because he was the constant target of flak from the rest of the lads and his defence was totally undermined by the fact his parents had come on the trip to support him. It was a long tour for Ronnie, made doubly uncomfortable by the presence of Family Regan, who even stayed in the same hotels. Their involvement was so complete, we invited his father to take part in the traditional end-of-tour court session on the basis that as they were with us on every other part of the tour they might as well join in on that. Ronnie's punishment from the tour court session was to be handcuffed to Adams for the final night so they could spend some quality time together and, hopefully, bury the hatchet. When they got handcuffed together, Ronnie's initial thought was, as obviously they only had one hand free, they could punch each other with the other. It was a case of who got the first punch in and that was Ronnie, who lamped Adams and continued the assault whenever the opportunity arose, with Adams only too happy to reciprocate. Thankfully, we decided to remove the handcuffs for the flight home.

Ronnie is a great character and always stands out in a group of 'normal people', but thanks to the quality of men in the Bristol dressing-room at that time, he sort of blended in. When you have great guys like Derek Eves, Peter Stiff, Andy Blackmore and Alan Sharpe, you have to be very special to stand out. However, Ronnie did his best to set himself apart with his everyday comments and actions.

The greyhound story is a good example of why so many tales have grown up around our Ronnie. By common consent, he is not the sharpest tool in the box and when I was eating one of those regular meals at the club after training, Derek Eves came along and explained he was organising a charity greyhound race night to raise money for the Colts tour to South Africa. He was asking the guys if they wanted to buy a dog for the race night, which would involve using old footage of greyhound racing. You would choose a number and that was your dog for the night and you could call it whatever you wanted. It cost around £20 and at that time it was about the cost of my weekly food bill, so I played the impoverished student card, which seemed to work pretty well.

Other, more affluent, players agreed to take a dog and Derek was pleased with this success and so he turned to Ronnie in the hope of securing another supporter for the cause. Derek asked Ronnie: 'Do you want to buy a dog?' and he said: 'I'll have to think about that.' Derek said: 'There's not much to think about, you either want to buy a dog or you don't, if you want to take part it's up to you, it's 20 quid a dog, let me know.' Ronnie was incredibly reticent – or would have been if he knew what that meant – and said: 'I'll have to get back to you on that one.' Derek persisted and in exasperation shouted: 'Can you not let me know now?' All he got from Ronnie was yet another: 'I'll get back to you tomorrow.' Completely frustrated, Derek wandered off to find someone who could actually make up his mind.

The following day, Derek continued his assault and was determined not to let Ronnie off the hook and after demanding to know if a dog would be bought, heard the following explanation: 'I have spoken to my Ma and she said we've got an Alsatian and we don't need a greyhound.' If it was a joke it would be funny, but he was completely genuine and clueless about what was going on and that made it even more enjoyable. I have brought this tale up on several occasions and this is one story he admits to being true.

On a recent Barbarians end-of-season trip, Kevin Maggs, our former team-mate at Bristol, was taking the mickey out of Ronnie 24–7 and the final evening was based around stories involving our mate. Maggsy was trying to get everyone to come up with a cracking story and Ronnie was giving me the evil eye throughout the storytelling, making it abundantly clear he didn't want to hear my voice. However, as the stories made him more and more angry and he became insistent they were all untrue, he challenged me to tell one that was fact, so I told the greyhound one. He replied: 'Yes, well, I was young and naïve.'

The 1993–94 season saw me heavily involved in a Bristol pack that was getting plenty of attention from the media. Having promised myself that I had to make more of my university life, I was throwing myself into the lively social scene, but not the lectures. As a result, I used to go out regularly with mates during the week, play at the weekend and go out again. I wasn't training as hard as I had done in my first year when I had a little bit too much enthusiasm and, as a result, the balance shifted completely the other way and I got a bit carried away with the whole university life and its excesses. I started to get expenses for attending various squad sessions at divisional level, so there was a bit of extra pocket money to spend. I made both the London and South-West squads and, to this day, I don't believe either divisional outfit knew I was also involved with the other. Having started my rugby in Surrey, the London side was very keen to have me on board, and playing for Bristol put me firmly in the orbit of the South-West squad. What helped me pull this off was the presence in Bristol of Rob

Smith, who would become head coach at Wasps, and I used to travel with him to London sessions, while claiming the travel costs as if I had used my own transport. Then, when I went to South-West training, I was claiming expenses for travelling to the West Country as if I was coming from London. As a result, I was making quite a good wage for a student, even though I didn't actually play for either side in that first year!

At Bristol, we had a very, very social team at the time and everyone enjoyed their beer. When I wasn't going out with my student mates I was going out with the Bristol boys, which provided me with an excuse almost every night of the week. We would regularly go to nightclubs, mainly Racks Wine Bar in Clifton, which was a Bristol rugby haunt and still is. This attracted a lot of rugby groupies and there was one particular girl who worked behind the bar at Racks whom I pursued for a while. Eventually, the young lady succumbed to my charms and, one night, uttered the wonderful words: 'It is your lucky night, after my shift you can come round to my house.' Buoyed by this major success, I got a bit carried away, drank too much and ended up somewhere completely different. I suddenly realised where I was supposed to be and made my way around to her house. Not paying any attention to the time – it was four in the morning when I got to her flat – I was throwing little stones up at the window when she popped her head out and uttered the immortal words: 'You had your chance, bugger off.'

This was all on a night when the city of Bristol, and the South-West in general, was soaked by heavy rains and, as a result, our local derby at Bath was cancelled. In fact, it had been cancelled, put back on, cancelled, put back on again and finally called off again. The Bath pitch at the time was in a pretty poor state even when the weather had been fine and so it was with some certainty that I had spent that Friday night on the sauce. It was the reason that I was standing, very much the worse for drink, outside the young lady's flat at 4 a.m. I had no money in my pockets for a cab and thought it was too far to walk home. Then I spotted a rickety old bike attached to a lamppost, removed it, jumped on the saddle and pedalled off down Whiteladies Road. Now, Whiteladies Road is very steep and there is a famous drinking challenge called 'The Cresta Run', which involves accepting a drink at every bar along the road – something I had probably done on that particular evening. I set off with the confidence that only considerable alcoholic intake can give a cyclist and, with the wind racing through my hair, life was sweet – for a short time. One moment I remember being on the bike and the next I was in an ambulance. It turned out that I had hit a concrete bollard in the middle of the road, had performed a somersault, landed slap bang on my head, knocked myself out, was found by the emergency services, bunged in the back of an ambulance and taken off to hospital.

I came round in the ambulance and I found myself strapped down with someone looking at me saying: 'You have a nasty bump on your head.' He then added the line: 'Don't worry, we'll recover your bike.' I ended up in Accident and Emergency, sat on this stretcher, strapped in, unable to get out. I asked one of the orderlies whether I could go to the toilet and he recognised me. 'Simon Shaw, isn't it?' 'Yes, yes,' I said. 'Aren't you supposed to be playing tomorrow?' I looked dumbfounded and managed to blurt out: 'No, no, it's cancelled.' He replied: 'No, it's not; it was back on the last I heard.' Very worried, I replied: 'You're joking. I've got to get out of here.' He said: 'No, you can't, you have got to be assessed by a doctor as you have had a very heavy blow. You won't be playing.' I said: 'I can't be seen to have been drinking the night before a game.' The orderly was not impressed and warned me: 'Well, you won't be released until you have clearance by a doctor.'

Somehow I came up with the idea that I needed to go to the toilet and the chap kindly, and misguidedly, unstrapped me. I tiptoed off to the toilets and, as soon as his back was turned, sprinted out of the hospital and all the way home. By this time it was 6.30 a.m. and I thought I had better get a couple of hours' kip as I was going to have to play a game of rugby – sore head and all – just a few hours later. I was living with Chad Eagle, a Kiwi and second-row forward at Bristol, and he woke me up saying: 'I don't know what you did last night, but the police are waiting outside, knocking on the door.'

I knew I had to get my story right, but on the basis that my head was aching, I was short of sleep and things couldn't possibly get any worse, I ran downstairs ready to confess all. I opened the door, but before I could come clean this very nice policeman handed over the bike I had stolen and said: 'We have recovered your bike, Mr Shaw, and hope all is well.' Smiling inanely, I took delivery of a very old bike with a severely bent front wheel, closed the door and put it at the bottom of the stairs, where it remained unused for the rest of my time in the flat.

I played that afternoon at Bath, we lost 10–9 and, amazingly, I felt great during the match. In fact, it was one of the best games I had played against Bath and I assume the only reason I got away with it was the level of rugby and fitness at that time. Remarkably, I have never really suffered from hangovers and I think that helped my cause that day. The monumental headache from hitting the tarmac was probably worse than any hangover I have ever had and, looking back, I cannot believe I pulled it off and, of course, the guilt of having been a bike thief still lives with me today.

Having managed to avoid being fingered as a thief and a player who turned out for major matches pissed, I was relieved to finish the season with my reputation intact. To celebrate a solid campaign, Bristol arranged a tour to Atlanta, Georgia, and it was the kind of trip that leading junior clubs still go on these days. You would never find a professional outfit playing the easy fixtures we were given or spending so much time interacting with the locals while holding a glass of gassy American beer.

The tone for the tour was set by our daily team meetings, which took place around the swimming pool every morning at 10 or 11. If you didn't turn up, you were fined. One day, I arrived back a little later than everyone else in a newly acquired pair of jeans I had on from the night before with my passport and all my money in the pockets. Maggsy promptly pushed me into the pool, which annoyed me greatly. While I accept I had been late for the meeting, Maggsy had failed to remember you need to show a passport to get served in any American bar. My passport was in the pocket of my jeans, along with around 100 dollar bills. I had no option but to carefully dry out my passport while laying out each of those single dollar bills on a wall in the sun. I promised I would get back at Maggsy while he assured me he would be looking over his shoulder at all times. Later in the tour we went to Savannah and played a game in around 100°F heat, which I would not recommend to anyone. Thankfully, the opposition were pretty poor and because the result had been so one-sided, I suggested to Maggsy that we jogged back to the motel rather than jump on the team bus. I sold him the idea on the basis that it would be the perfect warm-down and he duly fell into my trap.

As we were jogging back, we had to cross a bridge that had a swamp below it. Just as we arrived at the bridge, I nudged Maggsy off and he fell neck deep into the swamp. I jogged on, merrily, saying, 'I told you I would get back at you,' when our local tour liaison officer came sprinting out of the motel screaming: 'Get him out of there, get him out of there.' Apparently, the swamp was full of various different types of snakes and other animals with fangs and teeth. Maggsy completely lost it and chased after me in a terrible rage, but I had enough gas left in the tank to save myself and we managed to patch things up over a beer or ten.

CHAPTER 8

I AM MARTIN JOHNSON'S REPLACEMENT: THE SHAPE OF THINGS TO COME

Although it may appear as if I was training for the England drinking XV, I was desperate to attract the attention of the national selectors and 1994 would see me break through on the summer tour to South Africa when I was flown out to replace Martin Johnson, who had been concussed by a punch from Johan Le Roux, the infamous Transvaal prop who would later be banned for biting New Zealand hooker Sean Fitzpatrick's ear at a ruck. I knew there was a chance of being considered by England thanks to the success of the Bristol pack. We were a formidable unit and gave Mark Tainton plenty of ball to kick away, which constituted, to a great extent, our gameplan. The win that really made people sit up and take notice came at home to Leicester when they turned up with a side containing the famous ABC front row of Graham Rowntree, Richard Cockerill and Darren Garforth and the living legend Dean Richards at number 8. Martin Johnson, now England team manager, was in the second row, while John Wells, the current England forwards coach, was the blind-side flanker.

The match provided me with increased media coverage thanks to the decision by our prop, Paul Gutteridge, to kick Leicester's scrum-half Aadel Kardooni and hurl a bit of abuse at him. Not surprisingly, he was sent off. We now needed a tight-head prop and our captain, Derek Eves, suddenly looked straight at me and delivered the bone-chilling words: 'Come on kid, get up there.' Now, standing 6 ft 9 in., I considered myself to be about a foot too tall for the front row, an area of the scrum that I was more than happy to leave to strange beings such as Ronnie. I said: 'What qualifies me?' Eves said: 'You are the youngest and you are the biggest.' It was an argument based on fact and with the other six forwards backing him up, it was a unanimous decision to throw the kid into the Lions den. So, never having propped before, here I was waiting to bend my rather long back and pack down against England prop Graham Rowntree, the current national scrum coach. As that scrum collided, it hit the turf, which was always likely given that I didn't have a clue what was going on. It would never be allowed today as we are more conscious of the potential for serious injury in the front row, particularly when a novice is involved. As I picked myself up, I was amazed to discover the referee had penalised Rowntree for dropping the scrum. What a result! I had to play in that distorted position for 50 minutes and recorded one of the most enjoyable wins of my career with Bristol. I still take great delight in reminding Wig Rowntree that I forced him to drop the scrum and was never in any trouble against one of the most renowned scrummagers in the game. Any fleeting thoughts that maybe I could be a success in the front row disappeared, however, when I tried to get out of bed the next day. I was in bits and completely knackered. Although Ronnie would never admit it, I believe he has always had grudging respect for me after that win over Leicester. The best he would ever say publicly was 'You're not bad, you're not bad' – no one was allowed to get bigheaded in the Bristol dressing-room.

I am always last man out of the dressing-room for any team and at Bristol over the years this allowed me to pull myself together.

It is assumed that rugby teams charge out onto the pitch baying for blood and in the 'zone'. More often than not, I would take to the pitch smiling at the latest gem from the lads who changed near me. Of course, Ronnie was there, along with Alan Sharpe, and they are two naturally funny lads. Trying to prepare for any Bristol game, I would find myself in absolute hysterics and, to this day, I have always been relaxed before matches. Sharpey is known as a hard boy, but he is a really, really nice guy with a very soft side. He was incredibly helpful in rugby terms, was kind to you off the pitch and his expertise as a fantastic prop helped the entire pack. It would be interesting to see what would happen if Andrew Sheridan, the strongest prop in the current England team, came up against Sharpey, who was also ridiculously strong. Ronnie and Sharpey used to be like brothers: one minute they would be having a great time together laughing and joking and the next, quarrelling and in tears in the back of the team bus complaining about what one had said to the other. You would have to separate them, chat it through individually and, eventually, they would give each other a big hug and keep on saying: 'I'm sorry, I'm sorry, mate.' How touching.

While the front-row boys were getting in touch with their feelings, Kyran Bracken, our outstanding scrum-half, was spending his days dealing with the emotional reaction of various good-looking ladies to his presence on the pitch or in local drinking establishments. Kyran was the darling of the university rugby team and already an England international, but we kept on pointing out that he only looked good on the pitch because the forwards were delivering all that ball on a plate for him. Kyran and I both loved Bristol's seemingly endless opportunities to have a good time, no matter what day of the week. There are cities that switch off from Monday to Wednesday and come alive on Thursday. I think Bristol has been the downfall of most of the guys that played for the rugby club, as the social scene is hard to resist. Alan Davies, who was our coach for a while, had to enforce an alcohol ban and stop everyone going out because we were doing so badly, although we tried to put up a counter argument that didn't really wash.

When you were as popular as Kyran, there was always the danger of being stalked and I was with him one evening when this girl came rushing up and became overexcited to be actually talking to the great man who was at least ten years away from donning a pair of ice skates to win the hearts and votes of a misguided nation. We were in a nightclub in Bristol and this particular girl was very young.

After a short chat Kyran said it had been nice to meet her and we had to go and join some friends. She immediately hit him with the line: 'Well you won't come and talk to me again.' Kyran said: 'Yes, yes, we will.' She said: 'No you won't, you won't. You have got to promise me.' Kyran said: 'I can't, I'm out with the lads.' In a plaintive voice, she asked: 'How can I guarantee you will come back?' He said: 'You can have one of my credit cards.' However, he actually handed over a Next charge card, and one that was out of date. She believed it was the real thing and swallowed the promise hook line and sinker, showing it to all her friends. Kyran forgot all about the girl, but she managed to find out where he lived and turned up outside his house clutching the Next charge card. Personally, I have always thought that charge cards are extremely dangerous in the wrong hands, particularly those belonging to a young woman.

Jack Rowell, who had turned Bath into a formidable team, was in charge of England having succeeded Geoff Cooke, and I knew he had noted my performances for Bristol in the West Country derbies between the clubs. He included me in an England squad for warm-weather training in Lanzarote after Christmas 1993 and I was desperate to make the right impression. However, I considered this to be a ridiculous time of year to hold a training camp. How could you truly celebrate New Year surrounded by dirty rugby kit in a sports-oriented hotel out of season in the Canary Islands? The game was still amateur, yet here we were training alongside Olympic swimmers and athletes from various other sports. I arrived ready to prove I was up for the challenge and found the first day's training involved a decathlon of events including the long jump, which I found extraordinary. I thought it was a very strange way for rugby players to train and this was confirmed when we finished with a penalty shoot-out. Very relevant to test rugby! Looking back on it now, I am still wondering how we got away with preparing for international rugby like that. The first day also included the dreaded 'bleep test', which involved running a set distance there and back before the bleep sounded. I was quite confident, being young and fit, although I never bothered to use a treadmill. I decided my best option was to stick with Dean Richards, the England number 8, and do the test against him, on the basis that Deano was never considered one of the quickest forwards in the sport. I dropped out after giving it my all and, although I was concerned about the end result, I took comfort in the knowledge that I must have lasted longer than Deano. As I recovered, I was amazed to see Deano still running up and down, when I had been conscious that he had been lagging behind me at every turn. I had a strict linesman who made sure I touched the line and when I took time to watch Deano it became clear he was being allowed to turn about two metres short. But, then again, he was a legend, while I was just starting out and desperate to join the international brotherhood.

It was clear on that Under-21 tour to Australia that Lawrence Dallaglio was the main man and a guy who was destined to play test rugby. Kyran Bracken and Matt Dawson were also, by common consent, heading for the top, despite both being scrum-halves. It would turn out to be one of the great head-to-heads, with both proving to be outstanding international players before embarking on post-rugby careers on celebrity talent shows. On reflection, I was totally unaware that Matt showed any potential as either a cook or a ballroom dancer, while Kyran kept his ice-skating potential totally masked.

In 1994, I was picked to play for England B against France at Leicester. At the time, I didn't really recognise too many names in the French side, but one guy did stand out because, after the match, he came into the clubhouse with a beautiful blonde on each arm. We had a pretty handy side and we had a very different attitude from the senior side, who built their gameplan around Rob Andrew's tactical kicking and a big pack. In the B team, our coach Les Cusworth encouraged us to have a laugh and to throw the ball around. As a result, it was a hugely enjoyable experience. We beat Ireland in Ireland, and then France, and I was receiving some very welcome plaudits playing in the second row alongside Leicester's Matt Poole. Even though I was part of a successful B team, I knew my test chances revolved around the success of the Bristol team and our outstanding pack. Jack Rowell, the England manager, had said some very nice things about the Bristol forwards, and about me in particular, and with a two-test summer tour of South Africa looming, I was hoping to be included. As it turned out, my name was put on the standby list, not a bad achievement for a 19 year old.

I finished the season and went back to Surrey planning on enjoying myself over the summer and, to be honest, I never really thought about being on standby. I never anticipated being called up and it was a real shock when the telephone call came. I was in the garden kicking a ball around – not a rugby ball but a football – and had just recovered from a weekend of boozing with my old mates from school. I ran into the hallway and picked the telephone up to find an RFU official on the other end enquiring: 'How are you doing, have you kept yourself fit?' My answer was: 'I've played a couple of games of tennis, but I feel all right.' Amazingly, this did not elicit a rebuke or the phone being slammed down and instead, I was ordered to: 'Pack your bags, you are on the next flight out to South Africa.' That was it. Suddenly, my afternoon of messing around became a mad dash, trying to find my kit. I had only a few hours to get my boots, passport and stuff together and head to the airport.

In a flash there I was sitting on a 747 heading to Johannesburg to replace Martin Johnson – it seemed very surreal. Before boarding the plane I had caught the television news and discovered Johnno was coming home because he had been punched out of the tour by John Le Roux, the Transvaal prop. The report said his replacement was not known – but I knew his identity! The RFU arrangements did not stretch to a business-class seat when I picked up my ticket at check-in, but when staff saw my height, an emergency aisle seat was handed over. Sitting in my seat with a silly grin on my face, all sorts of thoughts were going through my head like: will the press be there at the airport (they weren't) and what am I going to do about kit? I was training in that new kit within hours of landing, because England had a key match against South Africa A in Kimberley and I was in the second row. I had an idea that it would be a memorable welcome to rugby in South Africa and this was confirmed at the first line out when Springbok lock Kobus Wiese upended me and I landed on my neck. I finished under a pile of writhing bodies and when a fight kicked off there was absolutely nothing I could contribute. I could barely move, let alone swing an arm.

It really was amazing how you could walk around the country wearing an England tracksuit and be greeted warmly by everyone, yet once you stepped onto the pitch the locals were intent on maiming you in any possible way. The referee just turned a blind eye to the punching, tripping and open warfare being visited upon the England players. You would be running across the pitch and suddenly get punched and tripped up from behind and, at that stage, I had never experienced anything like it on the pitch. I was just running on adrenalin, which was probably a good thing given that my fitness level was based solely on those two games of tennis. Despite having been in the country for barely two days the altitude wasn't a problem and I seemed to have a pretty good game amid the carnage. There was humour even in that match thanks to an impromptu call to arms issued by Steve Ojomoh, our Nigerian-born back-row forward, who had even more reason to believe the locals wanted his blood. We were gathered together behind our posts while waiting for a conversion and Steve was banging on about not letting these Afrikaaners get the better of us etc. . . .

and it was going really well until a very ripe orange hit him smack between the eyes. Evidently, we were too close to the crowd and Steve had become the victim of a drive-by fruiting. Still, it gave us a laugh in a gallows-humour sort of way. After the match, sitting in the dressing-room, I felt pretty good and was glad to have come through my first senior England game without my head being taken off. It was a violent initiation but I, wrongly, assumed things could only get better. Then came the Battle of Boet Erasmus.

Jack Rowell was always OK with me, but I was aware other players found him strange. However, no matter what you thought of his coaching and management, there was no avoiding the fact he was very quick-witted. He was far too clever for Louis Luyt, the South African RFU president, who viewed the sport in that country in 1994 as his personal fiefdom . . . and boy did he like the sound of his own heavily accented voice. After we won the first test against the Springboks 32–15 in Pretoria thanks to a 'full house' from Rob Andrew – a try, conversion, penalty and drop goal – we had to listen to the post-match speeches. This involved Jack and Luyt sharing the same podium and it became a very funny double act in which the South African RFU president was the straight man totally unaware of the jokes being made at his expense by Jack. The entire England party was chuckling away, thinking how Jack was making him look so stupid. I thought Jack was a bit weird at times but I liked him, which is not surprising, as he liked me.

There was a huge party after that first test victory and it was right to celebrate a rare English success on South African soil and, even though there was a midweek game against Eastern Province and the second test in Cape Town the following weekend, we made sure it was a memorable night in Pretoria. The main circus masters during the evening were Martin Bayfield and Dean Richards, two highly trained police officers! What sticks with me now – all these years later – is just how quickly I linked up with the London Wasps players on the tour, guys like Lawrence, Dean Ryan, Steve Bates and Damian Hopley. I seemed to spend a lot of time drinking with these guys, who were also part of the midweek side, although the significance of this choice of mates would not become obvious for a couple of years.

Arriving in Port Elizabeth, we were warned that the locals were coached by Grizz Wylie, the former All Black who had a reputation for 'not taking prisoners' when he was playing and who seemed to have created a team in his own image. The stadium in Port Elizabeth is strange because at the top of a big open terrace is an old railway carriage, while another section was made famous on the 1974 Lions tour as the area where the non-whites were allowed to watch behind wire fences. The Lions received fantastic support from the non-whites that day and it was still the part of the ground non-white fans used when we turned up all those years later. I do remember a strange atmosphere at the stadium before we kicked off. It was a night game and the floodlights seemed very, very poor. It meant that as you ran across the pitch, it was hard to make out who was who, and that only added to the danger. You would get slotted in the eye from behind and not know how it happened. You looked around to spot the person who did it, but there was just a dark mass of bodies. In the first few minutes you thought: 'Christ, this is going to be fairly ugly.'

As had happened in the South Africa A game, the referee just turned his back on what was occurring and let the Eastern Province players run the match. The violence just got worse and worse and while there were a couple of guys on our side who were known for being pretty forceful characters in the English game, it didn't mean anything to the opposition. Our cause was not helped when Dean Ryan, one of the hard men in our team, broke his thumb in the first minute. It left me wondering: 'Christ, if he's going off with that, what is going to happen to me by the end of the game?' I had no option but to gloss over what was happening all around me and try and help win the game. Graham Dawe, the Bath hooker, took a fearful amount of hammer, but refused to come off despite being kicked all over the place. He knew he had to protect Brian Moore, the test hooker, who was pacing the touchline desperate to come on and take revenge on the locals. Dawesy and Brian didn't get on at all, but there was a discernible change in their relationship after this match because Brian realised what Dawsey had taken to save him from punishment just days before the second test. When some of the young guys like Lawrence were twatted, it was Dawsey who would come along and get retribution on the local hit man. I, on the other hand, was concentrating on self-preservation. I had never played in a match like it, and haven't since, and along with every other England player, was shooed mercilessly whenever I hit the deck. You could see where the studs had torn the jersey on people's backs and left red streaks down the skin. The referee, a South African, wasn't interested in anyone alerting him to the fact that they were being gouged or kicked and it was as if he were condoning the violence. It was that bad. I was on the floor at one point being kneed and then whoever it was just left their knee on my head and put their entire bodyweight on my head. That's incredibly dangerous and frightening, because you are pinned to the ground feeling the intense pain of an opponent's knee pushing into your skull. It is someone's life you are talking about and that kind of incident has never had a place in rugby and never will. While I didn't take a backward step in the match, I knew the priority was to somehow get back into the dressing-room without sustaining a serious injury.

Then, we had Tim Rodber sent off. He had come onto the pitch to replace Ryan and was dismissed for throwing around 20 punches into an opponent who fully deserved everything he got. Unfortunately for Tim, it didn't happen in one of the many mass fights but to one side with everyone watching and the referee believed he had no option but to send them both off. A desperate situation had suddenly become even worse and what happened next would have dramatic consequences for Eastern Province rugby. Jon Callard, the Bath full-back, was raked on the head so badly he needed 25 stitches to close the awful gash to his forehead. He came frighteningly close to having a serious eye injury and, quite rightly, the management took JC to the after-match press conference to show off the damage caused by opposition boots. When we came off the pitch it was very, very dark and subdued and I can't remember anyone shouting three cheers for the opposition. The dressing-room was like a casualty clearing station with players looking at one another's war wounds and the more seriously injured being treated by the medical staff. The test players, who had been watching from the stands, came into the dressing-room to congratulate us for getting through that nightmare and there was a real bond formed that night between those who had stuck at it despite unbelievable provocation.

The Battle of Boet Erasmus created a very bad atmosphere going into the Cape Town test, although we were buoyed when Tim avoided a ban for his sending-off after Jack had gone into the disciplinary hearing and told them exactly what he thought about Eastern Province, Grizz Wylie and the appalling standard of refereeing. It was made clear to the locals that something unacceptable had taken place at Boet Erasmus and they had better not compound their problems by handing Tim a ban. There was a doubt over Martin Bayfield for the second test and I assumed that Matt Poole, who had been on the England tour to Argentina in 1990 and who had more first-class experience than me, would be the man on standby. However, in a team meeting after we arrived in Cape Town, Jack read out my name and I thought: 'Oh Christ.' It was quite difficult to stop smiling and to get on with training because I was so excited. I wanted to run with every ball and hit every tackle pad. Dewi Morris, the England scrum-half, congratulated me, but it proved to be premature because Martin recovered. Tim went down with food poisoning and his loss hit everyone because he had played so well in the first test. I think he was a player the South Africans feared and his omission was a big plus for them and a big loss for us.

Not being required for my test debut, I was free to join the dirt-trackers – the non-test players – on a big night out in the Waterfront area of Cape Town. We tried to convince the injured Dean Richards to join us, but he was a forlorn sight and was very upset about missing the chance to beat the Springboks for the second time. Lawrence, Hoppers and I threw ourselves into the party at the Sportsbar and everything we wanted was free, including trays of shots. As a student, I was uniquely qualified to make use of this free bar and got very excited. I have this recollection, halfway through the night and very blurry eyed, of seeing what looked like an outline of Deano walking through the doors. A huge cheer from the rest of the boys confirmed the great man had arrived. Together with Deano, I took on two of the bar's employees at two-on-two basketball, making use of the hoop that had been installed in an area of the bar. There wasn't a lot of skill involved in our tactical plan and, basically, Deano charged through one of them, passed it to me and I, to wild cheers, just popped it in the basket. Thankfully, I did take a brief enough rest on the drinking front before meeting President Nelson Mandela prior to the second test.

One of the fascinating aspects of the tour for me was the reaction of locals to the black players in our team, like Victor Ubogu, Paul Hull, Steve Ojomoh and Adedayo Adebayo. Now, we are talking about four guys who love a good time and they were thoroughly enjoying the whole experience in South Africa and the local ladies were certainly enjoying making their acquaintance. They were strutting into nightclubs, which, even at that stage in the post-apartheid era, black South Africans didn't dare enter. The local whites were not enjoying it at all and I spent most of my time worrying about whether it was going to kick off in the nightclubs as much as on the pitches. There was one incident in Pretoria at a nightclub where two distinctly Afrikaans guys with big orange beards were sitting at the bar having a drink. Suddenly, Adedayo appeared, slapped them on the back and said: 'Hi, what are you having to drink?' They turned to him and I thought: 'Oh, shit, it's all going to kick off now,' but nothing happened and we all enjoyed a pleasant drink. It was a regular occurrence throughout the tour and somehow we always found a way of keeping the locals happy. During the tour, we made a number of trips to townships to do charity work and help with rugby training. For one session, Jason Leonard, our prop, decided to fit in with the local kids we were coaching by taking off his trainers and going barefooted. He was very enthusiastic about this decision and kept on shouting: 'Come on, lads, we've got to muck in, when in Rome . . .' Jason, much to the delight of the locals, was barefoot on a clay pitch without any grass doing his coaching session. When he came back to get his trainers they had gone; one of these kids had run off with them, leaving him to yell 'Thieving bastards' to no one in particular. The Cape Town test was lost 27–9 and we drew the series, although it was obvious that our chances of taking it 2–0 had been fundamentally undermined by that problematic build-up to the second test. However, we had put a marker down just 12 months before South Africa hosted the Rugby World Cup and had proved we could mount another formidable challenge, following on from our appearance in the 1991 final.

I brought a couple of crates of wine back from Stellenbosch and celebrated my return from the tour with a barbecue at the student house I was sharing in Bristol. It was a bad move because after lugging the wine all the way back from South Africa, those bloody students downed the lot in barely two hours. After worrying that stepping up to England senior level would mean a fundamental change in my rugby lifestyle, I had discovered on tour that the players still had a great time and that you could have a boozy night out with some pretty famous guys. In the early stages of my career at Bristol, both Will Carling and Brian Moore found out I had once donned the Harlequin shirt and made numerous attempts to try and lure me back, but they failed. I was a Bristol boy and where else could I enjoy such a lively off-the-pitch lifestyle?

Jack Rowell was to assume total control of the England team following that tour when Dick Best, the head coach, was relieved of his duties. Dick had a reputation for giving players a 'beasting' and I got mine on that South African tour. I knew Dick from the London Division squad days and, after being the subject of horrendous abuse for everything I did in one particular training session, I trooped back into the dressing-room and asked one of the lads: 'What was all that about?' Someone turned round to me and said: 'It's just because he likes you.'

Amid the post-tour wine-devouring celebration, one thing was clear in my mind: I was within sight of a first England cap. Prior to this period, I had always felt it would take me another couple of years to break through and now I was letting very different thoughts enter my head. Being young, I worked out that if I could get that first cap I had a chance of being around for ten years and had a chance of becoming the most capped second row of all time. The thought process went along the lines of: 'I've got to get that first cap and once I get that, I will be away.' I remember holding on to that belief as I started the pre-season work and I was determined to do a hell of a lot more fitness work than I'd done in previous years. That included going up and down the steps of the main stand at Bristol and I started getting into weights more, something I'd never felt inclined to do before because I was blessed with a natural strength. It was also my sandwich year and I had to prepare for what was going to be a year in industry. Because I was doing International Business Studies in Spanish, I was supposed to go away to a Spanish-speaking country and work there. Originally, the plan was to go to Argentina and spend a year playing rugby in the country while working for an Argentinian firm, but that had all changed because I was now in the England squad. I didn't want to give up the opportunity of winning a first cap and felt it was my time and there was no point being out of the shop window playing rugby in South America. I pleaded with the university to alter things and they were willing for me to stay in the UK, but my degree would no longer be classified as International Business Studies in Spanish. It was changed to 'and Spanish' and I was happy to agree to that.

I used one of the contacts I had made on that England tour to South Africa and linked up with Courage, the brewers, who were now sponsoring English rugby. Under that deal, every member of the England squad received ten cases of any of their products once a month. I had moved in with a couple of mates of mine who were not university guys. They had come to Bristol from Cranleigh and were ecstatic to discover their housemate received a delivery of ten crates of lager, bitter or Guinness at the flat each month. As a perk of my sandwich-year job with Courage, I was given the option of buying an extra five or six crates for next to nothing. We had 15 crates of beer coming in every month. At this point, it was assumed that I would be going to the 1995 Rugby World Cup in South Africa as a member of the England squad and the Chief Executive of Courage, Bristol, was a big rugby fan and he just wanted me to be involved with the company and use the job as a way of pushing the brand during the World Cup. I was playing in the middle of the lineout for Bristol, which meant I offered England the versatility of jumping there or at the front and this increased my worth in terms of World Cup selection. I could see myself playing alongside Martin Johnson and I wasn't too worried about the starting position, I just wanted to get my first cap.

I knew I had a pretty good chance of going and it was just a matter of keeping my form at Bristol, who were playing pretty well at the time. I put myself in the World Cup selection mix, playing for England A and just when it appeared I was going to experience the biggest tournament in the sport I was struck down by serious injury and it cost me a place in the 1995 World Cup squad. The whole idea behind Courage employing me was to maximise the benefits of having a member of the England squad in South Africa on their books to reflect well on the brand. I obviously missed the World Cup, which came as a massive blow, not only because I desperately wanted to be out there playing in the World Cup and being a part of the World Cup, but also because I spent the rest of that year promoting the tournament from an office in Bristol. It used to pain me every time I looked at the posters and TV campaign that was promoting Courage and here I was, with a leg in a cast instead of running out onto the pitch. After the operation I was in a cast for two months.

SIMON SHAW

Despite being a rookie in terms of international exposure, I was invited to play for the Barbarians and it brought me into contact with Kenny Logan, the Scotland wing, who was to become a close friend after he moved south and joined Wasps. At this stage, I had no idea who he was, but was intrigued by the attention he was getting in the Baabaas dressing-room before we played a special game against his club Stirling County. Gavin Hastings was the Baabaas captain and when we gathered around for a rare team talk – this was the Barbarians after all – he announced that a key part of the tactics for the day would be silencing Kenny, the local star on the wing. Hastings' call to action went along the lines of: 'Right, this is the gameplan. If anyone can get a shot on Kenny Logan I'll buy them drinks all night.' This was mildly interesting, well, the idea of a Scotsman buying me drinks all night was certainly unusual, and I was conscious during the early stages of the match that Kenny kept on chatting away to his own players and the opposition. He really knew how to make a racket. Stirling had a penalty move that was pretty traditional at any level of rugby, but they obviously felt it was in keeping with the spirit of a Baabaas game, even though it was hardly original. It involved the front row standing with their backs to the opposition and the scrum-half would tap the ball and give it to this human shield while runners came from all different directions in an attempt to totally confuse would-be tacklers. Knowing how the move worked, I took the decision to wipe out the three guys acting as a shield and, after causing mayhem, discovered that the ball had found its way to Kenny, who flew off and scored under the posts. I was very irritated by this and when they did the same move again, I thought there was absolutely no way they would pass to Kenny. Unfortunately for Kenny they did and I slotted him, knocking the lad out with, I hasten to add, a totally legitimate tackle. As a result, I got great applause from Gavin and all my team-mates, who took great delight in patting me on the back as they thought I had done a fantastic thing. Then, the tackle got a mention in a speech by Princess Anne made after the match – she is patron of the Scottish RFU – and she congratulated me for shutting Kenny up for five minutes. I had a few beers with Kenny afterwards and there were no hard feelings and it can't have done him any harm as he went on to play 70 tests for Scotland, got to marry Gabby Yorath and appeared on *Strictly Come Dancing*. Maybe I knocked some much-needed sense into him!

As a result of my contribution to the Kenny Logan Appreciation Society, I was invited to play for the Baabaas in their prestigious Dublin match to mark the end of South Africa's 1994 tour of Europe. I was the traditional non-international picked by the most famous club team in the world and found myself packing down with All Blacks legend Ian Jones, who was to later join us at Wasps. It was a pretty big deal for me and I was amazed to get this unique opportunity to experience rugby at this level. Obviously, there had been talk about my potential, but I hadn't thought it would come this early, in terms of an international-class game, and my excitement level was at an all-time high. In my own mind, the way the Baabaas had dealt with the Stirling match was going to be totally different from taking on a Springbok side that was extremely powerful. How wrong I was. I had already played against some of the South Africans on the England tour and been whacked by quite a few of them and so I was ready for similar treatment as the new kid on the international block, even though this was a special fixture. Once, again, the Baabaas' way of preparing for matches constituted a couple of runabouts, a bit of touch rugby, a few beers and a chance to chat about life with some of the biggest names in the game. What a breeze. I thought we were going to get absolutely thrashed, but as is the Baabaas' way, it somehow works out because of the quality of the team's players.

Prior to the match we went on a tour of the Guinness factory in Dublin and drank a fair bit of the black stuff. I was pretty nervous as the kick-off approached and with about five minutes to go, I found myself standing in the Lansdowne Road tunnel with the rest of the team. Then a thought struck me. We didn't have any lineout calls! I turned to Ian Jones and said: 'I'm fairly new to all this, but I'm sure that we should have some lineout calls – after all, we are playing the Springboks.' My rationale was that shouting my name or Ian's was going to be a bit of a giveaway, although I had played with Ronnie in matches where he had just yelled 'Oi Shawsy' and thrown the ball at me. After a quick chat, we decided to go back into the Baabaas' dressing-room and come up with a very quick system to give us a sporting chance of actually winning some ball against one of the best teams in the world. I came up with the idea of using Thames Rowing Club with anything involving the Thames letters going to the front, Rowing to the middle and Club to the back. I looked around and found All Black legend Ian Jones and the Irish front-row pair of Keith Wood and Nick Popplewell all nodding in agreement with this kid. Woody said: 'Right, that is what we do.' So we trooped back out there again to play the Springboks armed with Shaw's patented lineout calling system. The match was amazingly quick and we managed to defeat the Springboks 23–15. One of the strongest memories I have of that match is the half-time break. I walked into the toilet area to find the front row all having a cigarette.

There were guys in the team who were just starting out on their test careers or guys like Australia's Pat Howard, who was on a backpacking trip around Europe when he was called up. He had no idea he was going to be playing in that game and had been drafted in when someone had mentioned to the selectors that this pretty useful Aussie centre was knocking about. The after-match function was just a blur, a continuation of what happened in the Guinness brewery and we were the toast of Dublin. I just followed the rest of the lads around the city until the early hours. I knew I would have to perform a song on the bus afterwards and was quite worried because I didn't actually know all the words to any. I ended up singing 'Waltzing Matilda' with Pat Howard and, although it was a bit of a cock-up because neither of us knew the verses, we somehow muddled through. Come to think of it, why didn't Aussie Pat know all the words?

I AM MARTIN JOHNSON'S REPLACEMENT . . .

For me, playing in what was effectively a test match had turned out to be merely an extension of my normal rugby life at Cranleigh and Bristol. You did a bit of training, played the match, had a great session at the bar and then came home! It just seemed like the best job in the world and I was having the time of my life. The England selectors had noted my involvement in the Baabaas game and had picked me for the England A game against Italy at Gloucester, which put me right in the frame for a place in the England squad for the 1995 World Cup in South Africa. I went into the match knowing I was already in the pre-Cup squad and was determined to make an impression. That is why I found myself running in support of Wasps centre Nick Greenstock, who kept on delaying the pass, despite my increasingly exasperated demands for him to hand the bloody thing over. He finally agreed to do that and I received the ball along with three Italian defenders and I got slaughtered from all angles with one of them putting my right knee out.

I knew immediately the ligaments had gone as there was a snapping sound. I stood up and then immediately collapsed because my leg just folded in. In that moment all kinds of thoughts went through my mind: could I crawl over and kill Greenstock? How was I going to play in the World Cup? The England medical staff rushed on and I was immediately taken to the medical room and it was patently obvious that I was going to need surgery to sort out the ligament damage. I needed an operation to pin the ligament back onto the bone to help the healing process, but was also put in a full leg cast. Looking back, I cannot understand why this was done and it contributed to a very frustrating two months walking around with this enormous weight of plaster on my right leg. If that had happened today, my knee would have been put in a brace to ensure it could move during the recovery period, but my leg spent eight weeks totally immobile which is why, when the cast was removed, I possessed an old man's leg: all grey and with a considerable amount of muscle wastage.

The cast went from my toes to just under my right buttock. I had no idea it would be such a huge cast and only discovered the full extent of my situation when I came round following the operation. I remember lying there with a ridiculously heavy leg that I couldn't lift. Whenever I come out of anaesthetic the first thing I need to do always is go to the loo. I looked around and there was a shiny bedpan next to me and I thought there is no way I am doing number twos in that and having some pretty nurse come in and take it away; it is not going to happen. I lifted my leg with the cast off the bed, and it was like a scene out of *Misery*, where he is in so much pain but he has got to get out of the house. The pain was incredible, but I needed to get to the toilet. I was sweating buckets, in agony and crying, because all the blood flow went straight down to my foot, which immediately started throbbing – so badly, in fact, I thought it was going to burst. I found myself face down on the floor, pulling my body and that bloody cast along using the carpet for grip – just to get to the toilet. I got into the toilet but because the leg cast came under my buttock there was no physical way of either sitting down or sitting upright. I managed to lift my leg up onto a window-sill – all this so as I didn't have to do a number two in a bedpan – which meant my leg was 45 degrees up in the air with this incredibly heavy cast and leaning on a window sill while I was sitting on the toilet. At that point the telephone rang and I guessed it was my mother calling to see how I was. It rang and rang and then stopped, which was a relief. I couldn't shut the door once I had dragged myself in, but I wasn't worried about that because no visitors were expected. Then the telephone rang and rang again and at this point, the door to my room burst open. Patently, all the nurses on the ward had been alerted that Mr Shaw wasn't answering his phone and, therefore, something terrible must have happened. It had. There I was with my leg in a cast, at 45 degrees in the air and stuck on a window sill with all my crown jewels on display to the world. It was a horrendous experience and one that still gives me shivers today. The nurses all had a great giggle and all I could think was: 'Why didn't I just have a shit in the bedpan?'

I was barely 21 and the World Cup was a constant reminder of where I could have been and the tournament was a massive incentive to get back into training. During the World Cup, I was watching Richard West play against Western Samoa and found myself thinking: 'How the hell is he playing for England when I should be there?' Then he played in the third-and-fourth playoff match against France and those thoughts kept entering my head again and it was so hard to take. I knew I could have been in the squad and that experiencing a World Cup would have been so very special. The pain was made even worse by the job I had with Courage, which involved me going around the South-West during the tournament promoting both our product and our link with the England team. I was a ridiculous sight, turning up to talk about being a member of the England squad with a huge cast on my right leg.

The cumulative effect of promoting a beer company was there for all my mates to see, because I was just getting bigger and bigger and fatter and fatter. I was still having numerous crates of beer sent to my home and the Bristol club had a guy called 'Tony the pie man', an absolute legend in Bristol rugby. He would join us on the team bus for matches and tell dreadful jokes. Tony owned all the pie stalls around the Bristol Rugby Club and Bristol City Football Club and he would always bring a crate of his pies on the team bus for those away games. On the way home from matches the bus would be full of beer and pies, which kept everyone happy, particularly this monetarily challenged student. Tony knew I was living with a couple of my mates from Cranleigh and would let me take whatever pies were left in the crate back home. For some bizarre reason, he also brought clotted cream on the bus as this was another of his sidelines and allowed me to take the unfinished huge pots of this back as well. On other occasions he would produce gammon steaks and those also formed part of my well-balanced diet as I continued my rehabilitation from the serious knee-ligament injury. The menu read: beer, pies, clotted cream and gammon, which meant all the key food groups were represented and those that I had missed were catered for by a local butcher in Bristol who used to supply me with prime steak.

I couldn't eat or drink any more and I was getting ridiculously overweight, reaching a peak at 22 st. That meant I was 2 st. overweight, a complete disaster. Then, having told everyone for years that rugby was going to turn professional it happened when I was in the worst shape of my career. Great! My time with Courage came to a natural end, which also enabled me to get out of a rather torrid relationship with one of the manageresses, and it was time for me to get my life back on track and to shed that unwanted weight and embrace professional rugby. This momentous move in September 1995 ensured that my studies would, once again, be firmly pushed to one side in favour of rugby.

The rehabilitation period was tough and I went to a number of early season Bristol games and found it really difficult to deal with the constant questions about when I would be fit. I knew the fans were being kind but, after so long out, I just wanted to get on with my career because I felt I was being left behind. I became more and more depressed and frustrated. Because of my rehab work, I didn't come across many of my team-mates, which only added to the feelings of isolation but there was a younger group of guys at that stage who included Mark Denney, Arwel Thomas and Garath Archer. They became more of a social network outlet because they enjoyed a good time and we became really close which helped.

Having shed that extra weight, I really put my heart into the training work I knew would be needed and I was able to start the following season with Bristol – the first one with the game fully professional, although the Rugby Football Union, in their wisdom, operated a 12-month moratorium in the belief that this professional thingy would go away. It didn't and the clubs signed up all the top players while the RFU waited to see what happened. It was a very strange time for everyone involved in English rugby, but I just kept my head down and tried to make up any lost ground caused by my injury. However, just as my life appeared to be back on track, I played in a match that would threaten my entire career.

Bristol had arranged a midweek match under lights against Northern Transvaal and practically everything seemed to go wrong that night. I remember the floodlights going out, the generator was put on and then clapped out, the lights came back on and eventually we were able to play. It had been raining heavily all day and the pitch was incredibly boggy and all I remember is taking the ball into contact, getting tackled, rolling a few times and then when I went to present the ball, found myself clinging onto it madly. I wasn't aware of any pain or anything wrong, but had the feeling something didn't feel right. I wasn't screaming or writhing around, just clinging hold of this ball and Kyran, who was playing scrum-half, suddenly came into view yelling for me to release the ball. He actually started tapping away at my hands with his feet because I wouldn't release the ball. Then I suddenly came round; I was in a zombie-like state, saw Kyran mouthing at me to release the ball and so I let go and just lay there still. Everyone else got up and ran off and so I turned round, looked at my leg and I couldn't see my foot. I then lifted my calf and I could see my foot dangling underneath where my heel would have been, with my sock stretched. It was almost like my foot had completely fallen off and was just being held on by my sock. At this point I yelled 'ahhh,' and physios and medics came streaming onto the pitch from all angles. Everything fell silent and there were 'oos' and 'ahhs' from the crowd while a couple of people fainted. Shortly after that the stretcher came on carried by St John's Ambulance volunteers and it appeared to be a relic from the First World War. You can't beat a good canvas stretcher. At this stage I wasn't given oxygen and all that happened was the throng of people around me decided I had to be carried off the pitch. The St John's Ambulance guys called for two or three other people from the crowd to help carry this huge weight and one of them let the handle slip. I fell off the stretcher. It meant I had to go through it all again in absolute agony. I then got shuffled to where the ambulance was waiting behind the old stand and they spent about five or six minutes discussing how they were going to fit me in the ambulance. By this time, I had started to lose the plot and had been given oxygen, but it wasn't doing anything for me, so I shouted some obscenities including a very helpful plea to 'get me in the fucking ambulance'. But they still dithered about. They tried me head first, lying down and virtually shut the door on the foot that was hanging off. Then they said: 'Oh no, that's not going to work' and decided to turn me around. I said: 'Well, I'm still going to be the same fucking height.' I was ready to blow my top, but held things together under great duress and came up with the suggestion: 'Why don't I just sit up?' All this, of course, came in the midst of me screaming and writhing around. I sat up and at this point they gave me morphine. They shut the ambulance doors saying: 'Don't worry, you'll be all right in a minute. We'll get you to hospital and everything will be all right.' They then reversed into a concrete bollard. I think I actually laughed because I had got beyond the point where I could produce any more anger. I just laughed out loud and thought this is just a debacle.

Eventually I got to Southmead Hospital and they carried me into the emergency ward. Nobody had taped my foot, so it was still hanging off and various doctors had turned up and couldn't understand why this hadn't happened. They were shouting at each other: 'Why hasn't this been relocated?' By this stage it was huge – the size of an elephant's hoof. Then someone really upset me by claiming the foot was so enlarged it was going to be impossible to relocate. The medical staff eventually decided they were going to have to relocate the ankle, and so they injected me with more morphine and twisted it round to the proper position. I'm not sure how to describe the action, but it involved my ankle being rammed back in by a doctor using his shoulder. I almost shot through the roof and passed out with the pain, even after having been given loads of morphine. I then got taken in for x-rays to check that there wasn't anything else. Obviously, I had broken my ankle as well and, when the x-rays came out, they said: 'We are terribly sorry, Mr Shaw, we are going to have to dislocate your ankle again.' I couldn't fathom it out but what had happened was that my foot had actually gone round twice: it had gone through a total of 720 degrees and so when they relocated it, all the ligaments and tendons were still twisted. I had to go through the whole process again. Luckily, because it was so swollen, the ankle was reasonably easy to dislocate again. I spent that entire evening listening to old-age pensioners pressing their alarm signals because they had peed the bed, while I raged against the injustice of the whole thing. While I never thought my career might be over, I was screaming things like: 'Why has this happened to me? Why did I deserve this?'

The timing was bollocks and the only way I could rationalise things was to hold on to the thought that I was still young and could come back from this awful blow. The surgeons had put a metal plate with eight screws into my ankle – it is still in there today. The plate and screws were supposed to come out about six months afterwards, but I was back playing well again and really didn't want to risk losing any more game time. The last thing I needed was to go through another few months of rehabilitation treatment.

During that period in hospital, immediately after the operation to insert the plate and screws, I woke up in bed to find I had visitors. I had been woken by yet another alarm going off, initiated by one of the elderly patients who, once again, had wet the bed. As I focused on Garath Archer, who was saying things to me like, 'Hope you get well soon' and 'You'll be back before you know it' and then stood up and started walking away. To be honest, I don't recall much of my time spent in the ward due to the need for painkillers. All the while I was worried that I might well have a career-threatening injury.

If I had played in any other position, one that required a huge amount of mobility and yardage, I don't think I would have been able to come back from the injury so quickly. I wanted to get back out onto the pitch so desperately that I just worked myself to a standstill. Being that crossover period between amateur and professional rugby, there wasn't any scientifically based rehab work to follow and I received virtually no aftercare. Bristol's one and only physiotherapist was my only help. One of the reasons Danny Cipriani came back so early from the broken and dislocated ankle he suffered in May 2008 was down to the fantastic medical back-up and physio help he received at Wasps. Unfortunately for those of us playing more than a decade earlier, such treatment was too hit-and-miss; chances of a full recovery from such a serious injury were dependent on the determination of the individual player. Having got myself back into shape to play, I decided to ensure my ankle was given the best chance of surviving contact with the addition of what amounted to a small cast. For every training session and match, I would strap up the ankle, put on a leather sock with laces and add more strapping so that the whole contraption was so tight the ankle could not move. I ran on my right leg and my left leg was almost like a stump, feeling more like a false leg. Despite this obvious impediment, I was able to play first-team rugby again the following season. Having suffered two serious leg injuries in the same year, there were experts who questioned my ability to play again, although I had no doubts. At one stage a surgeon told me, 'You'll be lucky to walk correctly again' – in terms of not walking with a limp – and others were saying, 'You might walk again, but you won't be able to run.' Such words seemed ridiculous to me and I vowed to prove them all wrong.

My parents were living in Barcelona at the time and when my mum saw my ankle injury on national television she was absolutely horrified. They used to come back here every other month to watch a game and stayed with my sister, who was still living in the house at Hindhead. My relationship with my sister had changed since we started going to different schools and it wasn't until later that we became good friends again. I have to say that I got a bit above myself for a period when I was getting selected for the Baabaas etc. . . . I didn't know it at the time but, looking back, I must have been a bit of a pain. I remember my 21st birthday when my parents had organised a party back at the house, had come over from Spain and ensured a lot of my friends from Godalming College and Cranleigh were there. I had brought a few mates from Bristol and while I didn't sense it at the time, I guess I was a bit aloof and spent more time with the Bristol guys and less time with my genuine mates. They are the guys I still speak to and keep in touch with now. My parents and my sister gave me a kick up the arse after the party and, while at the time I was in denial saying things like, 'I don't know what you are talking about,' I can now see they were right when they were saying I wasn't the same person. Their words hit home and I thank them for being so honest. I needed to get my priorities right.

One of the reasons I lost perspective was due to the way Bristol treated their players who achieved success at international level. If you played for England, or had a higher rugby profile than playing for Bristol RFC, it was a big deal. You were a big fish in a small pond. It's something you don't get in London, where football is king. In Bristol, at that time, you got recognised everywhere you went, received free drinks in pubs and clubs and it seemed as though people wanted to be associated with you. Clearly, I didn't hold back and embraced all of this attention and that is what my sister recognised. She is 18 months older than me and, at that time, despite the fact we had grown apart, I still respected her. Getting stick from her probably meant more to me and it had a greater impact than if it had come from my father, because he has always been telling me I'm too big for my boots.

CHAPTER 9

RICHMOND MAKE ME A £250,000 JOB OFFER

I was fully aware of what was being offered at the Hilton Hotel at Heathrow in late 1995 as around 50 English players packed into a room to hear details of a proposed professional circus that would change the face of rugby. It was backed by Australian entrepreneur Kerry Packer and was grandly titled the 'World Rugby Corporation'. Together with Ronnie – he was driving, or rather aiming, his car up the M4 – we had gathered to hear the details of a deal that had already convinced hundreds of international players to sign up.

All the best players in the world had joined for one very basic reason: they were offering us lots and lots of cash. The amount on offer was based on your international standing at the time. If you had over 50 caps, you would be in the £250,000-a-year category; just capped was worth £200,000; and if you were in the international set-up it was £150,000. I was in the £150,000 group and you can imagine the rush to sign up at the end of the presentation. We were all grabbing papers and signing them because, whether the circus happened or not, you were still guaranteed £30,000. The idea wasn't that we were going to break away completely, it was designed, so we were told, to force the Rugby Football Union's hand and make them confront the new professional era. The organisers didn't need to ask for a show of hands, the cacophony of 'hoorays' and 'yippees' showed that everybody was in favour of selling their rugby wares to the new game in town.

When I walked out of the room with Ronnie, it was all extremely exciting. There was a rumour the press had got hold of the story and were waiting outside for us. It was a case of getting out, sprinting to the car and avoiding speaking to anyone. As a result, we dashed to the cars giggling our heads off and pretending that it was some really big deal. We then waited for a cheque to arrive to see if it was all real. Bristol were aware of what was happening at the time because Paul Hull, Ronnie and myself were at the meeting and, to be honest, it wasn't a very well-kept secret. I guess that was designed to force the hands of the ruling Unions.

The cheque for £30,000 duly arrived – Happy Days – and we all assumed it was happening. Everyone banked the cheques and got the money straight away, which proved it was definitely a runner. However, the competition that was supposed to change the rugby world didn't get off the ground because the South Africans and New Zealanders didn't go through with it. The best part of the deal was that no one asked for the money back and a certain 22 year old wasn't about to ring up the now-failed organisation and offer to hand it over. If someone is kind enough to pay me £30,000 for signing a piece of paper in a room at the Hilton Hotel at Heathrow then it would be impolite to do anything but spend it. So, I put the £30,000 down as a deposit on my first flat in Bristol. I haven't got a clue what Ronnie did with his, he probably spent it on Coke bottles. I was expecting some kind of backlash from the RFU, but the silence was deafening and the only evidence that it wasn't a figment of my imagination was the cheque. The money was tax-free – a fact confirmed by my accountant – and I couldn't help feeling that life was pretty good and, what's more, that it was about to get even better.

I was then offered £250,000 a year to join the new professional team at Richmond and, because it was so huge, I thought the offer was a bit crazy. I had a meeting with John and knew that Ben Clarke had already signed. John, the director of rugby, had a piece of paper with a description of each of his players, but not the name as he tried to give me an idea of how the squad was shaping up. It was really funny because next to 'scrum-half' was a description of an Argentine who they couldn't name but was obviously Augustin Pichot. Then it said: large Welsh number 8, so you pretty much knew it had to be Scott Quinnell. I believe that sport is about longevity and history and that you can't buy results. This was always going to be a major factor in deciding where I was going to move after Bristol.

Bath, Leicester and Wasps were the big three and I knew I wasn't going to sign for Bath. I spoke to Bob Dwyer, who was in charge of Leicester at the time, and they offered me very good money and said they would pay me the same as Martin Johnson, but not a penny more. To be honest, I just couldn't see myself living in Leicester. Besides interest from English teams, there were offers from Wales. Cardiff came in and offered me various different deals, including shares in Cardiff Airport! I then received a brochure from Treorchy Rugby Club with a letter from the Chief Executive saying they were going to offer a lot of money to a host of top players. Despite being a club that had not broken into the top echelons of Welsh rugby, they were adamant funding was there to close the gap on the big clubs and their main selling point was that I would get a car. I turned to the back page of this brochure; it was all very professionally done, to see the car that was on offer. It was a Ford Mondeo covered in Zebra stripes, to mirror the club strip. If anything was going to stop me from signing for Treorchy that was it.

Why was I prepared to leave Bristol and all that the club and city offered a young rugby player with a big appetite and thirst? Well, my first contract with Bristol was for about £50,000 which, coming straight from university, is outstanding money. I was, at long last, being paid to do what I loved, although the effect of professionalism on the Bristol club was hard to register. We were now being paid to do two weights sessions and a couple of rugby sessions a week and I thought it was some kind of dream, but it was true and ridiculously exciting. I couldn't think of anything better, although it was obvious to me that Bristol were never going to compete with the offers coming my way and, much as it pained me to leave, I could see the writing on the wall in terms of where Bristol were going. They didn't have the structure in place to survive and this view was supported by the decisions of Martin Corry, Arch and Kyran to leave.

There didn't seem to be any massive effort to retain any of those guys. Ronnie was Bristol through and through and would never leave the club, but other guys wanted to hear the right things from the Bristol management and when that didn't come, it seemed blatantly obvious what was going to happen. I went into a meeting with the club and said: 'I understand you can't compete with what I am being offered, but can't you just make it a little bit more?' If they had, I would have stayed, even with my reservations about how they viewed professionalism, because I loved Bristol so much. However, all I heard was 'we just haven't got it' and so the decision to leave was effectively made for me.

Throughout this period, I was trying to keep focused on my game because I was desperate to regain my England squad place. I had no intention of thinking about anything other than the job in hand, which was to keep Bristol in the top flight and to avoid relegation – an aim we achieved. However, the club went down the following season and the whole thing started to crumble. Leaving was the right decision in the summer of 1997, but it was still a gut wrencher.

I am proud to have won my first England cap as a Bristol player. There was a lot of hype around our pack in the 1996–97 season and, despite only playing a limited style of rugby, we were challenging the top teams. Any side that came down to Bristol was going to have to face the mighty Bristol pack. I was back playing regularly in the second row and getting a lot of headlines week in and week out for my lineout work. Along with either

Arch or Andy Blackmare, we pretty much demolished most sides and I was getting a lot of praise for what I was doing in broken play and was referred to as performing 'like a fourth back row', which was unusual for a second row – our lot in life was supposed to be jumping and pushing and not an awful lot else. I think a combination of my form with Bristol and that match with the Barbarians in Dublin, when I got the chance to run with the ball a number of times against the Springboks, worked in my favour with Jack Rowell as he looked to put together his England team for the 1996 November internationals.

I got the impression from day one with Jack that he was eager to get me into the team and he never lost faith in me despite those two serious leg injuries. I had worked very hard to get myself back into shape and whilst I had trimmed down from 22 stones, I was still very big, between 20½ and 21 st. However, because I had embraced the concept of weight training now that the game had gone professional, I was a lot stronger. The boys at Bristol had taken a look at what the rugby league players were doing as professionals and had come to the conclusion that all we needed to do was lift more weights. Simple really. My legs weren't a problem, despite wearing that special protection on my ankle, and I felt I was operating at a level that would get me back up towards England selection. Because the game was different at that time, being 21 st. was an advantage; you couldn't lift in the lineout and so being that tall and big allowed me to use my physical presence to manipulate the lineout, always done within the laws, of course. Also, because I was a mobile 21 st. forward, ball carrying and running through people came easily to me.

I couldn't operate like that in the current game because I would be too heavy to deal with all the other requirements of being a second row, but back then, I was very much fit for purpose, even at that large weight, and Jack wanted to utilise me for England. My first cap came at Twickenham in the November against Italy, who at that time were not part of a Six Nations Championship competition. They were still on the outside knocking on the door.

I expected to get the call-up, I suppose, which meant I wasn't as stunned as I expected to be when my name was read out for the first time by an England team manager. This rather low-key reaction was understandable: my parents didn't come to the Italy game, preferring instead to watch me turn out for England in a non-cap match against the New Zealand Barbarians a week later – a team that was, essentially, the All Blacks with only a couple of changes. When people ask if the first cap was the highlight of my career, I have to admit it didn't feel that way. Yes, I still had the nerves beforehand and older players were saying it would all be over in a flash, but nothing happened like that in that game. It didn't feel that way at all: in comparison to playing for Bristol, it felt quite an easy game. It seemed everything was a bit slower paced and, while I am not going to say it was a breeze, it didn't feel like a proper international. We romped it 54–21.

It was a very different story the following week against the New Zealanders and, although it probably sounds terrible to say, the Italy game didn't even compare with playing for the Barbarians against South Africa. As a new cap, I had to sing on the team bus after the Italy win and, having messed up so badly in Dublin, I had learned a song called 'Peaches and Cream'. I actually got an encore, so I followed it up with 'Tooty Fruity'. I was a bit of a Motown/rock 'n' roll buff in those days and sitting right opposite me during my performance was Jack Rowell. I can still picture him shaking his head and frowning.

Jack had made various comments about me in those days, saying I was a showman and so forth – he liked to do a bit of mickey-taking. I followed that vocal triumph with the traditional ritual of having a drink with everybody in the squad. As a result of this enormous alcoholic intake, I ended up all alone trying to catch up with some university mates in Camden and not getting anywhere very quickly. I got into a cab, completely blasted, and woke up in the middle of Camden with the driver yelling: 'Right, this is where you get out.' I managed to gather my remaining brain cells into a group and worked out that stepping onto an unknown area of London totally pissed was a bad idea. I got the driver to take me back to the Petersham Hotel in Richmond where we were staying, knowing it would cost me an arm and a leg. In fact, although it should have cost me an arm and a leg, when we got back to the hotel I just got out of the taxi, completely oblivious to having to pay the guy, walked up the slope to the hotel and proceeded to be sick in the lift. I was then sick in my room and appeared to have been sick everywhere. I woke up in the morning minus my first England cap – which had been presented to me earlier in the evening – and missing my new England tie. I'd left them in the taxi and the driver wasn't going to give me them back as it transpired that I had been sick in his cab as well. I had to pay to clean up the vehicle as well as for the taxi ride to Camden and back. It was a bit of a disaster all round. To add insult to injury, I had to grovel to the RFU to buy another cap and tie as well.

Given the nature of my international career with England – I have always appeared to be caught in a revolving door operated by various coaches and managers – it seems remarkable that I won my first six caps in successive games and that they were all alongside Martin Johnson. We started with that underwhelming win over Italy, came through a real test against the New Zealand Barbarians and then took on the Argentine pack. It has always been difficult up front against the Pumas who are big men with a deep love of clattering into you at high speed. The Pumas match at Twickenham was a scrappy 20–18 win and the media climbed into the team because it was felt we should have achieved a much more comfortable victory. The crowd was booing Mike Catt for periods of the match, something you rarely hear at any Twickenham game, and I felt for him as the pressure intensified and we struggled to contain the Pumas. You feel a cumulative effect after 80 minutes of close contact with Argentine players. They test you to the physical limit, preferring to look for contact rather than space, and stemming the constant tide of blue-and-white hooped shirts can make for a very long day in the office.

I was, at this point, England's first-choice middle jumper, having started as a youngster with Guildford & Godalming and Cranleigh as the front jumper. When I first went to Bristol, the excellent Andy Blackmore was playing in the middle and I was directed to the front and happily caught, deflected or flapped at whatever was thrown my way and remained the nearest jumper to the hooker, including when I was called up for England in 1994 as replacement for Johnno in South Africa. When Andy Blackmore moved aside, I went to jump in the middle, which took me back to the very first days of my rugby career when my coach positioned me there because I was so much bigger than anyone else. Now I found myself operating in that role again and realised that, because Johnno was the man in possession of the number 4 jersey, this represented my best chance of securing a run at test level.

Jack Rowell gave me that early series of matches and our captain was Bath's Phil de Glanville, who was a good man, but who faced constant questions about his worth to the team. Phil didn't let the pressure get to him and I admired his mental strength during that period. He was a really nice guy and that is the way he came across as a captain, just nice, but certainly nothing really to write home about in terms of making my hair stand up when he spoke. That was Phil's way and he was a popular guy.

It is often said that the best second rows hunt as a pair, which implies they have a very close working relationship. It was never that way with Johnno. Before a match, Johnno would just come up and ask me if everything was OK. He wouldn't offer up a huge amount of advice, it would just be the odd word here and there, nothing major. We weren't bosom buddies and, at that stage, I wasn't terribly involved in the squad. I was fairly new to it all and I had my own group of mates, people who had just come onto the scene, like Andy Gomarsall and Paul Hull. I wasn't in the thick of it in terms of being part of the more experienced group, which included stalwarts like Jason Leonard and Brian Moore. I kept myself to myself a bit and I was always very laid back before kick-off, so I didn't speak to anyone really, just twiddled my thumbs in the corner until it was time for kick-off. Johnno would make his way over, give me the usual 'you all right, everything all right?' and I'd be 'Yep, yep, no problems' – funnily enough, it is still like that now when he is prowling around the dressing-room before the game as team manager, with the same exchange: 'Everything all right?', with my inevitable 'Yep, yep, fine' reply.

Johnno and I couldn't have been more different as personalities. He was a former bank teller from the Leicester club, while I saw myself as a worldly-wise bloke who loved travelling abroad and who had been born in Nairobi. I also had the attitude that Leicester was a very insular club – a view shared by every other team in the country – and while it may seem as though we were barely on speaking terms, that wasn't the case at all. I have never had a problem with Johnno, either when he was my rival for the position, playing alongside him or listening to his words as a team manager. I know people will find this hard to believe, given the number of caps I could have amassed if he had stayed in New Zealand all those years ago when he had a season with King Country. Our relationship never evolved into anything so extreme: we played and trained together, had a beer after matches and indulged in probably the most mundane pre-match chats in test rugby history, but once we got onto the pitch for England, we gave everything for the cause. I never believed Johnno was a better player, we had different strengths and weaknesses, which most people recognise, but he was the captain and I couldn't compete against that! If there is a major difference between us it would be our eyebrows – I have two of them.

I was hugely excited about the 1997 Five Nations Championship because there was a Lions tour to South Africa at the end of the season. With Ollie Redman and Martin Bayfield either out of favour or no longer on the scene, I was in the unusual position of believing that it was my England jersey to lose. If I kept performing for Jack, I was going to have a good run of matches and would be right in the selection mix for the Lions. We won every match except for the now-famous French game, when they produced one of the most amazing comebacks in tournament history to win 23–20. Did I marvel at their flair and ball skills? Did I hell. I was mightily pissed off that they had ruined our chances of Grand Slam glory.

Jack had a very strange sense of humour and I am the kind of player who likes to mind his Ps and Qs when it involves team management. I tried to avoid catching his eye and give him an opportunity to unload one of his caustic comments. One of the main reasons I agreed with everything he said was my response to the bizarre comments about players and tactics he came up with. I realised very quickly that the best way to deal with him was just to say 'yes', because most of the time I didn't have a bloody clue what he was on about.

I still take the view that as the man in charge of the team, the manager or head coach (the title really isn't that important), they are the boss and you don't need to aggravate them, annoy them or give them any reason to drop you. Then again, having been dropped by every manager or coach who has been involved with England, I may have adopted the wrong attitude. Maybe, I should have been a right pain in the arse, given them hell, argued over every selection decision and thrown my toys out of the pram on a regular basis. Being true to my own values and beliefs about how you should play and act, however, I still managed to earn more than 50 caps for my country, which is something I take understandable pride in achieving. And who knows what might have happened if Johnno had stayed in New Zealand . . .?

CHAPTER 10

SOUTH AFRICA 1997: YOU'RE TOO HEAVY TO BE A LION

During the 1997 season, I was invited to attend a rugby dinner as the guest of Fran Cotton, the former England captain and the man who was going to manage the Lions tour in South Africa that summer. The invite came out of nowhere because I had never met Fran before, but at the dinner he praised the way I had been playing that season and pretty much intimated I would be on the tour, barring any injury or disaster. I wasn't surprised the Lions appointed Johnno as captain for the tour; there were rumours beforehand and he had always got a lot of column inches in the papers. I took the view that if Johnno went as captain, it would probably help my cause and that chat with Fran made it clear I was going to have a very busy summer back in Africa. England's successes in the Five Nations had been based on a very strong pack and it was felt, by the experts, that we would supply the Lions front five. It didn't turn out that way. For England, Jason Leonard and Graham Rowntree were the props, Phil Greening or Ronnie hooked and Johnno and I were the locks to complete the front five. Lawrence wasn't first choice at this point and battled it out with Neil Back, Richard Hill and Tim Rodber to complete the pack. I got the impression that Lawrence wasn't one of Jack's favourite players and the team manager seemed happier when my Wasps mate was out of the side.

I was hugely excited about returning to South Africa as a possible test player rather than as a late replacement, as had happened on my previous trip with England. I had weighed over 20 st. during the whole of the Five Nations and my size had never been questioned. In fact, it was considered a real asset. So I joined up with the Lions totally unaware that my weight would become a serious issue. For now, it was a case of getting to know all the guys from the other Home Union nations and the Lions used a company to devise team-building exercises designed to get you working together with players you might have been belting the hell out of you only a couple of weeks earlier.

It was all aimed at seeing who would step up to the mark in terms of leadership and who would just get on with their job without saying too much; all the usual management mumbo jumbo. It was obvious right from the start who was going to step up, but it was a good time and we had a bit of a giggle. One of the major differences between this Lions tour and previous trips was the availability of former rugby league players now that the union game had turned professional as well. The arrival of men like Alan Tait, John Bentley, Scott Quinnell, Allan Bateman and David Young was greeted enthusiastically by the rest of us, because they had all started in union before moving to league and had returned with skills and information that would benefit all of us who were still coming to terms with what being a professional rugby player was all about. We used these players as a benchmark and fed off them throughout the tour. In short, they became a huge part of what we were trying to achieve in the test series against the World Cup holders. What they all possessed was confidence and this shone through in every case. It was great to be around players who had a such a fantastic work ethic and enthusiasm for everything they did in training and during matches. It must have made them feel special to be so important to the entire squad and Ian McGeechan's decision to include the league boys was a masterstroke that would underpin the entire tour. Initially rugby wasn't the prime concern during the pre-tour camp; it was all about getting to know one another and having a bit of crack. There would be a couple of rugby sessions – not terribly taxing – followed by a lot of talk as you met up with players for the first time in that kind of situation. I always had a beer and a chat with my opposite number after a match, but didn't get around the whole opposition team and now, here was a unique opportunity to mix with everyone.

Inevitably, groups of like-minded souls started to form, including Jerry Guscott, Jason Leonard, Lawrence Dallaglio and Scott Gibbs, who would remain great friends long after the tour ended. I had got on with Gregor Townsend and Doddie Weir before the tour and, while I was fine meeting with those guys again, as a personality, I had grown into myself a bit. It took me a while to open up and, while I was comfortable in this team-bonding atmosphere, I didn't embrace the concept as readily as others. However, those first couple of days made me feel very comfortable, the time we spent away from training really broke down any barriers and the good vibe was cemented by a big booze-up on the last night. Now, we were really talking!

I think there is a tendency for higher-profile players to stick together and the lesser-known, quieter guys to do their own thing and gravitate towards one another. I pretty much stuck with Ronnie (who is not in the quieter gang but inhabits his own special place in the grand scheme of things), Taity – because he knew Kenny Logan – and Gregor Townsend, which on reflection seems all rather Scottish. One thing I am fairly uncomfortable with in any rugby situation is the whole idea of rooming with someone I don't know. No, I don't have any strange habits or traits, it's just a case of preferring to have my own room. I am social and happy to mix in with anyone, however, I love to be able to head back to my own room and shut the door for a bit of peace and quiet. I like to have that haven and I was a little worried that I didn't know a lot of these guys and that we were going to spend a lot of time together. My initial thoughts were: 'Oh Christ, how bad is it going to be if I get a rotten one or someone I don't particularly get on with?'

It was made clear at an early stage that, as part of integrating the squad, we would be changing sleeping 'partners' every time we moved hotel and that everyone had to get on with it. My first room-mate was Dai Young, the Wales prop who had just returned from rugby league. Despite not knowing Dai, he had me in stitches from the moment I walked into the room. I immediately changed my views about room-sharing, although it was to prove the lull before the storm. My next roomy was Jeremy Davidson, the man who would be chosen ahead of me for the test series. At this point, though, we were just two second rows trying to making an impression on the management and, having enjoyed a Welsh room-mate, it was now time to experience life with an Irish lad. Davidson was particularly bad because it was like being his wife! He expected me to do pretty much everything in the room – no, not that – but I was having none of it. I don't know if it was just a test to see what he could get away with, but it failed to impress me and I was delighted when we moved hotels, because I then shared with Gregor followed by Neil Back, both of whom were great and also Tom Smith.

The Lions tour was being filmed for a special DVD that would become one of the most successful 'inside stories' ever produced. We were well aware that the whole thing was being taped and the guys in charge of the filming were a really good bunch. They paid for us to go on special trips, including shark diving and safaris, and mucked in as part of the squad. It also provided the group with people who were not solely interested in rugby and who could talk on different subjects, which is useful when you get so wrapped up in something as intense and important as a Lions tour. It may seem strange to admit this, but it can get a bit boring after a while. Despite all the wonderful footage the crew shot, I really wish they had put a camera in Ronnie's room.

On any tour, because food is available night and day as you are constantly training, you are going to gain some poundage. I admit I did enjoy the steaks and social drinking as we made our way around the country, but it affected neither my training nor playing. Nobody had said I was too big in terms of being supported at the lineout, but I was aware of comments that had first started as a piss-take but which then became a real irritation. Lifting had just come into the game, but players were only allowed to use the palms of their hands and were not allowed to support a jumper below the knee. In our first real training session, I remember being held up by the palms and a few comments started to fly around, from Dai Young especially. It was all tongue-in-cheek but, at the same time, it was all a bit annoying because I felt it created a perception and hearing large prop forwards wincing and moaning about supporting my jump wasn't helping my test-match cause.

For me, it hadn't been an issue before the tour because it was all about winning lineout ball and that was something I achieved on a consistent basis. Being able to use my size and physique had got me into the Lions squad in the first place and now, all of a sudden, it was something that was provoking both comment and debate. I was perplexed and worried. My demeanour was not helped when Davidson stole a few opposition lineout throws in the matches leading into the first test and I had to accept he was playing well. There were around six players – men like Johnno and Keith Wood, our hooker – who knew they were definitely going to make the first test side, but another nine places were still up for grabs and I desperately wanted to make the side. The England front five were still very much in the picture, until we lost 35–30 to Northern Transvaal in Pretoria. It was a game that saw us absolutely trounced in the scrum and it proved a turning point in terms of selection. For the test series, Ian McGeechan and forwards coach Jim Telfer decided that the props would be Tom Smith and Paul Wallace either side of Woody and that Johnno would be joined in the second row by Davidson with Lawrence, Richard and Tim completing the back row. You learned your fate when an envelope arrived under your door from the management, but Geech had already given me a heads-up. It was a huge blow. However, I put my own disappointment to one side and got on with training and that was the case throughout the tour for the guys who didn't make the test-match squad. It is vital for any tour that the players who are not involved in the big games remain united and do not become a problem. Yes, you would put an extra bit of effort into the first training session after receiving the bad news and that is something that happens in rugby all over the world.

During the tour our scrum became a focus for Jim Telfer and he delighted in using a new machine that had been taken out especially for the Lions to work with . . . because it pushed back. It would be the bane of our lives for eight weeks. Jim obviously loved it and I found myself spending hours battling with this bloody heavy piece of metal. Johnno had arrived on tour with an injury, which meant I had to play in the first six games. I played Saturday, benched Wednesday, played Saturday, benched Wednesday, so I had no real rest apart from having a few drinks after each game. At one point, my cauliflower ear – yes, it came on tour with me – completely burst and inflamed, and the delightful moment when I got it syringed was captured in all its horrible detail by the film crew. I went from having it syringed and bound to having to endure yet another bloody scrummaging session.

From a training point of view, I had never experienced anything like it because the sessions were extremely hard. I can't imagine there will be many tours in the future that will be so intense away from match days, because coaches now spend more time working on keeping players fresh rather than flogging the life out of them, although given that we won the test series 2–1, the means certainly justified the ends in South Africa.

The most upsetting part of the tour for me came when Rob Howley dislocated his shoulder and was ruled out of the trip. Rob was extremely popular within the squad and was an outstanding scrum-half who would later move from Wales to join Wasps and score the try that won us our first Heineken Cup trophy at

Twickenham. With Rob now ruled out, we needed a scrum-half to emerge for the test series. It was my old England Schools team-mate, Matt 'Shrinking Violet' Dawson, who became the first-choice number 9, having started the tour as probably the third choice in that position. Daws had real pace and throughout his career produced a little bit of magic on the really big occasions, just as he did in the first test with a wonderful solo try. No wonder we allowed him to join Wasps near the end of his illustrious career. We won that first test 25–16 and from that moment on the tour really took off.

I didn't know much about Jim Telfer at the start of the tour, other than his reputation for fearsome training sessions, and that proved the case throughout our time in South Africa. However, as much as Jim is an incredibly hard taskmaster on the training pitch, he is a bloody good laugh off it. During one of the visits to Cape Town, I sat next to him during a meal in Camps Bay. My initial thought was, 'Oh Christ, it's going to be a nightmare for two hours,' but it was very entertaining. I then bumped into my parents, who were following the tour and who were at the same restaurant with a bunch of Scotsmen at the bar. My parents informed me that the guys were former team-mates of Jim and they proceeded to try and drag stories out of me about his training methods and what classic lines he was coming up with. Initially, I avoided revealing any behind-the-scenes stuff, but eventually cracked as everyone was in such a great mood. They kept egging me on and eventually I started and almost didn't stop telling them anecdotes about Jim's coaching techniques. During a warm-up session whilst running lengths of the pitch, he ordered that we 'run as fast as ye can and then sprint!' On another occasion he informed me that I was like a lighthouse in the desert – bright and fucking useless! I carried on for about half an hour and all the time Jim, unknown to me, was standing behind me.

One of the best performances of the tour came in midweek as the party prepared for the second test in Durban. We flew in a special charter plane to Bloemfontein to take on the Free

State and produced an outstanding match that showed the remarkable depth of talent in the squad as we triumphed 52–30. My performance drew plenty of plaudits as I was able to get the ball in my hands and charge about the field. However, the match will always be remembered for a sickening injury suffered by Will Greenwood, who had yet to be picked for England and who was on the tour because he had impressed the Lions with his club form. Will was tackled and banged his head heavily on the rock-hard pitch and you can always tell the severity of an injury by the reaction of the medical staff. James Robson, the hugely experienced and popular Lions doctor, raced onto the pitch as soon as Will hit the ground, recognising just how serious the situation was. When someone is knocked out, it is always a worry and then seeing Will taken off on a stretcher was upsetting. As players, you have no option but to concentrate on the game. We recorded a great win and then it was a case of getting into the dressing-room as quickly as possible to find out how he was. It was the tour's darkest hour. However, the minute we discovered he was making a good recovery and that any element of danger/disaster had passed, someone inevitably made a joke about it and we moved on.

The moment Jerry Guscott kicked the drop goal to beat the Springboks 18–15 in that amazing second test is a cherished rugby memory. You are sitting there as the stadium erupts – well, the travelling Lions fans went barmy anyway – suddenly aware that you are part of a Lions squad that has just clinched a test series against the reigning world champions. The only acceptable reaction, of course, was to go out and get absolutely plastered. We got caught up in the craziness of the barmy army, who were following the tour, and it was sheer madness after the game. I went straight out to the car park at Kings Park where they always have traditional, if rather dangerous, barbecues – red-hot coals, alcohol and cars full of fuel – and found my parents in one of the large tents that had been erected. Ronnie's parents were in there along with Lawrence's mum and dad and within minutes we were all treated to the sight of Ronnie standing on a table drinking, two pints at a time. To a certain extent, we could have packed our bags and gone home then because the series was won and it was time to enjoy ourselves. It meant the final week was incredibly long for everyone, but we had two more games to play and so the party hats were put away.

Tim Stimpson was attracting a lot of attention after he pulled Miss South Africa at a pop concert having been the only one of us prepared to dance and make a fool of himself. I scored a couple of tries in the final midweek game as we thumped Northern Free State 67–39 and felt my level of performance had been good throughout, except for the disappointing loss to the Bulls. Before that hugely significant loss, Woody had been kind enough to suggest my rugby warranted a place in the test side, but it didn't happen. While I didn't have any real animosity towards Davidson, the same cannot be said for Ronnie and his rivals. Because Woody was always going to be the test hooker, it meant Ronnie was up against Barry Williams, the young Wales hooker, for the replacement's position in the big matches. Ronnie has got this bizarre thing about earning your stripes. I think he felt particularly aggrieved that Barry had come out of nowhere to make the tour and there was a joke going around the Welsh boys with them calling him 'Barry Three Tours' because he was speaking like a man who had a wealth of experience behind him instead of someone who was actually only on his first tour. I think that rubbed Ronnie up the wrong way, although it hardly needed anything else to wind Ronnie up about Williams. It came to a head – quite literally – in a training session at East London when Ronnie butted Williams as they went down in a practice scrum. There were some good punches flying in, but the rest of the party were just trying to split them apart and Jim probably had a smile on his face.

Ronnie has always made things very personal against his opposite number and would have seen getting on with his rival as a sign of weakness. I think Ronnie, while he has got a lot of bravado on the outside, is actually quite insecure on the inside and when he believes someone is, perhaps, better than him, he is willing to take a back seat. That was the case with Woody, but it didn't stop Ronnie fighting for that chance to get a test cap . . . and it duly came in the third match against the Springboks.

The great thing about Ronnie is that no matter how bad the tour gets, how depressed you are, whether you are selected or not selected, or whether the team is winning or getting thrashed every week, he always has the ability to make you smile and laugh. It might not necessarily be intentional, but it will happen. I was travelling in a glass-sided lift with Ronnie in Pretoria and, as we made our way to the top of the building, I just happened to mention that it was another lovely clear blue sky without any cloud . 'Of course it's clear,' came the reply from Ronnie. Intrigued, I asked him to explain why he wasn't surprised at the absence of clouds. 'Well, it's obvious. We're at altitude. That means we're above the clouds.'

John Bentley, one of the league returnees, had a great tour and the funny thing about Bentos is that if you look at his game in general, he is not a great tackler, which is strange for a man who did well in league after playing for England. He quite regularly used to miss tackles and be put on his arse by a hand-off, but made up for this with very strong running. Given his defensive problems, it was remarkable that he made such a big impression on James Small, who saw himself as the hard man of the South African rugby team, even though he played on the wing. Every time Bentos got near to Small in the second test he belted him and produced an outstanding performance of controlled bullying. Small was shot to pieces and didn't know what to do: he was being made to look a fool by former police constable Bentos.

By the time the final test came along, I was already demob happy and had been told I wouldn't be required for the third match with the Springboks. I came back into the team hotel in the early hours of match day, very much the worse for wear and in a great mood. There was a belief within the squad that, as we had already won the series, those players not involved in the first two tests should be given a cap in the final match. However, Geech and Jim wanted to go home with an emphatic 3–0 record in the test matches. You can imagine my grave concern when, as I lurched towards the lifts, I overheard a discussion between Jim and one of the medical team about someone suffering with flu and that either myself or Rob Wainwright would have to be put on standby to play. I think it was the first time in my life when I thought, 'Whatever you do, don't pick me,' because I was in no fit state to try and lace up my boots. If I had been breathalysed, I would have failed miserably.

When you are involved in something as fantastic as a Lions tour, the friendships you make remain long after the party has dispersed to their own countries. I still keep in touch with Alan Tait and always have a word with Neil Jenkins, now the Wales kicking coach, when we bump into each other at matches. I could barely understand a word Jenks said when I was on tour with him, but since then he seems to have been going to English lessons.

It was a happy tour and whatever anyone says about Geech, after he has finished coaching, one of his great strengths is enabling a team to enjoy what they are doing. That may sound pretty simple, but I have worked under plenty of coaches who don't allow it to happen. I think that has a profound impact on how players go about their actual job and how comfortable people feel on a day-to-day basis. On a tour of that nature, and that length of time, it is absolutely imperative that you have that joy and pleasure, otherwise people just lose it. They go off on their own and the passion dissipates. You have got to bear in mind how many people are fighting for a test spot and what a difficult task it is to keep them happy for such a sustained period. Some guys will know after just a couple of weeks that they are unlikely to get a test spot and it is essential they remain part of the squad until the very end. It is an incredibly hard job and getting it right is one of Geech's many strengths.

If I have one major regret – besides failing to make the test side – it would be having agreed to be a tour court enforcer and being filmed wearing tight trousers and a string vest, with my hair slicked down and sporting a heavy-duty handlebar moustache. It still gives me the shivers when I look at it and has been interpreted as some kind of homage to Freddie Mercury. I have no plausible explanation for my actions. It was a schoolboy error, but these things happen on tour.

CHAPTER 11

LONDON WASPS AND HOW TO RELOCATE TO A HOTEL PENTHOUSE

The London Wasps recruitment machine constituted Rob Smith, their head coach, giving me a lift to those London Division training sessions and bending my ear for long stretches of the journey up from Bristol. As I have mentioned, I did have offers from various other clubs and had been to see Bob Dwyer at Leicester, although I knew I wouldn't be heading to the Midlands, even though I could have formed a club second-row unit with Johnno. Smithy and Nigel Melville, who had become the Wasps director of rugby, continued planting the idea of coming to Wasps in my mind through a series of telephone calls, and I soon came to the conclusion that moving to London was the only viable option. I knew a lot of the guys at Wasps, they were the English champions and winning trophies was one of the major motivations for me – if the decision had been purely about money, I would have accepted that amazing offer from Richmond.

While I was on the Lions tour in South Africa, Malcolm Sinclair, the Wasps team manager, who was enjoying his part-time role as a tour leader with one of the major supporters' groups, had been pestering me to sign the contract he had taken to South Africa with him. Eventually I gave up and signed a deal that was worth £100,000 less than the one Richmond were offering – a huge amount really. The Wasps contract was still for a very nice £150,000 a year and I was absolutely delighted, even though I knew that the practicalities of being a member of the Wasps squad meant dealing with some of the worst training facilities in England. I had experienced the training ground before because I had endured various London sessions at Sudbury, but I had absolutely no idea of where to live or what life in a major city would be like. The Bristol club knew I would be leaving because I had been very upfront about the offers that had been placed on the table and, with their own limited finances, they were unable to come up with any kind of counter-bid. They just said thanks and I left the club on very good terms. I have never had any barracking or trouble when I have returned to the Memorial Ground and I am sure that stems from the fact I helped keep the club in the top flight that season. It was important to me that I left with their good wishes. Every time I go back, the people who remain from my time in the club office welcome me and I have a drink with the fans; that means a lot to me. I didn't break the news to Ronnie personally because it was pretty common knowledge and he had been with me on the Lions tour and understood my reasons. A few guys had left Bristol the previous year: Bracken, Archer and Corry, so it was inevitable that others would follow and soon after, after Bristol were relegated, Ronnie headed off to Bath. I don't feel any responsibility for Bristol's relegation and I am sure the other guys feel the same way. It is significant that all four of us became England regulars while playing for our new clubs.

Of course, leaving Bristol meant waving goodbye to my university days and it will come as no surprise to learn that I didn't gain any qualification from my course. A key aspect was the production of a dissertation based on my year in industry and, as this dealt with the Courage debacle, I had offered nothing in terms of a thesis. So I walked away with a large student debt and no university qualifications. Yes, I should have made more of my time at university, but my head and heart were elsewhere and I was only interested in professional rugby. I kept the flat in Bristol and a couple of the rugby club guys rented it off me, which helped with that debt.

Thankfully, when I moved to London, Wasps gave me a relocation fee, which came in very handy. The idea was that I would rent somewhere while I worked out where in the capital I was going to live. It was quite an attractive package and I have to admit the whole idea of coming to London was quite a daunting one because of the sheer size of the cty. I didn't know any of the areas and my only point of contact at the time was Chad Eagle's girlfriend who lived in London. She had a work colleague who said I could stay in her flat in Maida Vale for a while with a German girl, who was very scary.

Wasps outside-half Alex King lived just around the corner, which was a real bonus, and I gave the area a trial period, but everything seemed to involve such a long journey – training, matches, meeting up with mates etc. . . . After a short time, I realised I was pretty much living alone, had very few friends and was operating a social life that depended on various lifts or public transport to enjoy. With that handy relocation fee in my bank account, I opted to live in the Crown Plaza hotel, which is situated just before you hit Kilburn High Road. I lived at the hotel for almost a year and it was very convenient because you could call down to the restaurant for food and room service delivered it a short time later while the maid service tidied up the room every day while I was at training. I thought I had hit the jackpot. I didn't let on to the other players, but some of them knew about my sleeping arrangements and I had enough room to take in those poor souls who had broken up with their girlfriends and had, as a result, become temporarily homeless. It was a penthouse apartment within the hotel, hence all the room for waifs and strays, while there was also a gym downstairs, frequented by Peter Andre. He used to be in the gym a lot, but I wasn't impressed with his physique and, to be honest, he appeared rather camp. I have to say I was very surprised when he ended up married to Jordan.

At the time, Wasps were playing their first-team matches at Loftus Road, and it was a ground I had enjoyed visiting with Bristol, because it was pretty small and that meant less grass for the forwards to cover. In my first season with Wasps, we weren't terribly successful and I immediately put it down to the fact that we weren't having enough of a social life as a squad. We weren't getting together and having a few beers, which had been the bedrock of the team spirit at Bristol and one of the main reasons why we had been able to take on the bigger clubs. For some reason this really worked for me although, looking back on my early days in junior rugby, having a great time off the pitch was something that came naturally. There were a lot of Wasps guys who enjoyed a few beers and a good time but as we played on Sundays it was difficult to get everyone together in the same place. The guys were spread out all over London – some in Fulham, others out in Surrey, while I was still in Maida Vale bothering room service and keeping a close watch on that Andre character in the gym. By the time everyone got home from Loftus Road, changed and were ready to go out again, you were left with about an hour of pub time. Kenny Logan and a few others went to the Pitcher and Piano pub, and we decided to make our way there as speedily as we could. We tried various venues, often heading up to the West End, but we always seemed to be ending up at the P&P. We opted to stay there most nights on the basis that we just couldn't be bothered to deal with the travel in London and, gradually, the P&P began to fill up on the nights we were in residence to the point where there were queues going down the road. There were only two married guys in the squad at that time and the rest of us were single young lads, and girlfriends would bring friends who would seriously improve the evening. Eventually, it became our Sunday night venue and the hub of our social life away from training and playing and it's still the same today.

When I arrived there was a group of young players who had started together at Wasps but who had become stuck behind guys like Rob Andrew, Dean Ryan and Steve Bates. Those experienced players all left at the same time to launch the professional club at Newcastle and the tyros – who included Lawrence, a key figure in this group of young players, and Gareth Rees, our Canadian outside-half – all enjoyed the social side of the game.

I was one of four locks at the club together with the Scotland second rows Andy Reed and Damian Cronin plus Mark Weedon, from New Zealand, and when I first got there, I had a chronic back problem, which meant I was sporadically in and out of the side until Christmas. The first-team places were shared between the four of us and the two Scots lads were big men who could be hugely effective. I really liked playing with Damian, although he would be the first to admit he wasn't too keen on the contact area. However, he loved to run about with the ball and I also enjoyed that side of the game, which meant we often linked up in the midfield.

In that first season, we got to the Cup final and lost to Saracens but, despite the bitter disappointment of losing to our London rivals, experiencing a big day at Twickenham was the reason I had joined the club. They were the words I had used to Nigel Melville when I had joined Wasps and he reminded me of them just before I ran out for the final at Twickenham. It may not have been a great season, but to get to a final at Twickenham was the reason I joined the club. Unfortunately, the match turned out to be a disastrous day for Wasps against a Sarries team that had a host of good players. Not long ago, I had a conversation with Julian White during a break at an England session about that Sarries side. Julian was the tight-head prop, Kyran Bracken was at number 9 and Danny Grewcock in the second row along with big names such as Michael Lynagh, Francois Pienaar and Philippe Sella. I told Julian that I couldn't understand why that side had been dismantled because it was one of the greatest professional teams ever assembled. A year later, however, it was gone. Julian was equally bemused and Sarries haven't really ever recovered.

The major difference between Wasps and Bristol – apart from the facilities – was the London club's attitude to professionalism. The training ground may have been pretty disastrous and we had a ropey old gym at the back of the training hall made up of about three bits of equipment that were rusty and wouldn't pass any health and safety tests, yet Wasps were the English champions. They trained one day here and one day there, but the attitude of everyone at Wasps was completely different from what I had experienced at Bristol. At Bristol, we were all happy, enjoying our new professional sport and carrying on as though it was just like the amateur days, except that we were getting a salary every month. At Wasps, there was a definite change of thought process and it appeared to have been born out of the dark days created by the departure of Andrew, Ryan and Bates to Newcastle. Their decision to leave the club came as a big kick in the teeth to those who remained and the guys adopted the attitude that they weren't going to accept the trio of big-name departures had damaged the club. The players wanted to prove this by becoming league champions, which they did.

By making Lawrence captain, Wasps created a leader who could galvanise the youngsters in the squad and it proved a turning point for the club – although we would still have to put up with those shocking facilities. My first three or four months at Wasps came as a huge culture shock and I have to admit that at the time I was thinking: 'Christ, I've made a massive error here.' London can be one of the loneliest places on earth if you can't pick up the phone and meet someone: everything has to be planned because the logistics of London living mean that you simply can't do things on an ad hoc basis. In Bristol, you would bump into two or three of your mates simply by walking out of your front door. You would go to the local restaurant for lunch and there would

Dad with nursey. He already had women looking after him and nothing's changed.

Dad's first experience of horseriding was no fun for anyone involved.

Me and sis in front of Mt Kilimanjaro. Poses need a little bit of work!

Christmas jumper!

My first sporting award,
probably for swimming.

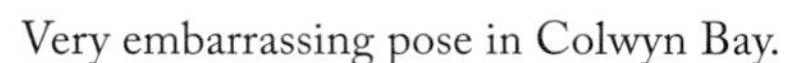

Very embarrassing pose in Colwyn Bay.

Fresh-faced youngster, aged 19, at Bristol.
Ears look remarkably good!

Me and Dad. People say they can see the resemblance, but I can't.

My wedding day in Tuscany. Slightly overdid the sunbathing the day before. Very happy, though.

The clan. Beautiful, aren't they? The kids all take after their mother, obviously!

New Year's Eve with Gabby and Kenny Logan. We were told it was fancy dress. Unfortunately no one told the rest of the hotel!

My first cap for England, versus Italy in a friendly in 1996 at Twickenham. Note the dodgy sideburns as Jason Leonard tries to stiff arm one of his own! (© Getty Images)

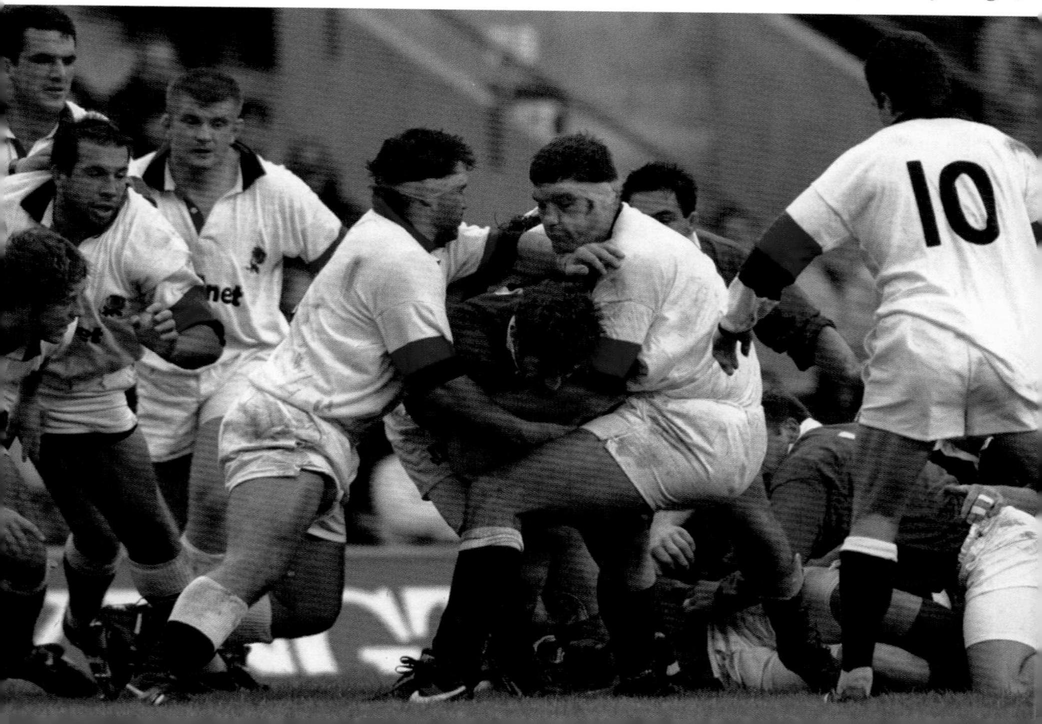

Scoring for the Lions in 1997, so long ago that Neil Back had hair! (© Getty Images)

World Cup winners 2003 – that's me on the far right of the middle row. Even when I met the Queen I couldn't get away from Ronnie, who, unlike Richard Hill, managed to do his tie up. (© Getty Images)

Lawrence Dallaglio, always more emotional on the pitch, shows his incredulity as I am wrongly sent off against New Zealand during England's tour in 2004. (© Getty Images)

The hard yards: Lawrence and I after putting our bodies on the line again for our beloved London Wasps. (© Getty Images)

Who cares that it's absolutely pouring down We are the Powergen Cup champions and it time to celebrate, Twickenham 2005. (© Getty Images)

A replacement Lion, 2005. Taking on Manawatu for the Lions 'Midweek Massive' led by Ian McGeechan – we remained unbeaten throughout the tour. (© Getty Images)

The desperation of defeat as my World Cup dream is shattered by South Africa in Paris in 2007. (© Getty Images)

Martin Corry's nose comes off second best as we take the fight to Leicester in the Guinness Premiership final of 2008. (© Getty Images)

Lions, Pretoria, second test. Clear proof – if proof were needed – that I can win quality lineout ball in South Africa for the Lions – something that hampered my cause 12 years earlier. (© Getty Images)

The calm before the storm. United at the st of the tour, still fiercely united at the end as prepare to beat the world champions in their backyard in the third test at Ellis Park. (© Getty Images)

'Geech' finishes his magnificent Lions career with a win and I celebrate my first – and last – victory in a Lions test jersey. Happy Days! (© Getty Images)

be three of your mates sitting at the table next to you and you would automatically join up with them. In London I would be sat in my penthouse waiting for the phone to ring and trying to come up with something to do. I would be searching for things, despite London having everything you could ever want – as long as you had someone to enjoy it with.

Nigel Melville and Pat Fox, who was our fitness guy, had a pretty strange arrangement for training, which meant that everything was over by around 1.00 p.m, so you had practically every afternoon off. I remember one period when Adam Black, one of our props, and I used to get together. He lived in Blackheath, and used to hate driving straight home after training, so we would head off to the cinema almost every day. One of the side-effects of this existence was that when I got together with my wife Jane, we would end up in Blockbusters trying to choose a movie for a night in with me constantly saying: 'Seen that.'

Clive Woodward had replaced Jack Rowell as England head coach in 1997 and it coincided with my chronic back problem and a virus I had picked up in South Africa – nothing sexual, I hasten to add. I first detected the virus problem when I agreed to put my entire body at risk by going on Ronnie's stag 'do' to Blackpool. Class! We travelled to Blackpool on a coach and I was feeling ill, which meant that by the time we reached our destination, I was in a terrible state. I said: 'Ronnie, mate, I'm really sorry, but I am going to have to go to bed,' which meant I received a torrent of abuse from him and the rest of the gang. All I could offer was, 'No, seriously, I feel awful,' and retired to my pit in a crappy B&B in the town. When I woke up, my famous cauliflower ear was plainly visible out of the corner of my eye, which is an image I had never previously had to deal with. I looked in the mirror and the whole of the right-hand side of my head was swollen to almost twice its normal size. I looked like the Elephant Man and had to cover my face with a hooded top. The last place I needed to be was at a Blackpool B&B, so I headed south, which meant having to take three or four different trains to get myself and my hideous features back to London. I was really quite ill for a period. It was diagnosed as a viral infection that might have got into my system via the cut on my ear. I saw the medical staff at Wasps and the antibiotics helped reduce the swelling in my face after two or three days. It is quite scary when you can see your own ear and, added to the disc problem in my back, I had endured a difficult start to my Wasps career.

I was invited to England squad sessions, but all too often I couldn't train because of the back pain. At the same time, there was a movement in the southern hemisphere to try and convert back-row forwards into locks to improve the pack's mobility, and Clive Woodward was looking at guys like Tim Rodber and Lawrence because they were slightly lighter and leaner. My own weight started to come down from the 20 st. of the Lions tour and this was due to the illness and the kind of training Wasps concentrated on compared to Bristol. With Bristol being a forward-oriented team, there was a lot of emphasis on lifting weights and on getting bigger and stronger. Wasps played a far more dynamic game that was all about fitness levels and mobility, playing with ball in hand, so at the start of the season I set out to lose a lot of weight and got down to 18 st. 7 lb. This had a major impact on what I could do on the pitch. I could no longer barge my way through, as had been the case when I was carrying that extra poundage, and it was a new scenario I had to come to terms with.

With the 1999 World Cup looming, players were starting to target the tournament, and while I hadn't written off being part of the England squad, I was happy to concentrate on getting my Wasps starting place nailed down now that the back had been sorted out and my head had returned to its normal size again. I needed to justify my transfer from Bristol to Wasps and the faith the club had put in me. At this point, Rob Smith was replaced as coach. It was a very difficult time, because he had been and continues to be, a great influence at Wasps, now overseeing the excellent academy system. As a squad, we felt we needed someone more dynamic and I remember having a meeting with the whole squad on the bottom pitch at Sudbury. We used to jog around the pitches as a warm-up and on this occasion we stayed on the bottom pitch and had a discussion, which then saw Lawrence, the captain, head off to the club offices to tell Nigel how the boys were feeling. The result was the arrival of John Mitchell, who had been player/coach at Sale.

When Mitch came in the impact was immediate. Before his arrival, the fitness levels had been fairly good up to a point, but the Pat Fox style was to make the guys undertake 32 runs of 150 metres on those back pitches at Sudbury and guys like Shane Roiser, our wing, was clearly a sprint athlete and not built for this kind of heavy work. It was more of a flogging than a fitness session and not a lot of science had gone into it. You didn't get any quality with those sessions and, as a result, the enthusiasm levels were pretty low: you simply turned up at training knowing there were going to be 32 sets of 150 metres and you just switched off. You certainly didn't train at your highest intensity because you knew how many of those bloody things you had to do.

When Mitch arrived he introduced game-related fitness sessions and emphasised the need to work together and pull one another along. It was all team-building stuff that we were doing as a group and it brought about a totally different attitude with an emphasis on playing hard and working hard. Mitch enjoyed socialising – something that perhaps he hasn't done in other jobs he has undertaken since leaving Wasps – but his attitude was that if you are going to work bloody hard, make sure you enjoy the rewards that it brings. If you work bloody hard all week and win a game, make sure you go out and celebrate.

The 1999 season took us back to Twickenham for another Cup final and, to the great delight of everyone at the club, we were taking on Newcastle. The build-up was all about the guys at Newcastle trying to rob us of our trophy and it was very much a case of payback time for Lawrence and the players who had stayed and helped rebuild Wasps. The week of the final was a complete nightmare for me because my bloody ear had flared up so badly that I needed to go under the knife three times in quick succession. If that sounds awful then let me tell you, whatever you are trying to imagine, it was worse. However, as always with my medical problems, there was yet another moment of ludicrous humour amid the blood and gore and this time it involved a tray of sandwiches.

My ear had been flaring up for a couple of weeks, constantly getting infected and full of dreadful stuff. Each time, they would have to release the infection and then close the ear back up again only for the problem to return. As a result, they decided to drill a hole in the back of my ear and insert a tap so that any fluid that built up was released. To enable the various operations to take place that week, I had been put under full anesthetic; you probably wouldn't be able to play these days having had that kind of intervention so close to a match.

They couldn't do the work at the private hospital because there wasn't any room and so I was put in an NHS ward attached to the private hospital. I have got the utmost respect for the NHS and what they do, but every person that came in to see me spoke a different type of English and got my birth date and name wrong every single time. I was panicking slightly prior to each operation thinking that if they were getting birth dates and names wrong, what else will they get wrong: will I wake up with my toe removed or have something else taken off by mistake? I remember going under once and saying: 'I am really hungry, can I get some sandwiches?' The nurse said: 'You can't have anything until after the operation.' I said: 'Can you make sure the sandwiches are here as soon as I wake up from the operation as I am starving and I haven't eaten for two days and I have a game at the weekend?' She said: 'Okay, fine, okay.' I made this point to several of the staff: 'I need to know there will be food when I wake up.' 'You will have to wait a while after you come out of the anaesthetic to make sure you are not sick.' I said: 'I have had operations in the past and every time I have woken up I have been starving and there have never been any issues of feeling queasy, so can you please make sure the sandwiches are there?' Just as they came to take me down to surgery, the staff from the catering department arrived and left a tray of sandwiches on my shins. The theatre staff carted me away with this tray of sandwiches still resting on my shins, but which seemed to be of no obvious interest to anyone treating me. The anaesthetist started speaking to me, explaining the dosage he would be using and what I would feel as it started to take effect and then he said: 'Have you got any questions or concerns?' I said: 'Why is there a tray of sandwiches still sat on my shins when I am just about to be operated on?' He glanced down and couldn't believe that I had got this close to the actual operation and no one had noticed the tray. Later, back in my room I devoured those sandwiches, even though they had been hanging around for rather longer than I had expected.

I had my last operation two days before the Cup final, which meant the ear was bloody sore. I didn't have any medical staff saying I was okay to play, it was just a question of 'get out there and do it'. The club medical guys had to devise a scrum-cap with a water polo-style ear fitting to try and minimise any potential damage. This proved a pointless exercise as my old mate Garath Archer stood opposite me for the entire match and spent most of the time trying to rip my ear off. I threw up straight after the game, just from the cumulative effect of the pain and, despite winning my first trophy with Wasps, it was a hellish day for me. I just hated every moment of it because I was in so much pain and the pills I took to mask the problem did absolutely nothing. After the match we went out to the Sports Café in the West End and I stood in the corner and sank a few drinks getting more and more depressed as everyone else was merrily enjoying themselves because I was still in agonising pain.

By this stage, no doubt to the delight of the room service staff, I had moved out of the hotel and had bought my own flat in Chiswick Green Studios, a warehouse apartment complex. I had a mini heart attack when they told me the price – £290,000 for a one-bedroom flat – given I had paid £120,000 for my Bristol flat, which was twice the size, but I was now on the London property ladder. I thought I had a keen eye for property and felt there was no doubt this place would quadruple in value and make me enormous amounts of money. I now had two places. When I told my parents I was buying a place in London, my dad said I had a screw loose and was absolutely mad. He had also told me to mortgage myself to the hilt, so I did just that. Parents always think your decisions are ludicrous: like the first car you get and they tell you that 'you should have got a sensible car'.

My parents came over for the Cup final win and my mum reacted to my ear problem in the usual way by telling me, yet again: 'You should give up this stupid game.' It doesn't matter what injury or ailment I've got, it is always: 'You should give up this stupid game.'

As part of the 1999 Rugby World Cup preparations, England headed to Australia for a training camp, for which I was not required. However, I did head to Oz for a holiday with a couple of mates, including Dugald Macer, our hooker. On our way up the east coast from Sydney we met up with Kingy who was taking a moment for a coffee away from the England sessions and he looked like he'd been put through the ringer. It left me thinking that perhaps I was better off out of it. They were patently having a tough tour, although when I bumped into Jason Leonard and Jeremy Guscott in Brisbane at the City Rowers Club at about 2.00 a.m. on a different day, they seemed to be coping much better with the demands of the England training camp. Maybe, Kingy was just going out with the wrong guys!

I love Australia, it's the attitude of the people, the weather, the great outdoors and, of course, their love of a good time revolving around large pieces of meat or fish and beer. Consequently, I wasn't in the greatest shape when I came back from the holiday, which didn't worry me until Clive called me into the final World Cup training squad based in Leeds.

Mitch was now involved with England, in charge of the forwards when I was recalled to the squad. I tried my hardest and did the best I could, but I wasn't quite up to the fitness levels they were expecting. It was during this period that England started handing out computers and occasionally letting you know your selectorial fate by email. There was an incident where Garath Archer handed back his laptop and walked away and I had hoped that might swing things in my favour, but he came back into the squad. Arch's reaction came as everyone was getting flogged – it was part of Mitch's way of weeding out the weak from the strong and working out who had the mental attitude to do it when it really hurt. We had a particularly hard session and, when it finished, Arch was then asked to do another session to prove his fitness because he had a slight niggle. Arch was adamant that to push it any further would only make the injury worse and he wasn't going to do it, but they insisted he carry on training. At this point he said, 'Bollocks, I've had enough,' handed in his laptop and walked away, straight out of the hotel, into his car and drove off. I was thinking: 'My chances of getting in the squad have now improved.' The thing with Arch is that he is not going to hold back on anything and calls it as he sees it and I respect him for that. He obviously put his side of the story forward and knew what his body could and couldn't take, which they accepted, and he was back in the hotel a short while later. The upshot of it all was that I was out again.

To be honest, I didn't pay any attention at all to the World Cup and just got on with playing for the club and while that may sound harsh, as the tournament was taking place in Europe, I was only focused on Wasps. Proving that some things never change, Wasps weren't the most consistent of teams in the Premiership that season: we were very up and down and that reflected on the management and coaching staff. I think everyone has a shelf life, especially in coaching, and once your ideas have been tried and tried and tried and things start to waver or fall off, then it's time to go. I think it was a point Nigel was fast approaching and he eventually left in 2001–02. We were still picking up trophies, but within the squad we had measured ourselves on our league form and needed to win the title with consistency, which was our biggest problem. We knew we could beat anyone on our day, but we never quite got it together over a series of games, which is the key factor in winning the league title or the Heineken Cup. We needed consistency and strength of character to be able to pull things out of the bag.

Our form can't have been too bad, however, because it provided me with a platform to regain a place in the England team and I played the whole of the newly expanded Six Nations Championship in 2000.

Johnno was out injured at this point and I was partnering Arch in the second row and we did pretty well as a double act. It is always best to have Arch alongside you rather than against you and while this big man could easily injure you as a team-mate, he could do an awful lot more damage to his opposite number. Arch had that intimidating factor that helps on occasions, but not always when it comes to referees. As a result of England's quarter-final loss to South Africa at the World Cup a few months earlier, England freed up a bit in terms of the way they looked at the game, and that is what Mitch and Brian Ashton, the backs coach, were trying to get across. We could no longer just play forward-oriented rugby and think it would be enough to win at test level. Brian also started coming into his own with free-flowing backs interlinking with the forwards and the whole team felt that the shackles had come off a little bit. We were able to go out there and play and no longer felt restricted. As a result, we racked up some good wins, knocking over Ireland 50–18, Wales 46–12, Italy 59–12 and then beat the French 15–9 at the Stade de France.

Defeating France initiated a party in the stadium hospitality box being used by the wives and girlfriends, which then became a boat trip down the Seine arranged by Clive's wife Jane, while the players and management attended the official dinner. My father and mother managed to get an invite on board the boat – something that turned out to be a really bad move for me. My father had been enjoying the booze all day and continued into the night on the boat and when Jane got up to make a speech – telling all the girls how important they were in the great scheme of things for the squad – her words were suddenly drowned by a large man standing up singing: 'Get your tits out for the boys.' My father continued with this demand until he was pulled back down into his seat. What made it even worse was that he was the only male on the boat! I had been sin-binned in the match and, despite our win, was in a pretty foul mood because it didn't reflect very well on me and I had put the team under pressure by being down to 14 men late in the match. The next day, I met Jason Leonard at breakfast and he shook my hand and said: 'It's been great playing with you, Shawsy, good luck in the rest of your rugby career.' I was totally bemused and, after a few more players had made similar cracks, I decided to seek out Jane (my partner not Mrs Woodward) who then proceeded to ruin my day by giving me every cough, spit and comma about my father's performance the previous night. Apparently, my parents ended the evening looking for a taxi and while my mother waited at the stand for a car, my father headed off on his own. The next time they came together was in the hotel room, where he had adopted a fully clothed starfish position on the bed, leaving her with hardly any room to sleep.

Having survived my father's attempts to kill my test career stone dead with his serenading of Jane Woodward, I was still in the team as we prepared to face Scotland at Murrayfield chasing a victory that would give us the Grand Slam title that had eluded the team the previous season. However, what unfolded was one of the blackest days in my playing career. I was under pressure before the match even started because there was a campaign to get Johnno back quickly and into the second row for the Scotland game. I felt it was very unfair and, in my opinion, against Scotland, I was one of the few forwards that kept on going and battering away until the final whistle. On that occasion, we didn't give the Scots enough respect. We lost in torrential conditions, with further problems created by our decision not to go up and get the Six Nations trophy. It wasn't a snub: the guys were frozen and in desperate need of a warm shower, not another long period standing around in the cold as Scotland went bonkers at having won the Calcutta Cup.

In the changing-rooms after the Scotland game the mood was one of utter disbelief that we had messed up the chance of a Grand Slam again and most of us just sat there, with our heads in our hands. The previous season, many of the guys had endured the loss to Wales at Wembley that had cost England another Slam chance. One year on at Murrayfield, the squad was experiencing the same feeling yet again and it was a very, very dark moment. It had been freezing during the game and I had never known anything like it. It was a difficult one because Lawrence had scored fairly early on and I think at that stage everybody thought we had everything tied up. Scotland obviously saw a chink of light and went for it. We were left to reflect on another massive opportunity thrown away.

The season ended on a high note for Wasps, who had to say goodbye to Mitch after he opted to move back to New Zealand, when we successfully retained our English Cup crown by defeating Northampton in the final to prove that at club level, at least, we could be winners. It had been a season of great highs and lows and cannot be allowed to pass without reference to my drop goal against Bath right at the start of the campaign.

I think we were about 30 points down to Bath at Loftus Road and apparently I had a three- or four-man overlap when I received the ball. I was just outside the 22 and hoofed it through the posts, turned round and found all my team-mates smiling and laughing. I then looked to the bench and saw Nigel with a horrified expression on his face. I was pleased it went over because I always start and finish training sessions by kicking balls, just drop and spiral kicking. Quite often coaches have joked that I should take the kicks to touch, but obviously I would never dream of putting myself forward because that would be the occasion when I would scuff it on the outside of my boot and put it straight into the full-back's hands. However, I remain the only second-row forward to have ever scored a drop goal in a Premiership match.

CHAPTER 12

TREVOR TERRORISES WASPS, WHILE CLIVE LEARNS TO CHILL OUT

Trevor Leota joined Wasps the same season as I joined the club and when I first saw him at training I thought he was an unusual sight: huge neck, short body and immensely powerful arms. Trevor came to Wasps with a bit of a reputation and we had seen a couple of videos of him putting in some pretty big tackles, yet on first appearances he seemed to be a really jovial guy, who loved to banter and chill out. Surely this couldn't be the same guy with the biggest tackle in the game? Before the first training session the boys were saying: 'Hear you are a bit of a big tackler,' and he said: 'Yeah mate, I put ten people in hospital last year' – a fact he was more than happy to reveal. We were a bit sceptical . . . ten people in hospital, whatever. Then, in the first session, he pole-axed Kenny. Initially we found it all hysterical and fell about laughing; a few moments later, however, we thought: 'Hang on a minute, Kenny is in a pretty bad way.' He really did need treatment and the medical guys raced over to my mate's prone body. In that one tackle we got a very clear idea of our new team-mate and what he could bring to the party.

Trevor didn't have many starts in that first season as his fitness was a slight problem and getting him into the right shape and keeping that unusual body of his ticking over was a constant balancing act. He had a sponsorship deal with a fast-food outlet that rewarded him with a bucket of chicken for every try, which didn't really help the fitness team at Wasps. He eventually brought his wife and kids over to London, she put him on the straight and narrow and he actually got fit for a period. When his family went back to New Zealand, it was felt he might go off the rails and so one of the fitness staff moved in with him to monitor his food intake. The impact he had was huge – I have never seen the likes of it since – and Big Trev became an icon for the supporters. He was also a human battering ram and it would take four or five guys to eventually put him down; his only flaw was his love of KFC and rum and cokes. His regular drinking haunt was the Red Back, which is about 100 metres from our training ground and he loved it there.

If you meet Trevor and start up a conversation with him then he comes across as a really nice gentle guy. If you got on the wrong side of him, however, or if he had been on the rum and cokes, he could be a handful. When he went home to New Zealand or Australia – where he had family as well – there was always a reason why he couldn't catch the flight back to the UK such as one year, his passport had run out and he was delayed a while in flying back from Auckland. His idea of getting fit was to play in the touch-rugby leagues around London. He would even play in a rugby league game on days before our Premiership or cup matches, with those appearances often leading to reports in the local papers that revealed: 'Trevor Leota plays stand-off for London New Zealand' – which didn't go down very well with the Wasps management. His rugby league appearances went unnoticed for quite some time until he pole-axed someone and put the guy in hospital. He was a beast of a player in professional rugby, so heaven knows how he came across in the amateur games!

TREVOR TERRORISES WASPS . . .

When Warren Gatland arrived at the club during the 2001–02 season, he took a good look at Trevor and understood that you had to keep him on a tight rein, maintain some sort of fitness level and keep him out of trouble. The fans loved him because he would go across to the main bar wherever it was – Loftus Road or Adams Park – and just cross the pitch afterwards to be with the public. It is probably not the best thing for a professional rugby player to do, but that is what he did and the fans loved him for it. I never got hit by Trevor in training because I kept out of his way. With Trevor, as long as you kept an eye on where he was when you received the ball, you could always sidestep him. The main thing was not to run into him. If you opted to take the contact and recycle the ball against Big Trev, you were destined for disaster.

I was in and around the England squad at that time, but wasn't really featuring a great deal and that scuppered any chances I might have had of going on the 2001 Lions Tour to Australia. It almost completely passed me by, although there was some suggestion I could get called up for Malcolm O'Kelly, but that came to nothing. With Johnno back in the England team, I didn't seem to feature prominently in Clive's plans. However, I was taken on the tour to Canada and the USA, which took place at the same time as that Lions trip to Oz. Clive was more laid back and the England trip turned out to be a lot of fun. It was the leftovers of the England team that weren't on the Lions tour and caps were awarded in the three test matches – two of them with Canada.

Initially, Martin Corry was on our tour before he received a call-up to join the Lions and went on to play a huge part in the test series. Generally, when the Lions tour is on you want to be touring, because there is always that chance of being called up, like Martin. Even if the call didn't come, those of us in North America figured it was a nice place to tour anyway. Canada is always good fun and we were given an opportunity to play a more expansive kind of rugby. We had new coaches involved with the squad, as Andy Robinson was away with the Lions, and that meant a first tour as coaches with England for two former Great Britain rugby league stars, Ellery Hanley and Joe Lydon. It was also a debut tour as forwards' coach for John Wells, who is still in that role.

It was interesting, especially with Ellery Hanley, because he had new ideas and delivered some strange sessions. He wasn't a huge fan of contact work, because the league guys believe you save that for the weekend fixture and saw no point in beating yourself up during the week. He used to have this drill where you stood opposite the same-sized player, second row or whatever, and you would give them a fireman's lift and shout, 'Stick, stick, stick,' which made you feel a bit daft. A lot of coaches have their own different shouts that become part of their sessions: shouts of 'up and in', 'turf wedge', or whatever it may be to signal that players should move forward and then start hitting or wedging; there are lots of different words, but Ellery's was 'stick'. As a result, you had a few jokers saying: 'I'm a stick, I am a stick.' It was all rather bizarre. Ellery used to like hugging everyone before a game as you went out onto the pitch. He also produced badges with '100 per cent' on them, which he would present after a game. If you missed a tackle you weren't a member of the '100 per cent Club', but if you got your 100 per cent then it was good enough for the special badge and up you went to receive it from one of rugby league's legends. Joe Worsley played in the first two games and in the midweek one he got his badge; on the Sunday, though, he missed a tackle and was made to give his badge back.

It was also a first England trip for Simon Kemp, the RFU doctor, with whom I had a difference of opinion because we had played the Baabaas at Twickenham as a warm-up fixture and I'd twisted my ankle. It is usually an injury from which it takes me about two days to recover and he immediately ruled me out of the following weekend's first test with Canada, a match in which caps were being awarded. I was very angry and said to him: 'I'll be fit, I'll be fine.' He said: 'I'll have to rule you out.' After discussions with the coaches, I was given longer to prove my fitness and was named on the bench and I eventually came on as a replacement against Canada and then played the second test, where I scored two tries.

The tour was good fun and plenty of new faces emerged on that trip. Steve Thompson, who would be England's World Cup hooker in 2003, was also on the tour. No one really knew him when he was taken out; he was being groomed as a hooker, even though he had played in the back row for Northampton. I remember him throwing a ball and thinking, 'That guy is never going to make it playing hooker,' because, at that time, he couldn't throw the ball into a lineout. The ball was moving from left to right or right to left by about five metres. He kept to himself for the entire tour and, occasionally, we found him drinking Guinness on his own in a bar. Obviously no one knew then how much of a key player he'd be in England's triumph in 2003.

With test matches in Toronto, Vancouver and San Francisco, there were plenty of opportunities for players to lose their way and become totally engrossed in the local culture. The Vancouver test took place on what looked like a bit of prairie, with telephone wires stretching into the distance and a rugby pitch in the middle of nowhere. Canada had featured in my rugby life a couple of years earlier when Nigel Melville told me there were two female Canadian writers who were going to produce a Mills and Boon-type book about rugby players and needed more of an insight into the game and how it all worked, and characters, etc. Nigel got me into his office one day and said: 'I need to speak to you, you seem like a sensible chap, do you mind?' I said: 'No, not at all.' They rang me up and it was all very, very bizarre, with these sexy, husky voices down the end of the phone, ringing from Canada at different hours of the day. Sometimes they would call at 1.00 a.m. and say they had forgotten the time difference. I was very cagey about the whole thing and thought: 'This just seems all too strange.' They said they were speaking to other players and that they were eventually going to come over and meet some of us, would we mind? I kept all my comments about rugby very tame and said we were all very professional now and the game had changed. They said that was all very strange because a few guys they had spoken to said they still led a very exciting life that involved touring and drinking. Some time later, I remember training at Sudbury, jogging around the pitches as a warm-up, when this car pulled up in the little car park next to the clubhouse, which you could see from the pitches. Out of the car got these two women, who must have been 6 ft 3 in. in heels, with massive fake boobs, ridiculous amounts of lipstick, and long hair – one was brunette, the other blonde – and I thought: 'Who in the hell are these two?' It turned out they were the two Canadian authors and I thought: 'Thank Christ I haven't divulged too much detail about what went on, because clearly this is a set-up.' They came into the club and spoke to a few of the lads, and it seemed to be some sort of plant from a newspaper, although nothing appeared.

Some of the players went out with them and, because they had enormous knockers, a few were very interested. Apparently, they came out with extraordinary stories about being ex-KGB spies, and knew all about self-defence, including five different martial arts. I thought it was all crap, although I do remember on one occasion, when we were in a club in Fulham with some women who were wearing particularly short dresses, one member of the club pinched one of the females on the bottom, she jabbed him in the solar plexus with her elbow and swiftly punched him in the face. He flew across the floor and ended up in a heap. It was an astonishing display of self-defence – I kept well away. Fast forward to the Canadian tour and, while jogging around the pitch before the second test match with Canada, I recognised the two amply proportioned women on the touchline. Needless to say, I stayed well away and I'm still waiting to read their book!

One of the many standout aspects of this England tour was just how many A-list celebrities we met along the way. None of the other players knew who it was at our first hotel, but Peter Ustinov was staying there and trying to explain who Ustinov was turned out to be a hopeless task – the boys were obviously a group of uneducated plebs. The cast of *The Matrix* was staying in the hotel in Los Angeles and Vin Diesel was out and about at one of the nightclubs we visited. It was quite a 'cool' tour and, thanks to Clive, no expense was spared. He made sure we were staying at all the nicest hotels and even booked us a private jet to fly from Canada to LA. The plane had what seemed like 50 big armchair seats and two air hostesses per player.

In the Vancouver hotel there was another lift incident with Ronnie. We walked into the lift – there were about four or five of us – and it was quite a squeeze with Ronnie the last man in, which meant we were all facing out while he was looking in. There was a chap in the middle of the scrum of players, who became totally surrounded with Ronnie staring him straight in the face. It was clearly a celebrity because, on a fairly warm day in Vancouver, he was wearing a scarf, dark glasses, a hat and an overcoat. I clocked him as soon as I got in, realising it was Liam Neeson. As Ronnie was staring straight at him you could see his mind ticking over and just before the lift pinged and we got out he said: 'It is, it is, Liam Neeson. Pleased to meet you, Mark Regan,' and shook his hand. Everybody else knew it was Neeson but left him alone; Ronnie, on the other hand, decided to go ahead and make his day.

One of the strongest memories of the tour was Clive's demeanour: he was so chilled compared to previous meetings and tours. It probably helped that we were winning comfortably and having a good time but it was still good to see. In the run-up to the last game against the USA in San Francisco, we ended up at the British Consulate and Ronnie decided to become the judge and jury and hold a little court session in the palatial surroundings. It was Player X's debut tour and, having won his first cap, it was a case of taking a drink from everyone, including Ronnie. We had left it to the end of the tour to initiate the new caps and shall we say they got slightly tipsy. We still headed to a bar after Judge Regan's court session, with Player X following along. Then, suddenly, he came out of nowhere and tackled one of the guys into a car, accidentally denting the vehicle. He carried on, before succumbing to his initiation and we packed him off to his bed a full-international! Happy Days.

CHAPTER 13

'DO YOU REALLY TRAIN ON THIS MUD HEAP?'

The desperately poor training pitches at Wasps were becoming a real problem at this stage and we had to start using the public areas on the other side of the clubhouse. To be blunt, the pitches were covered in dog crap, left by the many four-legged residents walked by their owners who couldn't be bothered to poop scoop. A few of the Wasps players picked up infections and illnesses because of the excrement, but we carried on suffering in silence until Phil Larder, the England specialist coach, came down to the club because we felt there was a problem with our defence. We warned Phil that it was a pretty messy pitch and his reply was: 'Oh it doesn't bother me, I'm a northern lad, I'm used to all this.' However, he couldn't quite believe what we were training on and, as a result of his reaction, it was decided to find training pitches more in keeping with one of the top teams in Europe. We headed to Bisham Abbey, where the England football team used to train, and the change in circumstances was amazing. We swapped a shit heap for the grounds of a stately pile and it was no coincidence that our fortunes started to improve. We finished runners-up in the league and while you can do without a state-of-the-art gym or a running track for sprint work, it is absolutely vital to be able to use a playable training pitch every day of the week. It was nice to have somewhere good to train and Bisham signalled a fresh start for everyone.

In 2000 we signed Ian Jones, the All Blacks lock, whom I had packed down with for the Barbarians against South Africa in Dublin four years earlier. Ian was great for us because, traditionally, we had a pretty poor lineout and it wasn't really an area we focused on. Ian's attitude was slightly different. He would almost guarantee us the ball without even having to do an awful lot. It always amazed me that he didn't actually use the lifting laws much to his advantage because he always jumped without them. One thing you learn when playing with Ian is that he never really plays outside his comfort zone and I know that sounds odd, but he does the things he knows he can do very, very well. He is light framed, so he's not going to go charging into contact and bowl someone over. He will take the contact, retain the ball, put it back on a platter and repeat that process as many times as you want him to. The same went for Craig Dowd, our long-serving All Blacks prop, who everyone knew wasn't going to pop up in the midfield and launch a charge like Phil Vickery occasionally does. Craig barely handled the ball, but as a one-out runner, just taking the ball two yards and producing it again, he was the best in the world. Over here, we tend to think that New Zealand players are terribly skilful and amazing ball handlers, while the truth of the matter is that they know their jobs and do them very well – it all fits in comfortably with the rest of the team. In England, however, we try and coach a player into doing something different compared to the job he undertakes for his club. Joe Worsley is a great example. For years England have tried to get Joe to be someone he is not. They decided they wanted a ball-running number 8 or number 6 who is able to pass with both hands, link up and offload. Joe can do that on occasions, but what he is extremely good at is knocking down anything that comes in his way. He is not going to be the guy who has got amazing hands and who links up with everyone, and the Wasps coaches created the right role for him. England thought they knew better and I was so happy that he came into the 2009 Six Nations Championship and played for England in the same way he does for Wasps and was outstanding. Equally he had a great Lions tour to South Africa and was very effective in our victory in the final test. I think England have been guilty of making the same error with a number of players over a number of years, even myself, to a certain degree. People are picked for a reason, because of the way they play for their clubs, yet they are selected for England either in a different position or are asked to undertake a role that is alien to them. And the selectors wonder why they don't perform on occasion.

CHAPTER 14

WARREN AND HIS 'DREAM TEAM' ARRIVE TO LAUNCH A REVOLUTION

The 2001–02 season was the last under Nigel Melville's management and I was aware of the talk about his going to Gloucester. We had a game called off because of under-soil heating problems against Gloucester that season and their supporters, who had travelled up, were shouting all sorts of things about Melville joining Gloucester. We were very much aware of the possible move, but it wasn't really an issue because everyone has a shelf life and Nigel's had clearly come to an end with Wasps. Change was in the air and, having benefited from a new training ground, we were happy to embrace anything that would make us a better team. There were rumours that former Ireland coach Warren Gatland was going to take over and he had done a good job turning Connacht into a force in Irish rugby. I felt Ireland played a better brand of rugby while they were under Warren's management and we were also aware that he could be a bit controversial. I had heard that Warren liked a drink with the players and knew that would fit in quite nicely.

When Warren turned up he brought fellow Kiwi Tony Hanks with him to do analysis and Craig White to look after fitness. Shaun Edwards had been in and around Wasps prior to Warren's arrival, and had also done some skills sessions with the England squad. Warren and Shaun hit it off immediately and so Shaun came on board with the new management regime. I think it was just one of those meetings of minds; they thought alike and got on extremely well. There was a completely different attitude, outlook and drive under this new management group and, despite Warren's track record with us and all the accolades he rightly received, I am sure he would acknowledge that Craig White was probably as influential, if not more, on the players. Craig raised the bar in terms of our fitness levels and what we could achieve. The Wasps players felt we were just about there, but Craig showed us just how far we still had to travel if we wanted to be at our very best. What we thought was the limit of our workload proved to be just a base level in his mind and we were finding we were able to reach a new level of play in the fourth quarter of a game because we had so much more strength, speed and fitness than the opposition. It almost became a case of us thinking: 'Well, we'll just have to keep playing and our strength and fitness will pull us through, no matter how far we are behind.' In the past, under Pat Fox and Nigel Melville, the approach to fitness was more of an old-school mentality, where you just worked hard and were flogged into the ground. Craig's attitude was to work us incredibly hard and take us to a very uncomfortable level, but in intense, very short bursts.

Craig believed in being able to recognise the moment where you feel you are almost at the point of exhaustion, yet wanted to continue to work hard because it was only for a short period of time. He didn't make you stand out there for ever and a day doing rugby, conditioning and sprinting. It meant that although we were at the club for three-quarters of the day, the actual sessions we had with him were very, very short. Come the weekend, while you might not think you had done as much work as in previous years, you would be so much fresher. Once you are out on the training pitch it was 'wham, bam', with everything done in under an hour and Warren had a lot of respect for Craig and vice versa. Ultimately Craig, not Warren, was the one who had the final say as to when the training session finished, regardless of whether it was a crap session or a good one. Even if the plan was to be out there for 50 minutes, if he felt that, for whatever reason, we looked sluggish after half an hour, that was it, we walked in.

Shaun accepted Craig's philosophy because Warren backed the same attitude. Warren was very much Shaun's mentor and Shaun was very respectful of what Warren said and did. It was natural for Warren to surround himself with people he trusted and who sang from the same hymn sheet, and I cannot understand why this doesn't happen more often at international level where a new coach or manager is often forced to work with people who are already in place. When Warren moved to Wales, he brought in the people he wanted alongside him and quite a few of those choices were guys he had worked with at Wasps. It means you have fellow coaches who understand your ethos, the way you want to go about doing things and who respect you for it and are willing to back you to the hilt. In the past, there have been situations at club and test level where, for financial reasons, certain people have remained in posts because it would cost too much to get rid of them. You could see when Warren went to Wales that he wanted everything absolutely right, otherwise he wasn't going to take the job. That is what football managers do when they go to a new club: they strip it back and say: 'I want this physio, I want this fitness guy.' Fair play to Chris Wright, the Wasps owner until Steve Hayes took over in 2008: he completely backed the board and Warren in almost every decision he made.

Obviously, at Wasps, Warren was restricted by financial concerns and things like the gym at Acton, where we moved after a short period at Bisham, weren't filled with the very latest weights or fitness machines. Wasps used other methods to improve facilities, like fining the players for various offences – turning up late, etc. – and that money was used for new equipment. There were lots of little things that all added up and helped maintain the team ethos that has always been so important to Wasps. It is often assumed by our rivals that we just deliver the club motto: 'Once a Wasps, always a Wasps' – because we have all been brainwashed. That's simply not true: the club affects you in so many ways and becomes a very special part of your life.

The real gem that had perhaps more of an impact on the morale of the club than anything else at this stage was the discovery of Paul Stridgeon, aka 'Bobby Bushay'. Bobby was formerly a featherweight wrestler who Craig helped train before competing in the Commonwealth games. After being beaten in the early rounds of that competition he decided that wrestling may not be his route to fame and fortune and joined Craig as a voluntary assistant in the fitness team at Wasps.

For the most part, Bobby's role was to provide the lads with water whenever it was required and hence he took on the name from Adam Sandler's film *The Water Boy*. Bobby is like a skinny Johnny Vegas – only funnier – and his responsibilities soon grew from watering and conditioning the lads to the club's full-time entertainer. Warren then gave Bobby the task of awarding a man of the match award, which would become known as the 'Bobby Cup'.

The award would only ever be handed out after a winning performance and it was entirely up to Bobby how he would present the cup. One week he would dress up as Sting, our club mascot and make a video of how Sting would spend his spare time. This would involve Bobby catching the tube into central London, dancing with buskers, going into pubs clubs etc. Other times he would involve academy players in mock ups of films or music videos, the most famous of these being *The Lord of the Rings* where Bobby plays Golum. There was also a *Bohemian Rhapsody* parody featuring England forwards James Haskell and Tom Rees. They would die if it ever appeared on Youtube.

The promotion of Bobby to the very esteemed position was a stroke of genius on Warren's part. It wasn't all just fun and games at

Wasps under Warren. Whilst there wasn't any doubt that Warren enjoyed a laugh and a joke, we also worked harder than we ever had, not just in training but also in the upkeep of our facilities.

We used to walk regularly around the Twyford Avenue training pitches clearing up rubbish left by other teams who shared the facilities. It didn't matter that we hadn't created the mess, Warren made us do it because it was our training pitch, our workplace and it needed to be kept clean. There would also be a bi-weekly gym clean which everyone had to take part in – some would be polishers, others sweepers, some with mops in hand, and others with hoovers. Before making our training home in Acton, we spent a very short period – thank goodness – based at Grasshoppers, very close to the Sky studios, in Greenford. It was shocking because the facilities were very basic. It was very open with just a little bit of a breeze seeming like a bloody whirlwind and the only plus side was that it wasn't too far away from my flat. However, I was more than happy when we were able to end our nomadic existence and finally find a permanent training home that didn't feature dog crap or howling gales.

CHAPTER 15

FAREWELL LOFTUS ROAD, HELLO ADAMS PARK

When I was at Bristol I loved playing away at Wasps, because the Loftus Road surface was fantastic and, being a very small pitch, it was the perfect size for a big lump like me. You felt you could get round it and, by not having to expend so much energy, came to the conclusion you were really fit. It was a great little stadium for rugby, but our attendances were woeful. This was partly due to the location in White City and fans weren't keen to drive there and leave their cars in that particular area of London. The transport links weren't fantastic either for people who had to travel on buses, trains or tubes on a Sunday when we played our games. There were occasions when the club did try a few promotional offers and we attracted crowds of 12,000 or 13,000, which created a fantastic atmosphere, incredible. However, when you got 2,000 or 3,000, the atmosphere in the crowd was pretty pitiful.

The players used to leave their cars in the BBC car park and then negotiate a couple of housing estates leading to the ground where some supporters had been mugged. It gained a bit of a reputation and our fan base – never that big at Loftus Road – dwindled quite rapidly. In 2002, the club came out of the Loftus Road PLC venture with Queens Park Rangers and Chris Wright, our owner, turned his back on football and stuck with the rugby side of the operation. QPR weren't very successful, but with Wasps Chris was able to enjoy regular league and cup success while never overdoing the 'I am the owner' bit.

I joined Wasps after Chris had come on board and I found him an enigma, because here was the owner of London Wasps who didn't appear to know much about the game. He was a huge QPR fan and rugby just seemed to grow on him. He was impressed by our play and also by our attitude on and off the pitch. Because he had a direct contrast between the football team and Wasps, it soon became clear where the fun lay for him. He would always pop into the dressing-room for a quick chat and would then be off again, although he did get more involved after we split from QPR and stood alone.

Wasps has never been a club with a massive crowd base and was always way behind city rugby clubs like Bristol, Gloucester and Leicester in terms of support. Chris's money kept us alive and while Richmond probably had a better foundation in terms of a ground and support for rugby in that area of South-West London, they didn't survive very long at all. Chris's prudence when it came to spending his money proved the correct course of action compared to the way Richmond just threw huge amounts at the game with abandon in those early days. Given Chris paid my wages, it may not come as a shock to learn that I have always been on the side of the clubs in their seemingly endless rows with the Rugby Football Union, because they are the ones who took the bull by the horns when the game went professional and the RFU has been trying to claw back the players ever since. The investment the clubs made in the players has been extraordinary. I don't believe the club owners, who have spent more than £150 million collectively to keep the game alive, have received the credit they deserve. There is no doubting that rugby would not be in its current strong position had it not been for the clubs. You could argue that men like Chris, Nigel Wray (Saracens) and Tom Walkinshaw (Gloucester) have been bonkers for ploughing so much of their money and time into giving England a professional club rugby system, but good on them for sticking around during all the bad times. The club game has gone from strength to strength and England have fed off this growth in attendances to the point where the sport is now emerging as a major force. We now have an Elite Player Squad agreement in place, although it really still needs tweaking to benefit both sides. Still, at least the interminable warfare died down for a short while.

Wasps' decision to relocate to Adams Park in Wycombe caused plenty of debate at the time, but seven years on, it has been a success and attracts regular crowds of 10,000. Getting in and out of the ground is a bit tricky, or it has been in the past, but improvements have been made. That first season in Wycombe coincided with the club winning the Premiership title and the Parker Pen Challenge Cup with a squad that now included Rob Howley, the Wales scrum-half. There is a general perception in the game that Welsh players don't like to leave Wales and that they get a bit homesick. Rob was very much like that and it took a lot of persuading for him to move to London. Once he was with us, however, he admitted it had been the right call.

I have been asked so many times to explain the iffy starts that Wasps continually make to the league season and I can't put my finger on it. The excuse I use is that a lot of our players go away on summer tours and, therefore, come back jaded and take a little longer to swing into action. I don't think that is a complete explanation for why it has happened so many times and maybe we need to give ourselves a mountain to climb after Christmas to prove the doom-mongers wrong. It is an easy excuse to say some of those poor starts were due to the various injuries that have interrupted Lawrence's career. There is no doubt that Lawrence added to the playing side in the past and has always added something to the dressing-room, but he is not the sole reason that we won games or lost them just because he was missing.

One of the features of Warren's regime was the way he handled the players and did not ask people to perform week in, week out. I think Rob found this strange to cope with at first, because Warren made it patently clear he would not be expected to play in every single match at scrum-half. Warren's words to Rob were: 'You're our number one and we want you to play the big games. We want you absolutely right for those games and firing on all cylinders, but we don't expect you to play week in, week out.' One of Warren's great strengths was that he knew when to give the players time off and when to crank up the pressure. We might have lost three games in a row, but we would still be given four or five days off. I am sure our critics felt this was a cop-out and that we should have been worked harder but, in the long run, there were real benefits to his approach. When everyone else was really struggling to put a side together because of injury or mental and physical fatigue, we were always fresh. We certainly believed we were fitter and fresher than everyone else as a result of those extra days off and we enjoyed Warren's sympathetic handling.

It can sometimes be a difficult process accepting a new regime and a different way of doing things, but we embraced Shaun's defence system the moment he arrived. He had no coaching pedigree when he first joined Wasps, but he quickly won us over with his amazing enthusiasm for the game and his eye for detail. When you speak to any of the Welsh players, they couldn't wait to take their first defensive session with Shaun after he was appointed to do that role alongside Warren. Shaun, a rugby league legend, gets very excited about the defence system, which is an odd thing to say given the physical demands this puts on your body and the concentrated effort required to get it right. Shaun was somehow making us get excited about tackling people and creating turn-overs and we fed off his enthusiasm, which remains to this day.

Our victory over Bath to win the Parker Pen Challenge Cup was important and a step in the right direction for the club, because it was the new regime's first bit of silverware. I know it was viewed as a minor final, but it was still a final and rugby is all about winning the big games. You don't want to turn up to a final and be happy with second best; if that was the case you might as well get knocked out in the first round. It was important that we won, but we moved on swiftly and that was the way everyone viewed it at Wasps. It set us up nicely for the Premiership final against Gloucester, after we had made an impressive charge up the table (yet again) to earn the right to battle it out for the title of English champions. Gloucester had finished top, which meant they hadn't been playing in the immediate build-up to the final, whereas we had been performing every weekend.

When Gloucester walked out onto the Twickenham pitch, I thought almost every single one of them looked as though they had their heads held low. It was almost as if they could taste defeat before the match had even started. They were clearly worried about not having played for a while; in contrast, we were in the groove and battle-hardened. An early try seemed to drain what little confidence they possessed and in rapid time we were being crowned the best team in England. Until Christmas, everyone was sorting themselves out in the league and then after New Year we pretty much proved we were the best side. There was almost as much bitching before the game as there was after the playoff final about who were the 'real' champions, but we were the ones with the trophy. I had joined Wasps to win things and now we were champions of England. However, despite being part of the country's most successful club, I still wasn't in the England team.

That summer, England had arranged tests with New Zealand and Australia as a key part of the World Cup preparation and there was also a midweek clash with the New Zealand Maoris. I went to New Zealand and felt I played really well against the Maoris, even receiving plaudits from the locals, which is almost unheard of. Initially, I thought we were going to be in for real problems and, after the first five minutes, I thought 'Bloody hell, this is going to be hell a of a game,' because they had lots of pace and power and we did really well as a team. The next day the New Zealand papers were full of 'Who is this Simon Shaw and why isn't he playing for England?' I met up with Warren and Tony Hanks, who had gone back to New Zealand for the summer, and they came to the test match, which I wasn't involved in. I had a beer with them after the game nonetheless and it was nice to see them and nice to have that backing. However, injury was to ensure I didn't have a chance of making the Australia test in Melbourne. I was forced to fly home early after losing power in my left arm.

CHAPTER 16

HOW TO BECOME A WORLD CUP WINNER WITHOUT PLAYING A MINUTE OF THE TOURNAMENT

I realised getting into the World Cup squad was going to be a difficult assignment and one made even tougher by the injury I suffered in New Zealand in the summer. I had various issues with my neck due to osteophytes (bone spurs) that come out the sides of the vertebrae. If my neck closes down on one side or the other, these osteophytes impinge on the nerve roots that come out of your spinal cord. As a result, it shuts down the nerve sensations and signals to whichever area of the body they relate – usually my left arm. That arm would, basically, just shut down and I wouldn't be able to lift anything or use it properly. I remember being in a gym with Phil Pask, the England physio, on that tour and could barely lift 5 kg above my head. It is not the sort of injury where you are put on a stretcher and get carried off the pitch; it just happens and is sometimes referred to as a 'stinger'. In effect, a stinger is a neural impingement, which sometimes sticks around for 20 seconds or so and then goes away. However, if there is sufficient inflammation that impingement can take a lot longer to subside and Jonny Wilkinson, who kicked the drop goal to win the 2003 World Cup, has got the same sort of thing. It is usually progressive, so if you get one stinger it is not so bad, two stingers and it gets gradually worse and sometimes you can get one that sticks around for months. I had this particular stinger from the summer until the start of the World Cup season, which meant I missed some early games. Simon Mitchell, a former Wasps hooker some years retired, suffered the same kind of prolonged problem and when I see him now, he has an arm that could be hanging off an 80 year old. The correct neural signs don't travel down the arm and I have always been aware of the potential problems the condition can cause. Jonny and I regularly have chats about it; our injuries have many similarities; another player who gets the same pain is Joe Worsley. I don't know whether there is any physical reason why certain players suffer from it more than others and the only good thing with an injury of this sort is that you can still run and keep fit. It is simply a case of waiting until the neural signals come back and, once that happens, it takes next to no time to get back to where you were. It is almost like turning the mains on in your house; once the signal starts coming through it is full power ahead – for a rugby player, it is simply a case of working the muscles back into shape for matches.

Leading up to the announcement of the World Cup squad, the players heard absolutely nothing about their individual chances of making the trip. We were all convinced we were going to be the fittest team in the world. We knew we had the talent, skill and stamina and, thanks to the most demanding training camp I have ever experienced, we would be stronger and fitter than everyone else. The training camp was intense to say the least: we were doing three sessions every day, starting at 7 a.m., and despite the workload it was good fun with plenty of variety to ensure we didn't get bored. We went mountain biking, which was probably the best part of it because they didn't want us to be running all the time and putting extra pressure on our very large joints. I think the forwards mountain biked more than most and everything was a competition, which included the static rowing sessions. I remember Sale hooker Andy Titterell really attacking one of the rowing machines, even though, as a small guy, he wasn't really built for excelling at the exercise. His reps per minute were ridiculously high but he was actually going nowhere in terms of the monitor and received all kinds of abuse from Julian White, who was standing behind him and screaming his head off at him. I was very aware that my role was to play second fiddle to Johnno, but I desperately wanted to take my Wasps form into the test arena and show what I could do for England – if given the chance.

I felt an enormous amount of pressure in the warm-up game with Wales but, at the same time, I was relishing the chance to express myself. Whatever thoughts Clive and the coaches might have had about me as a player, I knew that if I could show my best form – the real me – then there could be a lot of pressure to include me in the squad. As it turned out, I received a lot of plaudits – which gave me a real boost. The team against Wales was made up of guys who had an outside chance of making the squad and we all wanted to go out there and play good rugby. There was a lot of skill shown. On that day I thought we had shown a different style from that being produced by the first-choice England team.

I had been so focused on producing something special against Wales that I had asked Jane to do the same that week. She was expecting our first child, who was due the same weekend as the Wales match, and I asked her if she would mind getting induced to ensure I could concentrate on the game. Being the wonderful lady she is, Jane got induced on the Wednesday and Samantha was born on 18 August. I stayed for the birth, met up with the team on the Thursday and played a game in Cardiff on the Saturday, returning in high spirits to Jane and Samantha that night. What a great week: our first child had been born and I had received lots of pats on the back for my performance. Life couldn't get any better.

England still had the two warm-up games with France to play before the final squad was revealed. When I came on as a replacement against France in the first game I played well again and for the first time allowed myself to think that Clive had to take me and was relishing another opportunity against the French in Paris. I was confident and happy with the guys around me and felt we could beat the French, although we lost narrowly. At the time I felt as though I had done enough to make the squad. We were then told to go away and rest up and wait to be notified by telephone.

Jane and I were living in a small house as I had moved out of my bachelor pad because she said it was far too much of a 'manly' home and that I needed to trade up. I temporarily moved to Acton and bought another place in Chiswick to refurbish. On reflection, I didn't really get the timing right: the arrival of a first child, refurbishing a new home and trying to clinch a place in the World Cup squad. Who said men couldn't multitask! We tried to refurbish it in time for the baby's arrival and it was a very close call, but we managed to complete all the work shortly after Samantha was born. I had promised Jane that if I went to the World Cup in Australia, they would have a house to live in rather than a half-finished site. That is why I was racing around in that removal van when my mobile phone rang. Clive said I had played very well, but that I hadn't done quite enough in the two French games. I was a bit startled by that and said: 'I don't understand what you mean. I thought I played very well in both games and toughed it out.' I couldn't believe what I was hearing and pulled the van over. I was stunned more than anything because, for the first time ever, I had allowed myself to adopt an optimistic outlook on my chances rather than be pessimistic and look for reasons to be excluded. I genuinely thought I had done enough and couldn't think of what reason he would have to leave me behind. The reason Clive gave – I hadn't played well enough in coming off the bench in the game against France and the second game with the same opposition – completely astounded me. I said: 'Clive, that's fucking ridiculous, what sort of reason is that?' I never like to use examples of other players, because I think everyone has their own individual case, but at the time I said: 'So and so didn't play very well, he was pretty crap, what are you going to say to him?' It was the first time I had ever done it, but I just felt so pissed off. I held the belief that if you were going to use the warm-up games as a selection platform, then certain guys who were going hadn't justified selection based on their performances. I never thought Clive's decision to leave me at home was personal as he then discussed with me that he was thinking that if Martin Corry was going then he could cover both lock and back row. To me it all pointed to a confirmation in my own mind that I simply didn't fit the mould that England wanted and, therefore, it was almost irrelevant what I did on the pitch because I wasn't fulfilling their criteria.

The worst aspect about being left behind was that when the players were called into a meeting and shown clips from those warm-up games to highlight what was wanted to unlock defences, I was featured in almost every clip. I had sat there with a smile on my face thinking, 'It's nice that they recognised my play,' and then Andy Robinson, who was giving the debriefs at that point, would tell the squad: 'This is the kind of attacking rugby we want to play. We want to be linking backs and forwards and off-loading.'

Andy had arrived with the England set-up after coaching Bath, who were all about set-piece play and lineouts. Those were the elements England were basing their game around: it was all about meeting pressure with pressure. If it was the opposition's throw at the lineout then we had to pressurise it. It didn't matter what you did in the game, if you didn't do what they were asking for in certain areas, that was it. What made it even tougher to accept was my fervent belief that England were going to win the 2003 World Cup, whether I was there or not. That almost made the whole situation worse.

Having put the phone down on Clive, I was left parked at the side of the road in this removal van looking very odd to passers-by. All they would have seen was a large, irate man swearing at the top of his voice, alone in the cab. When the anger subsided, I thought,

'That's it then,' started the engine and got back to moving home. I know it may seem like a strange way of dealing with such a heavy body blow, but I had a newly arrived baby daughter and a house move to complete and this was simply a case of having to overcome yet another rugby disappointment, something I was uniquely qualified to do. Of course this one was as bad as it gets and I did share my thoughts with close friends who were forced to listen to more swearing, but my overwhelming thoughts as I put the van into gear were: 'It's a fucking joke and they are fucking idiots.'

In her own mind, Jane also thought I would be selected and she was a huge help in helping me come to terms with the bitter disappointment; my baby daughter Sam, on the other hand, just gurgled away wonderfully, blissfully unaware of her father's predicament.

I remember reading an article in which Clive said the most difficult decision he had ever made was to leave myself and 'Wig' Rowntree out of the World Cup squad. I knew I was playing well too. I had won the Players' Player of the Year award at Wasps, which gave me real confidence, and with club fixtures set to continue during the World Cup, I threw myself into my rugby and was motivated by a 'to hell with them' attitude. I honestly didn't watch any of the World Cup build-up or any of the early England games and was more than happy to put all of my effort and thoughts into my new family, the refurbished home and the club.

On 11 September, I received a letter from Louise Ramsey, the England Team Manager, which informed me I was on a standby list in case of injury but still it came as a shock to be told Danny Grewcock had suffered a hand injury and that I was needed in Australia. I had been enjoying my early season rugby with Wasps and had scored a hat-trick of tries against Saracens when the call came from Louise telling me: 'You need to get your passport and bare essentials, boots etc., and get yourself off to the airport ASAP. We need you out here tonight or tomorrow.'

It was a repeat of the rapid deployment operation I'd had to undertake in 1994 and, suddenly, I was saying farewell to Jane, Sam and my parents, who had come over from Spain to see their granddaughter. They would all make the trip out to the World Cup – Jane is Australian – after she had sorted out a passport for Sam. The added complication was that Jane and I weren't married, having agreed to wait out my turn at Wasps. Myself, Will Green, Kenny Logan and Peter Scrivener were all having weddings in successive years, and it really was a case of waiting for the right moment when everyone could turn up. Because Jane is Australian, Sam automatically got an Australian passport, but I had to sign a form to ensure Sam was given a British one and that had to be done at the British Consulate after I arrived to link up with the World Cup squad.

I arrived in Sydney at the team hotel close to the beach in Manly and was immediately taken into a press conference. It was all very surreal and, while I can't remember what I said, there were quite a few giggles from the media guys who had all spoken to me when I had been originally left out of the squad and knew the kind of language I had used while telling Clive exactly what I thought about the situation. I don't know if they were trying to avoid me, but I didn't see any of the coaches for quite some time and had already met up with almost the entire squad before Clive loomed into view, shook my hand and said: 'I knew you would get out here.'

When I arrived to join the World Cup squad, it was clear that the guys were supremely confident, although those outside our group would no doubt have described the attitude as arrogance. I don't necessarily think that was the case: it was just that all the individuals involved were supremely confident in their ability to win a game. It was almost irrelevant how they went about winning, they just knew they were going to end up victorious and this attitude would underpin the whole campaign. I didn't think England, because of Jonny Wilkinson and his amazing ability to kick us to victory, were a one-man team, but what we did on the pitch created opportunities to keep the scoreboard ticking over. The brand of rugby we tried to play was never going to produce lots of tries, but we were almost impossible to beat thanks to our amazing fitness levels and our unwillingness to give up. This particular England team was almost like a prizefighter who was going to battle to the death and, to me, Australia seemed to have the same kind of aura. New Zealand and France were playing all the rugby, in terms of scoring tries, and were more fluid and free flowing. With Australia and England, on the other hand, it was a case of having to play incredibly well to beat either of them, because they had so much resilience in defence and every member of their team was seemingly unbreakable. Even when Samoa and Wales put England under an extreme amount of pressure, it was our dogged refusal to be beaten that got us through such demanding games. England didn't play particularly well against either of them, but they toughed it out and got the all-important win. I watched the 28–17 quarter-final win over Wales from the replacements' bench having been allowed to change into the match kit for the first time since arriving in Australia. It was quite strange to be sitting there in the number 18 jersey having wanted to be involved for so long and now, here in the Suncorp Stadium in Brisbane, I was going to fulfil my rugby dream. I had worried that my time with the squad would be spent holding tackle bags in training, but being put on the bench was a really positive thing and when the two locks – Johnno and Ben Kay – became so knackered they could barely stand or run, I was convinced my time had come. I was raring to go, but still no one came over to me and said: 'Get ready to go on.' I kept waiting for the call, but it never came. It was yet another kick in the teeth and just confirmed my own view that the coaches didn't have confidence in me or believe I could help close out the game. The one thing I don't think I have ever been criticised for was my defence and that is what England had to do for pretty much the entire game against Wales.

I wasn't included on the bench for the semi-final with France, when Clive opted to include Martin Corry, and I was resigned to my fate. In that Wales game, Clive had the opportunity to put me on for ten or fifteen minutes and didn't take it, which meant I spent the rest of the tournament having a few beers with Ronnie. I managed to get out and see Jane a couple of times at Doyle's, a fish restaurant at Watson's Bay in Sydney Harbour, which raised my spirits and, despite a lack of match action, I continued to throw myself into the tournament. Having missed out on the previous two World Cups, I was determined to soak it all up. It was great to see hundreds of people hanging around the team hotel morning, noon and night trying to get a glimpse of a player – probably Jonny! I just thought to myself, 'You might as well enjoy being here as you are not going anywhere and you are not playing,' and it became a very nice three-week vacation. I was training as a member of the squad throughout that period and I knew I had a job to do for Wasps when I got back, so I made sure I just didn't switch off.

On the day of the World Cup final there were nine of us with absolutely nothing to do once we got to the Olympic Stadium, although we all had to wear our England tracksuits and take our boots just in case anything happened to one of the players in the warm-up. For the game, we had seats a few rows back from the pitch and it really was a relaxed atmosphere as pre-match nerves as a player didn't apply. We were all getting excited because it was a tight game and Ronnie, in particular, was jumping up and down one minute and looking a bit concerned the next.

As the final headed into extra time, all nine of us were jumping up and down, screaming and shouting while also working out how much we could charge for after-dinner speaking as members of England's World Cup-winning squad! We all knew the game could have gone either way, with Elton Flatley's amazing ability to kick goals under intense pressure largely forgotten because his heroic efforts were eclipsed by Jonny's last-gasp drop goal – the most famous kick ever struck by a rugby player. People tend to forget that Jonny missed a couple of drop goals before he nailed the final one but who cares, he made the one that mattered and at the final whistle, we all rushed on the pitch, jumping up and down.

Then, in that wonderful moment of euphoria, it suddenly kicked in that I hadn't been involved in a single minute of a World Cup campaign that England had won. The other guys going bonkers on the pitch had earned the right to celebrate, because they had all played their part. The guys who played in the games and recorded the wins leading up to that final had all played their role, whereas I had just tagged along at the end like some competition winner. All I could think is: 'Why am I hugging anyone? I haven't really done anything.'

I joined the rest of the squad to receive my winners' medal, one that was supposed to go to the injured Danny Grewcock, back in England, who had to wait ages for his to be delivered. Basically, I had nicked Danny's and when they put the medal around my neck, I had a look and noticed it didn't even have the word 'winner' on it and was just a silver thing with a badly engraved World Cup. I remember thinking that if I had gone all that way and got the crap beaten out of me in order to win this thing, I would have been a bit pissed off. That is the kind of stupid thing that enters your mind when you are going through the kind of mental turmoil I was dealing with that night. I took the medal off pretty much as soon as I got into the changing-room and stuck it in my kitbag. Obviously, there were a lot of things happening in the changing-rooms. People were popping bottles of champagne and slapping one another on the back, and various members of the Royal Family turned up. Three or four of us just sat outside the room, because unless you are actually playing in the final, you don't really feel part of it. There were other guys with similar feelings to me – Stuart Abbot, Kyran and Ronnie – and we sat just talking to one another. Zara Phillips and Prince Harry joined the party and, due to the press conferences, drug testing and everything else that happens after a big game, we didn't get out of the stadium until almost 2.00 a.m. It all seemed to drag on for ever.

Eventually we got to the nightclub that had been booked for the squad at the quayside in Sydney and all the wives and girlfriends were there. As it was so late, I only stayed for a quick beer and never saw the start of the Mike Tindall–Zara Phillips romance. Jonny only stayed for an orange juice before heading back to the Manly hotel and just before I left I made sure Ronnie and Kyran were up for a proper celebration drink later that day. My parting words were: 'You're going to get plastered tonight, so just make sure you're up for it.'

The following day, after breakfast with Jane at the team hotel, we went to her sister's to say goodbye – her flight left later that day – and then I returned to the hotel to prepare for a real blowout with my mates. I got the taxi to drop me short of the hotel, which was being mobbed by fans, and I sneaked in the back way, which meant I missed the police van turning up with some of the lads inside who had managed to convince the officers to give them a free taxi lift back from Kings Cross. I changed and left the hotel and linked up with Ronnie, Kyran and Stuart in a nearby bar. We had time to kill before the official presentation evening in the city and, with a potentially boring night in prospect, drinking all the way through seemed a sensible option. It wasn't long before word got around that there were a few England players in the bar and, suddenly, a queue of autograph hunters stretched out of the bar and around the corner – our quiet beer was over. Ronnie was pretty hung over and not in the best of moods and we were encouraging fans to keep asking him for an autograph: 'I've had enough, zero tolerance, zero tolerance,' he kept shouting. I hadn't drunk much at this stage and was very sprightly, which meant I took in the tale being given to us by an English couple who had saved all their money and got married at the World Cup. They were flying back that day and were very fresh-faced and excited. It was a lovely story and they only wanted a few things signed, but Ronnie, now totally irritated and unaware of the couple's love story, greeted their arrival in front of him, plus details of their wedding, with, 'Yeah, what do you want signed?' He got into the mood when we pointed out what had happened and happily agreed to sign eveything.

The flight back to London was made special because, as the 'extra' player, I wasn't in the original booking and ended up in seat 1A in first class. What a result. All the boys had turned right when they got on the plane and I was the only one who turned left. Obviously, I didn't go back to liaise with the boys, because you tend to keep contact with riff-raff to a minimum when you are that far up the front of the plane! Most of the guys only kept going for half the journey before sleep kicked in, which is not surprising as, apparently, they were playing a game involving drink and sleeping tablets. It was all about who could stay awake the longest and, although a couple of guys suggested trying to match David Boon's drinking record, too much alcohol had already been consumed in the previous 48 hours. On arrival at Heathrow we put on our number ones (a suit and tie) and I didn't anticipate anything like the reception we got. During one of the coach journeys after the final, Jonny had asked me what kind of reception we could expect when we got home and, having joined the trip late, I was able to tell him that the country hadn't seemed particularly bothered about the World Cup when I left. 'There wasn't really much of a furore about what was going on down here, so it might not be that bad.' I was, of course, completely wrong. The place was overrun with fans and we had an amazing battle just to get out of the terminal because so many people wanted to catch a glimpse of the men who had won the World Cup – and that Shaw bloke who had won his own battle just to be part of the squad.

In the days that followed our return, I didn't really have to deal with many fans wanting to talk about the Cup victory, which was in stark contrast to the Gloucester and Northampton boys. There were stories about Phil Vickery, the tight-head prop, being unable to leave his house because fans were besieging it and the same interest followed the Northampton contingent. Unlike Gloucester and Northampton, rugby isn't a main focus for people in London, and those of us living in the capital have always been able to just get on with life. I have seen Kylie Minogue and Madonna in restaurants and people just let them have a quiet meal. I think it is just the nature of London: people just don't tend to bother you.

I was asked how I valued my medal and where I kept it. My

answer – 'To be honest, I haven't got a clue' – was interpreted as Shawsy not caring about his World Cup medal. A story started – which kept going for years – that I had lent it to a mate who kept it in the glove compartment of his car. That wasn't true. I genuinely didn't know where it was because we had moved house and lots of important things were in drawers to be sorted out later. I knew it wasn't going to get lost and none of the medals I have been fortunate enough to win were on display at home. They are still in their presentation boxes, a shoebox or drawer somewhere around the house, but that doesn't mean I'm not proud of each medal.

There had been talk of a special open-top bus trip around London and the chance to meet the Queen and have a reception at 10 Downing Street. Eventually, all the various strands came together and we were given an amazing itinerary that would take in all those exciting elements. We didn't have a clue how many people would turn up in Central London and we were blown away by the reception given to all the players and management that day. There was plenty of talk about what sort of numbers might turn up, but figures didn't really mean anything until you actually saw it. What's more, it was unusual to be back together as a squad. If you win the Six Nations in April, the next time everyone is back together again, if there isn't a summer tour, could be November. However, just weeks after winning the Cup, here was the entire England squad on two buses travelling around the packed streets of the West End. Looking back, I loved every part of the day, it was an amazing experience, but at no point did I hold the World Cup as it was passed around. I actively didn't want to hold it because, as I hadn't touched a ball during the tournament, I thought it was hypocritical. I have a photograph with me and the World Cup, but I'm not holding it and have never picked it up – not even during the 2007 tournament when I played a full part. Danny Grewcock felt the same and we both stood at the back of the bus while most of the guys, who were part of the team, were right at the front with the Cup. Ronnie got up there a couple of times, while Jonny joined us at the back, which is more an indication of his character than anything else. Clive told us we were not allowed to wear coats and it was bloody freezing, so there we all were, standing on an open-top bus, shivering our bollocks off and drinking beer and champagne. Of course, these old red buses didn't have any toilets, but the drink was flowing and the players had no option but to find another use for the champagne bottles once they had been emptied of their original contents. It is a mystery to me why there have never been any photographs showing players peeing into bottles, because the sky was full of helicopters with cameramen, there were fans everywhere taking pictures and live television links covered the whole route.

We were given an audience with the Queen, in which everyone stood around the edges of the room while Her Majesty greeted us one by one. Everyone was getting slightly nervous as to what they might say and what they had to do. The instructions had been to greet the Queen as 'Your Majesty' and thereafter to call her 'Ma'am'. We had been told about this etiquette beforehand and you could see people crapping themselves thinking they might get everything wrong. While we were waiting, a few in-house jokes flew around about Zara and Mike Tindall – this is where he could be getting married, etc. – when the doors opened and in ran the corgis. The Queen spent about two seconds with you, asked you a question and before you had a chance to answer was about three or four people down the room. All that nervousness thinking about answers was a complete waste of time and when she had completed the line of quivering players, we headed into another great hall for a reception. As we walked through, we were approached by this chap – who had all the regalia, the medals, the red jacket and the gold trim – who said: 'Earl Grey, Sir?' Ronnie replied: 'Mark Regan, pleased to meet you.'

CHAPTER 17

HOW TO GET SENT OFF FOR ENGLAND AND WIN THE HEINEKEN CUP

A week after meeting the Queen, a group of Wasps players, including myself, Lawrence and Josh, flew to Rome to meet the Pope. We had been scheduled to meet him during an England match in Italy, but the appointment had to be cancelled. It was a unique experience and one I will never forget. Having met our Head of State and then the Head of the Catholic Church, I was a bit stuck for something to do the following week, and so opted to head back to training! Once the madness of the post-World Cup period was over, it was a case of getting my head down and helping Wasps.

With so many guys away on international duty, the squad had performed a minor miracle by keeping us in the top three of the Premiership. For the first time, I felt as though we had real strength in depth, something that has always been tough to achieve on a limited budget, but our academy system is outstanding, producing a conveyor belt of talent, while Warren had brought in new faces like Johnny O'Connor from Connacht, another in a long line of

Irish flankers seemingly impervious to pain. If Johnny had been kicked into the medical room, then Paul Volley would step up to the mark, and after Johnny suffered a serious injury, Volls became a vital cog in the machine as we attempted a league and Heineken Cup double. Because I had played most of the early season club games – before joining the World Cup campaign – I only missed around three weeks and after not having expended very much energy in Australia, was raring to go.

Our Heineken Cup challenge had started to gather real momentum and the team was supremely confident under Warren and Shaun. We earned the right to take on Munster in the semi-finals at Lansdowne Road in Dublin and you could see on Warren's face that this was going to be a very special day for him. Warren had been dumped by Ireland as national coach – a victim of political manoeuvring he couldn't control – and we all knew he was desperate to mark his first game back at the home of Irish rugby with a special performance, one that would make a very public statement about his quality as a head coach. Warren had purposely planned a lineout session in the car park of our hotel to ensure the Munster fans got an early look at us and the whole atmosphere around the game was memorable.

We have always been able to rely on a hard core of Wasps fans who travel all over Europe to give us support, but they really struggled to be heard that day as there were more than 50,000 red-shirted Munster fans in the ground. When you looked into the crowd it was a sea of red and it would have been very intimidating if we hadn't already come through a similar match in Perpignan earlier in the tournament. On that occasion, our small group of fans was in the French stadium singing their hearts out, ringing bells and waving Wasps flags, while the locals really cranked up the intensity and created a very intimidating atmosphere. It had been a pretty brutal game and perhaps on other occasions when we had played in Europe, we would have come off second best. However, this was a different Wasps side and our physicality allowed us to stand up to anything the French players threw at us and we won the game 34–6. That performance became a benchmark for the rest of our season. Guys like Big Trev, Volls, Joe and yours truly helped impose our game on the locals and our performance was underpinned by the self-belief provided by our fitness. We could take everything they threw at us and had the capacity to come back with even more. In many ways, the 2003 England World Cup-winning team had exactly the same mentality and belief: at Wasps we knew we were the fittest team in the Heineken Cup. This belief certainly got us through the semi-final against Munster, as we won a tremendous game 37–32 to hand Warren the win he so desperately wanted and book our place in the Heineken Cup final.

We also possessed players like Alex King and Rob Howley, who could control a match and put us into a winning position. Kingy wouldn't do anything magical all season, just get on with his job and use his pitching-wedge left boot to knock over the three points every time he lined up the ball. Kingy didn't have a great range, but was fantastically accurate when the kick was within his capacity – admittedly, not very far! Then, when you got to a match like the semi-final with Munster, Kingy would find another level of performance. It had happened in every final Wasps had appeared in: he consistently upstaged the opposing number 10 when it counted most, including Jonny Wilkinson. The problem for our follically challenged outside-half was that, like a number of us, he didn't fit the mould required at England level. Perhaps not being able to kick off both feet was a factor and he probably didn't have the same speed through the air with his pass as Jonny, or any lightning pace, but give him a really big match when the pressure would be white hot and decision making had to be spot on, and Kingy was the best.

It also helped that Kingy was on the end of Howley's wonderful pass from scrum-half, as this gave him that extra split second to make the right decision. He was also brave in the tackle, despite not being the biggest guy on the pitch, and spent much of the final falling in front of Isitola Maka, the 20 st. Toulouse number 8, and trying, legally, to trip him up. The fact that a number 10 was prepared to put himself in harm's way for the team set him (and Johnny) apart and we have all played with number 10s who have been more than happy to wave a big forward through and hope the cover defence picks up the pieces.

The win over Munster was one of the greatest days in the club's history and even though victory meant we would have to take care of Toulouse – the most powerful team in Europe at the time – in the final, we were supremely confident. How could you be anything else having just gone to Ireland and faced down one of the hardest teams in the competition and silenced their vast army of fans? As the match came to an end, we started to hear the Wasps supporters singing – it was a great moment. The dressing-room was one big party, with everyone acutely aware of just how significant the result had been for Warren. Knowing there were so many Irish Rugby Football Union officials knocking about outside, we let rip with a long and raucous: 'One Warren Gatland, there's only one Warren Gatland . . .' His broad smile said it all.

The perceived wisdom among the critics was that Toulouse carried too much firepower for Wasps, but we revelled both in that verdict and in our perceived role of underdogs. Toulouse saw themselves as the Kings of Europe and had a playing budget that meant the match-up was akin to Tesco taking on a corner store from Acton, but we didn't care. Warren gave Joe the job of cutting down Maka every time the big man got the ball . . . and what followed was a masterclass from the best man-marker I have ever played with. In the semi-final and final, the stats showed that Joe made 52 tackles and didn't miss one. That is an unbelievable statistic, and with their talisman being chopped down before he could get up any head of steam, Toulouse couldn't function properly. The French side had dominated their games coming into the final because they consistently broke the gain line and fractured defences, but with Joe in world-class form, we didn't buckle. He had been given a job and he stuck to it brilliantly.

It had got to 20–20 and extra time loomed. I was seriously

worried because I had absolutely nothing left in the tank. I simply couldn't imagine playing any longer. It is in these seminal moments that you hope that someone will produce a moment of individual brilliance . . . and we got it from Rob Howley. Now, anyone who sees Rob stripped off to the waist will assume he hasn't eaten anything for weeks and his striking resemblance to Stan Laurel is also somewhat disconcerting. However, Rob is a player who has consistently produced something very special when his club or country have needed it and on this occasion he chipped ahead to the corner and gave chase like a man possessed. Clement Poitrenaud tried to gather the bouncing ball or usher it into touch, but his hesitation proved fatal and, in a flash, Rob had touched the ball down.

He is one of those players you look at in training and wonder how he manages to produce such world-class moments, but there is no recipe for what makes a great rugby player – some are born with that brilliance. I like players who don't just get out there and do their job, but who think about the bigger picture and what will and won't work for the team. Rob was constantly thinking about the game and while he was doing his job with an incredible work rate, still managed to find the time to recognise how situations were developing and how we could capitalise on them. With Rob at scrum-half, Kingy at outside-half and Lawrence up front, Wasps possessed a world-class 'spine' at 8–9–10. Thanks to Rob's moment of individual brilliance, Wasps were now champions of Europe and, having made 26 tackles in the final, I had just enough energy to enjoy the lap of honour. We were parading the trophy around the stadium as the new Kings of Europe.

It really had been a massive battle and on the slow walk around Twickenham I found myself thinking, 'How the hell did we win that?' because we seemed to have spent the whole game defending. As a club we had never previously played to our full potential in the Heineken Cup, but that had now changed and the victory was the end of a chain of events that had started in Perpignan, took in Dublin and now culminated in London. Warren wanted to celebrate the victory and so did the rest of the boys, although we were acutely aware of the Premiership final against Bath in six days' time. Warren's attitude was: 'We have won this bloody thing and we have done it the hard way, so let's go out and celebrate and worry about Bath later.' And so we did.

The build-up to facing Bath consisted of one training session and a team run. There has always been an edge between the Bath and Wasps players and I am sure our West Country friends thought we were a bunch of London show ponies, the glamour boys who featured in the pages of *Hello* magazine. It was all rubbish, but the perception was alive and well and we didn't care. Lawrence knew he was a high-profile target and loved every minute of the attention. He is also the kind of character who likes to voice his thoughts and opinions 24–7. As a result, the opposition gets fed up hearing his London accent; he gets under the opposition's skin by saying things and constantly winding them up. I admit that he is one of the most cocksure people I know and that can grate on people. Warren is another character who doesn't mind winding people up and the combination of those two, along with Shaun throwing in his own very unique observations, would get backs up all over England.

The final against Bath was an incredibly hard match, and Big Trev was having one of his wayward days at the lineout with the ball going all over the place. Something drastic was needed. Warren took him off, Ben Gotting took over at hooker and the change was dramatic. We were suddenly winning our own ball and the doom-mongers in the Wasps backs had possession to play with on a regular basis. Kingy and Fraser Waters used to have a joke that whenever we had the ball to throw into a lineout, rather than set up in a deep 45-degree attacking line, they would come up flat ready to defend on the basis that we lost the throw 90 per cent of the time. Fraser was massively overlooked by England and I rate him as the best centre I have ever played with. He was a key figure in our famed defensive system and an underrated attacking threat. The true nature of his play was brought home to me during his testimonial year. Every player enjoying this honour asks for a tape to be put together of their best moments – although the one Ronnie had done featured virtually nothing of note! Fraser's is, by some way, the most impressive highlights video I have ever seen. It showcased the breaks, tries, numerous massive tackles and the only area not covered was any shots of him kicking – I had told him constantly he needed a decent boot.

We finally subdued Bath and thanks to that improved line-out, we won a close match 10–6, and were able to take another lap of honour around Twickenham as the double champions of England. In two seasons, despite working to a tight budget and with our now-famous limited training facilities, Warren and Shaun had helped us accumulate four trophies. The club had risen to the top in Europe and it was time for a party to celebrate that fact – along with my award as the Premiership Player of the Season.

I had very little time to savour our achievements, however, because England had arranged a tour of New Zealand (two tests) and Australia (one test) to focus the mind. I had played very little part during the 2004 Six Nations Championship with Clive still in charge, but went on tour confident that my success with Wasps, and Johnno's post-World Cup retirement, would level the selectorial playing field. Having spent time reflecting on everything, I started coming to the conclusion that it wasn't necessarily Clive and it was more the forwards' coach Andy Robinson who might be making the call. The one season under Clive when I had enjoyed a good run in the side came in 2000 when Jonno had missed the first four matches of that Six Nations through injury.

Maybe the fact that Wasps were double champions and I had been named Premiership Player of the Season finally gave Andy an opportunity to take a look at my attributes, because he picked me alongside Danny Grewcock in the test matches against New Zealand. We lost the first test in Dunedin, but still felt we could produce something to unsettle the All Blacks up front in the second match in Auckland. We were more confrontational than we had been in the first test, were better in the contact area and came out with a real determination that we were not going to allow them to dominate us. However, after just 12 minutes, my rugby season hit a very public low, with referee Nigel Williams sending me off – for the first time in my rugby career – for use of the knee in a ruck. I know exactly what happened and it certainly wasn't what touch-judge Stuart Dickinson reported to the referee.

In the first test we had struggled to get clean ball from the ruck area and we weren't going to stand for that again in Auckland. We were going to ruck players out of the way and not dither around allowing the All Blacks to lie all over the ball. That is exactly how we started the match and it was enabling us to dominate the first few minutes. Then, I arrived at a ruck that had piled up to above-normal height because there were two or three people on top of one another. Lock Keith Robinson, who is one of the worst culprits for lying all over the ruck, had his head and shoulders all over the ball. As I approached the area, I went to ruck for the ball and realised it was far too high. It was going to look ridiculous if I tried to ruck and when I put my foot back down, I glanced Robinson's head with my knee. There had been no intent to knee him in the head and what really sparked this incident off was that the All Blacks outside-half, Carlos Spencer, having seen what he thought was a knee, came charging in and shoved me. Lawrence, the England captain, took Spencer out and it all got a bit unnecessarily vicious. Robinson certainly didn't stay down there and didn't grab his head in pain. He probably didn't even know what was happening above him. Dickinson, the Australian touch-judge, came onto the pitch and said: 'I think I have seen one of the England players stamping on Keith Robinson's head, or kicking him in the head.' The fourth official was then asked to use video to identify the number of the player Dickinson thought had committed the foul play. Having been given my number, the referee then sent me off, something that is not allowed – the fourth official is not allowed to give this kind of information; his role is clearly defined in the rules and it was completely out of his jurisdiction.

It was immensely frustrating because I had never been shown a red card in my life at any level and couldn't believe I was being sent off for England, having waited so long for my chance to start in the second row again. However, you cannot stand there and argue or protest, you just have to take the lonely walk off to the side of the pitch. I was completely alone and I sat there isolated and in a world of gloom for the rest of the game.

Clive had voiced his anger at the referee's decision in the post-match press conference and I was told to prepare to appear before a disciplinary hearing the next day as we were about to head to Brisbane for the test against Australia. We had a QC travelling with us on every trip – one of Clive's moves – and I went back to the team hotel to review the match tape with him and work out our argument for the hearing. In my mind, I was thinking this was an utterly ridiculous situation because as far as I was concerned there was no case to answer and so I ordered some beers and asked for them to be brought to the video room. It was a pretty stupid idea. I sat down with the QC and the incident actually looked a lot worse with the camera angle appearing to accentuate the contact I had made with Robinson. I thought, 'Oh Christ,' but the QC said it was irrelevant, because the whole procedure had been completely wrong, there was nothing to worry about and we were going to get off on those technical grounds. But I still wanted my name cleared because I am not that kind of player. The QC, however, insisted that it would be a lot easier, and quicker, to follow his advice and that we would emerge from the disciplinary hearing with a rap on the fingers, so I agreed.

At this point, Clive walked through the door, severely pissed off, only for the waitress to walk in with the beers. He said: 'Who ordered these?' I said: 'I can't imagine.' It was all very bad timing. Clive was very supportive during the whole affair and when I arrived for the hearing, I saw Dickinson who had made the original error. The hearing was all over pretty quickly once the

QC had highlighted the issues and he got Dickinson's back up hugely with his analysis of what had occured. Dickinson thought he had been completely in the right and then we made it clear there had been an infringement of the rules. He was a little bit pissed off to say the least. I have had, over the intervening year, a couple of games under his jurisdiction and he constantly barks at me about the offside line etc but it is all water under the bridge and I'm sure he bears no ill-feelings. The panel were all Kiwis and they were all trying to stay on the 'did he knee or didn't he knee' issue, which is exactly what our QC said would happen. However, he stuck to his guns and they didn't really have an answer. Eventually the red card was cleared from my record. As we left the building, I found Grewy in his England suit, waiting in reception and said: 'What are you going in there for?' Grewy had been spotted by the independent citing officer illegally using his boot on an opponent, was banned for six weeks and had to go straight home.

Fraser Waters had played at centre during that Auckland game at a time when England were short of talent in the position and I was sure he would keep his place. However, following our World Cup win, there was quite a bit of confusion about how we were trying to play the game. This was not aided by it being a difficult tour at the end of a Rugby World Cup-winning season on the back of many injuries and retirements. Despite what may have been written about the Clive era, the players were just as big a factor to England's success in a successful partnership. The team meetings moulded a unity of purpose and the players would implement the overall plan agreed. There were changes for that 2004 tour with various retirements and also injuries to key players not helping. When new faces come into any side they want direction from the coaching staff and to be told what is required. Due to those factors, I don't think there was that feeling of leadership on this tour that we had had in 2003 and that isn't just down to the coaching. Warren had travelled back to New Zealand and had invited some of the boys to a barbecue in Auckland. Later some comments that had been made to him about the way we all felt appeared in a local paper. It talked about how the players were hearing the same old things from the coaches, that meetings went on for too long and that training wasn't interesting. It was all largely true but the fact it came out that way didn't really help the Wasps boys in the squad as Warren had made the situation ten times worse and we were pissed off. The main difference within the England set-up was that while we were hearing the same stuff repeated again, at least it was said with a real sense of conviction and purpose at the World Cup. Now, it was all a bit half-hearted, with the coaching staff just going over the same points we had heard so many times before. It just didn't feel convincing and was in stark contrast to the way Warren handled things. With Warren everything was always really positive; the tone used by the England coaches, in my opinion however, was quite dour in comparison.

The match against Australia was an unusual one and while they may have viewed it as payback time for the World Cup final loss, we were fielding a much-changed side. The 51–15 scoreline indicates they gave us a hell of a beating. It was a very strange match and one that seemed to go extremely quickly and, from a forward's perspective, we were all over them. I thought I was having a great game and it seemed very, very odd to come off the pitch having suffered a beating like that. The Australians are always a very difficult side to beat on home soil, extremely cocky and self-assured, and once they get on a roll that is it. They are good at putting the knife in and finishing you off.

Many of us felt a change must be in the air following the tour defeats. The press and media were speculating too that he had problems with the Rugby Football Union hierarchy, who were not delivering on his demands to ensure that England stayed ahead of the rest of the world, which to a large degree encompassed the welfare of the international players. This put Clive at loggerheads with both clubs and the RFU alike. These demands have now become reality in the EPS scheme. He had been knighted by now and shortly afterwards he would be heading off to Southampton FC and the British Olympic Association safe in the knowledge that he had at least delivered the ultimate prize.

CHAPTER 18

GOODBYE CLIVE, HELLO ANDY: ALL CHANGE, BUT THE SAME OLD STORY

When Clive decided to leave the job, I believed it was a golden opportunity for the Rugby Football Union to start afresh. Therefore, I was surprised to discover that, basically, it was going to be the same system, with Andy Robinson now moving into the head coach role. In my opinion, he didn't have the presence needed to do the job. I felt, with the power the RFU possessed and the money generated by the World Cup victory, we now had a great opportunity to start afresh in this post-Woodward era. The RFU had the clout to go out and get whoever they wanted and clear the decks but they obviously felt Andy deserved a shot seeing as he had been a key part of a successful team.

When I had my first session with the not-so-new set up, it felt as though nothing had changed. In terms of training, it was the same and the only obvious difference Andy made was to create a more free-thinking, open environment, where we were encouraged to express ourselves and enjoy being with England.

Under Andy, things started to loosen up and we had normal

social situations away from rugby rather than what I considered to be the 'compulsory fun' Clive believed in. Whatever one could say about Clive, you had to admit he made an impression and possessed a personality you couldn't ignore, no matter how hard you tried! Some players felt that with Andy, from a rugby point of view, we were hearing the same things and it had less of an impact. It just wasn't coming across with the same substance. It was simply a case of: it worked before, so it must work again – but with a bit more fun thrown into the equation.

With Clive now out of the picture, Lawrence retired from international rugby too as he decided to concentrate his efforts on Wasps, where we were joined by Matt Dawson, who had quit Northampton after a long career with the club. I had known Matt since our England Schools days, although I didn't consider him a great mate.

Having been England's World Cup-winning scrum-half, 'Daws' now needed to find a new club and Wasps has a reputation for taking in all kinds of waifs and strays. It is one of the club's great strengths that, no matter what kind of reputation you have as a player on or off the pitch, if you are prepared to work hard we don't care about anything else. Your social life is your own affair. Although Daws was a proven international scrum-half, I had real doubts when it came to putting him together at half-back with Alex King, our playmaker. Daws didn't have a particularly good pass off both hands and Kingy liked guys with a quick delivery, which gave him that split second of extra time to work his magic. With Kingy, if the ball was hard to catch, he used to deliver this stare back at the scrum-half that would seriously concern anyone. We just thought: 'Christ, there'll be a few of those this year,' but, fair play to Daws, he worked his nuts off at everything: passing, fitness and gave 100 per cent. This changed a lot of people's views about him as a player and I believe moving to Wasps took him out of the comfort zone that had existed for him at Northampton, where he was never going to get dropped. At Saints, he was a big fish in a small pond and a bit of a show-boater, but he changed all of that at Wasps.

Shaun Edwards, for example, firmly believes that every missed tackle, or defensive error during a game is as much his responsibility as it was the players and is so brutally honest with his players that it sometimes comes as a shock, but at least he's up front with you. Matt Dawson, instrumental in the World Cup victory, knows only too well the blunt honesty with which Shaun will sometimes address his players.

After one of Matt's early games in Wasps colours, we had analysis meeting to look at the good and bad points from our most recent encounter. Matt believed that he had filled the shoes of the recently retired Rob Howley and, in particular, kicked extremely well. Shaun, on the other hand, had a different view of Matt's performance.

Roll video footage. Matt executes an extremely long box kick out of our own 22 and into touch some 30–40 metres down the pitch. Matt turns to the rest of the squad with a beaming smile on his face, clearly very pleased with his effort. Shaun then shows three more similar incidents involving Matt doing box kicks into touch and then addresses the squad . . . 'Surprise, fucking surprise, Matt Dawson kick's another ball straight into touch! What do you think you playing at Kid? We want to keep the ball in play as much as possible, Kid. You've just let them of the hook there Kid! Kick to compete Kid, kick to compete!'

Daws's arrival at the club gave us two world-class scrum-halves, but very soon we were down to one, after Rob Howley was kicked on the hand during what turned out to be his last game for Wasps. The break proved too difficult to mend – in terms of being able to play – and when it was explained to him that being able to pick up his children could become a problem if he played on, his decision to quit became a no brainer. Everyone felt Rob's loss because he had become a popular and hugely influential member of the team and had won us the Heineken Cup with that individual piece of brilliance at Twickenham. However, professional rugby being as it is, we all moved on and now it was Daws who had to dominate the number 9 jersey. He rose to the challenge with real enthusiasm.

The defence of our Heineken title ended in controversy against Biarritz, when a miscalculation saw us trying to score four tries when a win would have been enough for us to make the latter stages.

We were heavily in control of the game in Biarritz, despite having lost Stuart Abbot to a broken leg, caused by Serge Betson's trip – who would have thought then that the same player would go on to leave the south of France, join Wasps and even captain the club a few years later? As we absorbed the news that Stuart's season was over, Serge wasn't particularly high on our popularity list. Having failed to defend the Cup, we were left to concentrate on retaining our Premiership title, with one of the key regular season matches coming at Welford Road, where we lost to Leicester. During the match, Johnno, in his final season, tackled me and, as we lay on the ground, he started laughing and said, 'Are you still all right for my testimonial game at the end of the year?', before pushing my head down and running off. I wasn't best pleased and didn't feel like getting into any banter because we needed the win. As it turned out, Leicester and Wasps met in the Premiership final, a match billed as the perfect way for Johnno to end his playing career at club level. All this talk only made the Wasps players even more determined to retain the title and, as luck would have it, I ended up on top of Johnno in that final and took great delight in saying, 'Yep, I'm in fine fettle for your testimonial, I'll be there with bells on' – which *he* didn't take too kindly to. However, we both had a joke about it afterwards and it was a good way to conclude our years of head-to-heads, with a smile and a handshake. I never really had any run-ins with Johnno on the pitch, which was a bit of a surprise given the length of our careers. I did have scuffles with Arch and Danny Grewcock, but then almost every second row in world rugby would say the same with that pair! I felt that as long as Johnno was playing, he was going be in the England team and that I would play second fiddle. That is not to say I felt he was a better player. My rationale for this was: we might have been on a level playing field as players but, because there was a perceived aura and magic about his captaincy, they were always going to pick him. End of story.

The Premiership final also signalled the departure from Wasps of Kingy, as he opted to end his career in France with Clermont Auvergne. Kingy had been a massive part of what turned Wasps into the best team in Europe, but it was the right time for him to try a new challenge. Those dodgy knees of his had taken a hell of a battering over the years and, given the pain and discomfort he endured, he did well to last that long. It was going to take a special player to fill the void left by Kingy, but we had already seen what Danny was capable of producing and now his time in the Wasps number 10 jersey had come.

We had also given Warren the perfect send-off with another Premiership title. Everyone knew he wanted to go home with his family to Waikato and build a house on a plot of land he owned near Hamilton. You could imagine that losing someone of Warren's calibre and trophy-winning ability would have left the club engulfed by depression, but that's not the way at Wasps. No matter who leaves, we just get on with the job and Warren's departure was always going to open the way for someone new to be added to the equation. The rumour mill kept throwing up the name of Ian McGeechan, the greatest Lions coach of all time, who was now working at the Scottish RFU after success with Northampton. Kenny Logan, who by now had retired from playing, was very much a part of getting him to Wasps and a lot of the younger guys who hadn't worked with Geech were genuinely excited about the prospect. Although, compared to Geech, Warren may have been fairly new to coaching, he achieved a lot in a short time and Wasps needed someone special to fill the void: there was no one more experienced to take over the reins than Geech. Of course, the fact that Shaun was still such a huge influence made the transition even easier for everyone.

I didn't hold out much hope of being selected for the 2005 Lions tour because the Six Nations Championship campaign under Andy Robinson had been a bit of a non-event. I felt England were stagnating. Nothing of any significance was really happening with everyone simply going through the motions. I didn't play for England at all in the Six Nations – not the best advert for anyone wanting to make the summer Lions tour – and the fact that Andy was going to be a part of Clive's management team seemed to seal my fate.

With any coach, I always look at what they were like as players and, more often than not, it tends to translate into their coaching style. Andy had been a winner with Bath as a player (and as a coach with their Heineken Cup win in 1998), and his playing style had been all about having a hard edge and, from a forward's perspective. But for me, he didn't give us many new ideas when it came to forward skills and how to break down defences. He retained Joe Lydon as a backs' coach (who had been brought in by Clive in 2004) and, although he is a lovely, decent guy, I have no idea of how good he was for the backs. In contrast, when Wales offered Warren the top job, he had a proven track record of success at elite club level and you couldn't argue against that kind of pedigree. Clearly, Wales looked at Warren's CV – plus the help of Shaun – liked what they saw and gave them a chance at test level. They won the Grand Slam in their first year and, although you might say that is a coincidence, it is certainly not a strange one.

CHAPTER 19

WELCOME TO THE 2005 LIONS TOUR FROM HELL

When I looked at all the plans for the 2005 Lions tour to New Zealand, my immediate thought was: 'This has got problems written all over it.' My reaction was based on all those years of listening to Clive's ideas about how we were going to play. I really couldn't see what this was going to bring to the Lions table that would be so very different from his time with England over the previous decade. Yes, those ideas had won a World Cup, but the England guys on the tour would have heard it all before and Andy had been using the same basic principles after Clive had waved goodbye. I felt that if Clive employed the same doctrine for the Welsh, Scottish and Irish players, they were going to think, 'What's this?', because some of his ideas were not what they were used to.

Clive had come up with a theme for the tour based on 'The Power of Four', and had sent a package containing his blueprint for the trip, along with a plastic wrist band with 'Power of Four' written on it, to all the likely squad members. Now, given that rugby players are a pretty hardheaded, cynical lot, did Clive really think we were all going to wander around with these wrist bands on? Clive also brought in a chap who had sailed around the world who gave us a talk about swallows and various other aspects of his life, and while all of this may have fitted in nicely in a corporate environment, we were rugby players, not executives.

Divisions and groups often appear in a Lions tour party. The normal assumption is that the England players are arrogant and stick together while the Celts often congregate as a group during the trip. I get on well with most of the Welsh, Scottish and Irish guys and found it illuminating to listen to their reaction to the Lions tour build-up and the motivational tools used. I spent an afternoon with a lot of the Welsh guys, who simply could not stop laughing about what they were hearing in the meetings and it was interesting to discover that players from other nations were finding all this stuff just as difficult to deal with.

I had missed out on the initial Lions squad and found myself listed as a standby player, which gave me the opportunity to take part in Martin Johnson's testimonial match. I was driving up to the game when my mobile rang, so I pulled the car over to take the call. It was from Louise Ramsay, Clive's team manager in charge of the Lions logistics who had been with us throughout the World Cup. Louise told me I was now needed in New Zealand due to injury and, not for the first time in my career, I heard the following words: 'Get all your stuff and make your way to the airport.' Having missed out on the 2001 Lions tour, it may appear churlish to admit that I sat in the car mulling over my decision. I genuinely asked myself if I really fancied two months in New Zealand being grumpy and pissed off. It is the worst place in the world to be if you are going to be negative about a rugby tour, because the entire country gets wrapped up in the sport and every man, woman and child has an opinion they like to offer. However, I convinced myself to join the tour and to arrive in New Zealand with a completely different outlook, one that revolved around having lots of fun and trying to forget about the test matches. I also thought it might be my last chance to play for the Lions teams which, amazingly, hasn't proved to be the case. I continued my journey and, on arrival, sought out Johnno and told him I was unable to play, only to hear him say: 'Oh well, no five grand then.' What a blow.

There wasn't anyone to meet me when I arrived at the Lions hotel in New Zealand and on this tour we all had individual rooms rather than sharing with other players, so I bedded down for a while as I assumed everyone else was at training. I took the opportunity to look down the squad list to see if I could find a good buddy to link up with and the first name I came across was Craig White, who had made such an impact as fitness coach with Wasps and who was doing the same role with the Lions. I went to Whitey's room as soon as he got back from training and said: 'Hey buddy, how is it going?' He said: 'It's not what I thought it would be like,' . . . and it was still in the first week of the tour! I had done all that work to ensure I was in a totally positive frame of mind mentally and now here I was being told by my mate that the tour was already a tough one. Whitey is normally such a positive guy and I couldn't understand his disappointment. Whitey said: 'Well, mate, I'm not in overall control and I'm not making any major decisions. I'm basically just one of the support team which isn't the real me.' After this chat, I tried to maintain my commitment to just playing rugby and, if a chance of a test place came along, to view it as a bonus. Very shortly after linking up with my fellow Lions, I was told to get myself ready to play against the New Zealand Maoris in Hamilton in the Saturday team alongside Paul O'Connell. I thought this was a very positive move, because the team included many of the guys who were expected to feature in the test series and I was raring to go. One of the priorities when you link up with a new squad is to get the lineout calls into your brain to ensure you don't make any mistakes at crucial moments. I am terrible at looking at the calls on a sheet of paper and prefer to go through the moves in a training situation, where they immediately sink in. I read the sheet prepared for the Lions Saturday team and was completely confused. I didn't have have a clue what was going on because there was no pattern. Clearly, the players and coaches had started with an agreed system and then incorporated whatever suggestions came along as they worked them through during the early stages of the tour. The end result was the most complicated set of calls and variations I had ever seen. I stayed up for two or three nights, unable to sleep, because I was so worried about the calling system and was convinced that on the day of the game, I still wouldn't have a clue about whether I was supposed to be jumping, lifting or acting as a decoy. I found myself constantly going up to people and saying, 'Please can you . . .' and they were like: 'Well, there is no real system, you just have to learn the calls.' I still couldn't get it in my head.

For me, the Maoris fixture was a nightmare. I couldn't concentrate on playing normally and my only thought was, 'Get the lineout right, get the lineout right,' because that is the one thing they are going to bring me up on. If there was a case for one player or the other and I fucked up the lineouts, I knew I'd be gone. We lost that game 19–13 – it was the only defeat the touring party suffered outside the tests – and our cause was not helped by the yellow card England prop Andrew Sheridan received for thumping Luke McAlister, who would later join him at Sale. It was the Maoris' first-ever win over the Lions. As a result, although the lineout hadn't been the cause of the loss, I was packed off to the midweek team and stayed there for the rest of a tour that now operated with two separate teams, both of which were looked after by different coaching groups. Nobody debriefed me about my first performance and, to be honest, I was much happier under the midweek coaching team of Ian McGeechan and Gareth Jenkins, of Wales. Clive was heavily involved with the Saturday team, while Ireland's Eddie O'Sullivan was the hands-on Saturday coach. I had the distinct impression that the Saturday gameplan was like a map: you went from this position to that position without anyone posing the question: 'What if something goes wrong?' When I got involved with the Wednesday side, there was a completely different attitude and feeling among those guys. It was like being on a separate tour.

The Saturday team, as far as I could make out, was stressed from the start. There was a real 'world on their shoulders' feeling among them, which I registered as soon as I got there. They were all very serious and moping around, while the Wednesday team, thanks to Geech and Gareth, were operating a 'let's give it a go' attitude. I spoke to my fellow midweeker Donnacha O'Callaghan and said I didn't understand any of the lineout calls. He made my tour by replying: 'Don't worry, we're going to get rid of half these calls, and you'll probably only have three or four to worry about.' O'Callaghan doesn't drink and is a bit mad in terms of his sense of humour, but he is totally professional and switched on when it comes to his rugby and cut out anything that was going to confuse us in terms of the lineout system.

With no disrespect to him, Gareth operated like your first Colts club coach; it was all about enjoyment and I just couldn't picture him as a Lions coach. That's not because he wasn't a good coach, it was just his personality: he was always good for a laugh, which was great. It was perfect for us and perfect for Geech and we just got on with it. With this coaching double act, we went through the tour unbeaten in the midweek games, culminating with a 109–6 demolition of Manawatu in Palmerston North in our final fixture. That day we were just too good, strong, confident and clinical for the locals and it could have been more.

It felt as though we were on one tour of New Zealand and that Clive was on another. We barely saw each other, because when they were training, we weren't. It became a case of the two 'squads' occasionally crossing paths: when they were finishing their lunch, we were just coming back from training. The tour was a complete contrast to my experiences in South Africa in 1997 when the midweek team knew the Saturday guys would be there to support them and it felt like a single unit rather than two different groups who happened to be playing in the same jerseys.

I had heard about Gavin Henson but didn't know him at all before the tour and my first chance to chat to him came at the end of a weights session in the gym. I thought he seemed a perfectly decent guy who didn't say a lot and who didn't seem 'up himself' at all. I remember coming away from meeting him wondering what all the fuss was about. Later on the tour, when he wasn't involved with the test matches, the press seemed to want to make a story out of him – whether true or not. He was obviously not happy about not starting the first Lions test, which was well reported at the time. I was aware that his girlfriend, Charlotte Church, had been in the country at one point and that the hotel we were staying at in Wellington suddenly became home for a group of his mates who, basically, were on holiday. They stayed in Henson's room and could be heard up and down the corridors during the night. Possibly he needed this mental break and after Charlotte Church and his mates had gone home, Gavin was back on song and played well and a lot of that had to do with the way Geech and Gareth handled him, too.

The midweek tour group had a few beers together and socialised after matches; it was a massive contrast to the way the Saturday team went about things. I felt as though the Saturday lads didn't want to go down that road because they were conscious that Big Brother was looking over their shoulders and making sure they were doing absolutely everything needed to win the test series. After we beat Otago 30–19 in Dunedin, I met up with a few mates from my Pirates days and ended up playing cards at their house until five or six in the morning. I remember falling asleep on the couch and waking up to discover it was already 7.30 a.m. and that we had a recovery session at 8.00 a.m. I knew my bearings, realised I was at the other end of town and decided to run the distance of around two miles in my normal shoes, tour jacket and trousers. People were pointing at me as I was running along the main street and when I got back to the hotel, I couldn't see anyone at all. My initial thought was: 'Christ, shit, this is a nightmare.' The best thing to do was to go for breakfast and I was the only person in the room until, you guessed it, in came Clive. I was eating my breakfast, head down, as he chose the seat opposite me and, before I could scoff all the food, he said: 'Simon, we are not travelling in number ones today.' This gave me the opportunity to say I had to get back to my room and put on the correct travelling gear. As I left the breakfast room, I bumped into three or four others who had also missed the recovery session and we all had a laugh.

When we got onto the midweek team bus, the shout went up that all the guys who had missed the recovery session – were scheduled to make a hospital visit. I knew the hospital, as I had been there before, and walked around feeling hungover, stinking of alcohol, terribly short of sleep and trying to make small talk. All the nurses, without a doubt, knew we were all hungover and obviously bleary eyed and seemed to take pity on us by bringing the visit to an end. However, they said there was just one more person to see and that it was a bit sensitive as it involved a hermaphrodite who was waiting for the operation to remove the extra bit of tackle. My reaction was a bleary eyed and slightly queasy: 'You can't be serious.' The nurse said: 'It is no laughing matter.' We all agreed and entered the room very sheepishly and no one could look the girl, who was in on the joke the nurses were playing, in the eye. We spent about five or six minutes looking at everyone and trying not to be the first to speak when they all burst out laughing. We had been completely stitched up.

This kind of fun moment lifted the spirits on a tour that was deeply affected by the injury suffered by Brian O'Driscoll, the tour captain, a week later in the first test against the All Blacks. I wasn't totally shocked at the way the All Blacks dealt with Brian, because there had been instances of foul play earlier in the tour that neither the media nor the match officials had picked up on. I just couldn't understand how a referee and two touch-judges could miss so many off-the-ball incidents and, in my mind, what happened in Christchurch at the start of the first test was a cumulative thing. The way Tana Umaga and Keven Mealamu lifted Brian up and dumped him down on his neck was a perfect example of this and, while they avoided any kind of punishment, Brian's tour was brought to a shuddering halt.

On a bitterly cold evening, we lost that first test 21–3 and the gloom increased when it became clear that Richard Hill and Tom Shanklin had both suffered injuries that would also rule them out of the rest of the tour. As a result of Brian's neck injury, the test team captaincy was handed to Gareth Thomas, the Welsh skipper. I knew 'Alfie', having shared a few coffees with him and the rest of the Welsh boys, and there was no doubt that he was the leader of their gang. He wasn't your stereotypical captain material, because leaders generally keep themselves a little bit away from the rest of the troops, but Alfie is into the piss-taking rugby players enjoy. I think the Welsh players respected him so much they did absolutely everything he said and he was a popular guy. The loss of Brian removed a huge amount of test-match experience from a squad already bereft of Lawrence, who broke his ankle in the opening game of the tour against Bay of Plenty in Rotorua. I wasn't surprised Lawrence had been picked by Clive, even though he had retired from test rugby. I don't think Lawrence was playing his very best rugby at the time, but his influence would have been a huge help in times of crisis on tour and losing Brian only compounded the problem. It also didn't help that the management became worried with their belief that New Zealand were using their SAS soldiers and special audio equipment to record the Lions lineout calls in matches and training. If they had asked me I would have said that, from my experience, there was no way they would have been able to understand them.

Despite the already complicated system, the response to the threat, however, was to change all the lineout calls 6 days prior to that first test. It is hard enough to cope with this kind of decision at club level, when you have two or three training sessions a week, but to attempt to do it over a season before the first Lions test was a big call. I was under the impression that Andy Robinson (together with the starting eight forwards) were the driving force behind the decision and I remember there were heated discussions between hooker Shane Byrne, Paul O'Connell and Andy about the system and whether or not they should scrap it. It was all due to this feeling that we had been compromised, which must have had an impact; the pack were still learning the new system when the second test arrived in Wellington. Paul hadn't been playing that well throughout the tour and now he had the added stress of a new system when he was the one calling the lineout moves.

Despite an early try from Alfie, we ended up trailing 21–13 at half-time in the second test. We then had to endure a Dan Carter masterclass as he scored two tries, kicked three conversions and two penalties to finish with 33 points in a 48–18 defeat in which we had actually played better than we had done in the first test. The build-up to the second test was made more memorable by the decision to ask Alistair Campbell to address us as a squad.

Clive said, 'Alistair wants to have a word with you,' and I found myself sitting there thinking: 'What the hell does this guy know about rugby?' He got up in front of the entire squad and said he had been in many battlefields and that he had seen the worst of the worst. He was, basically, comparing us to soldiers and saying that soldiers were willing to put their lives at risk and that we should be prepared to do the same. Had there been a soldier up there who had lost a limb and who could actually speak from the heart it would have had an impact on us, but this was Alistair 'King of Spin' Campbell and he really seemed to think his words would lift us – quite extraordinary. The only person who didn't come away bemused by it all was Josh Lewsey, who enjoyed chatting for hours with Campbell during the trip.

Now that we had lost the test series, I thought some of the players from the successful midweek team would be given a chance in the final test in Auckland. But the management team sent all the midweekers off to Queenstown for three or four days and I chose not to go, because I had arranged to meet my wife's friends who lived in Auckland. It was a nice break, but only served to highlight the fact that two different tour parties were travelling around the country. We only got back together for the final test, which we started brightly only for Umaga to score two tries to help register a whitewash over the Lions with a 38–19 win. Lewis

Moody got a try for the Lions – it was only our third in the series; the All Blacks, on the other hand, had amassed 12.

As I boarded the plane home, the general feeling within the squad was: 'Thank God that's over.' From Geech's perspective, I think he had done his job and, together with Gareth, had made his area of the tour a success. He handed out T-shirts bearing the logo 'Midweek Massive' for all the players who had been under his control – it was little things like that which set our tour apart from the Saturday side. When we were on the team bus going to matches, people would be on the mike, having a laugh, taking the piss and this just wasn't happening in the other side. I felt sorry for the guys in the test group. They had to stand on the pitch before each test match and listen to the ridiculous 'anthem' – 'The Power of Four'. I thought it was an absolute load of codswallop and I think everyone else felt the same. Hopefully, it will never be used again.

Having promised to maintain a new outlook on my rugby life during the tour, I felt a sense of achievement because I had enjoyed myself. Having only been used as a replacement during the previous Six Nations Championship, I knew I still had a major problem convincing Andy I could be an asset, but I was never going to follow Lawrence's lead and retire from test rugby. This is how I viewed it: if you stop playing international rugby while you are still capable of performing at that level, you lose an edge. You are no longer fighting everyone, fighting the selectors or fighting everyone's opinion to be out there. You don't get the media coverage because you are of no interest any more. I think one of the things Lawrence missed more than anything was being away from these big international matches and I wasn't surprised at all that he made himself available for England again.

CHAPTER 20

ANDY GETS THE BULLET AS WASPS BECOME EUROPEAN CHAMPIONS AGAIN

My return from the Lions tour signalled a patchy period in the international squad for yours truly. Although I was in the squad of 22 for the 2006 Six Nations, I only managed one start (against Ireland). Andy never sat me down and told me I wasn't much of a player and I had lots of meetings with him over the years where I would air my views and he would generally agree with my points. I never had a heated debate with him: it was a situation, which, understandably, was frustrating as I was competing for a position where we had world-class cover. I was a fringe player, when I believed strongly that my club form waranted an extended run in the starting XV.

In one sense I did think the appointment of Brian Ashton was a positive one, but I did wonder whether he was going to be a hands-on coach or whether he would get someone else in. He kept the same people in place, which always baffled me and I have always wondered if it was down to financial stricture from the RFU. Clive had convinced the RFU to invest money – which did yield the World Cup – and, after he went, everything was being cut back. You could no longer put tea on your room bill and on a tour you weren't allowed to get in-house movies.

Brian was put in charge for the summer tour to South Africa and I wasn't part of that squad. I had spoken to several people while Andy Robinson was in charge in his last season and I was trying to get explanations and reasons for my absence. I wanted to know what could I do and how could I improve my game. In the past I had never been that proactive, even though I knew other players used to send in videos of their games to Clive and Andy but I was of the opinion it shouldn't be down to me to sell myself. I felt he should be watching the games and making up his own mind rather than having propaganda shoved in his face. In the past, because I thought it was a crazy thing to do, I had never bothered, but it was getting to the stage where I thought I had to do something. I wasn't getting any younger and I needed to speak to someone, so I had a word with Mike Friday, the ex-Wasps scrum-half who was in charge of the England Sevens squad and, for some reason, part of the selection meetings for the senior squad. I asked him: 'What has been said about me, what is it that I am doing so badly?' He said: 'I don't know really. John Wells will be completely honest with you.'

During Andy's last season in charge, I rang Wellsy and said: 'What am I doing wrong?' He was fairly honest, but didn't give me a whole lot to work on. It was the same old stuff: 'You need to improve your defensive lineout.' So I said: 'Is that it, is that what has held me back the whole time?' It was frustrating. He added: 'But there are occasions when you play for Wasps and you are absolutely outstanding, you are everywhere, you are all over the pitch and you are noticeable, you do a great job and there are other games where you just drift in and out of the games.' I could accept that, because there have been occasions when I had played with a niggling injury where I just wasn't full throttle. At least Wellsy had given me something and, later, it was Wellsy who rang me up to tell me that Brian wanted to involve me.

It was great to hear after having felt as though I was stuck in a one-way street.

When Brian Ashton came back into the picture I think it suited the way I wanted to play, interlinking backs and forwards in a style of play where the number on your back wasn't so important. Andy had been very much a part of the Clive era and, even though he tried to make it more relaxed, the basic building blocks were the same. He had almost tried too hard to make the environment a more chilled one, but when Brian took over, it just happened naturally. You would never see Clive wandering around the hotel with a bag of dirty washing over his shoulder, but that's how you would find Brian. The atmosphere was different straight from the off: if you wanted to go out and have a big lunch in town rather than eat in the hotel you could do it. Under Andy we went up to Loughborough but it was a bit of a throwback to England Schools days, where you felt you were being looked after while you were away on a school trip. It was very much institutionalised whereas when we were down in Bath, Brian's choice of venue, it was far more relaxed and you could pop into a local cafe for a coffee and chill. Wellsy's training sessions were pretty intense and long but, once you had finished, you were given the freedom to spread your wings. The shackles may not have been completely off, but I felt a lot more comfortable in my role; I had a freer rein to do things as I saw them on the pitch.

That was very much how I played with Wasps and the departure of Warren didn't unsettle the club because Geech was such a top-quality replacement. One of the biggest things you have to stop Geech from doing at Wasps is spending too much time on the rugby pitch. He loves training sessions and when things go well he gets carried away and wants to spend the whole day out there. We were used to doing everything in a short and sharp manner and always within 50 minutes. Having taken over from Warren, who had won the league and Heineken Cup, it had been important for Geech to pick up the 2006 Anglo-Welsh trophy in his first season and, with the 2007 Six Nations Championship out of the way, we were at full strength and looking good. Young guys like James Haskell, Danny Cipriani and Dominic Waldouck had emerged, while experienced old hands like Lawrence, Raf Ibanez, Fraser and myself were playing really well. I was happy with my form and was enjoying the momentum we had built up and the chance to add more silverware to our trophy cabinet. Raf was absolutely desperate to win anything and had cried after we won the Anglo-Welsh Cup. We were all standing round going: 'Well, it's all right, but it's not that good.' Raf, on the other hand, was saying: 'You don't understand, I have never won anything in my life.' He had certainly come to the right club to change that state of affairs!

Raf had arrived at Wasps from France via Saracens where he had some serious problems. I played with Raf for the Barbarians and the story went that he made it clear to Sarries coach Steve Diamond and fellow hooker Matt Cairns that if they didn't release him, he would beat them up endless times. He confirmed this story to me over and over again and I thought: 'I am not sure I want this guy at the club because he sounds like a psycho.' After a few beers on that Baabaas trip, however, I realised Raf was a really great guy and, before injury forced him to retire at the end of the 2009 season, he proved a wonderful player for Wasps. He was a class act and I still can't understand how Saracens failed to get the best out of him.

With guys like Raf around, there was a huge amount of confidence within the Wasps squad and having just one trophy from the previous season spurred us on to great things. Knowing that despite Warren's departure we still had a steady ship under Geech and Shaun was also very comforting. Even though we felt equipped to try and win all the main trophies, it was the Heineken Cup that appeared more within our grasp than the Premiership, where we finished a disappointing fifth that year. At the start of the season, there had been plenty of talk about how strong the Welsh and Irish teams had become, but when it came down to the semi-finals, it was English clubs that dominated. We defeated

Northampton 30–13 at Coventry, while Leicester accounted for Llanelli 33–17 to set up yet another battle between the clubs. We knew from a historical perspective we could beat any of the English sides, and knock-out games suited our mentality. We almost felt invincible in a one-off game and there was a brilliant atmosphere at Twickenham, that saw a world record crowd of 81,000 turn out. Fraser was Man of the Match in that game and had been incredible all year – how he avoided winning more England caps is a mystery to me. He was the most disruptive centre in Europe, his defence was brilliant and he was creating and scoring tries at will. We all expected him to have a big say in the final. We had highlighted a few things before that game in analysis sessions, particularly Leicester's problems winning ball at the front and back of the lineout. These had become weak areas because they were so hell-bent on stealing the ball in the middle through my England team-mate Ben Kay. There is no way of covering every angle at every opportunity in a lineout and on that day pretty much everything we planned worked. Raf and Eoin Reddan scored tries from short throws to the front of the line where I was operating and by exploiting the gap at the front we were able to grab the points we needed to deny Leicester the treble. Kingy chipped in with 15 points and we were able to parade that huge Heineken Cup trophy around Twickenham again after a thoroughly deserved 25–9 win. Tom French, who had not even started a Premiership match, had been handed the awesome task of playing loose-head against England tight-head Julian White and produced a truly remarkable performance.

At this time we also had Peter Bracken, from Ireland, in the front row and he was a guy who always looked tired just running onto the pitch and I have never come across anyone like him on a rugby pitch. When he ran with the ball he looked awkward, when he scrummaged he got in some dangerous positions and I felt couldn't talk to him on the pitch because he sometimes seemed to be in a fluster. We went into one game in which we decided to change the lineout calls for him to aid him to retain information.

SIMON SHAW

We went back to a really simple system of calling, which meant the third number in a series of four would be the number that dictated where the ball was going. If two was the third number that was going to me, if it was four it was going into the middle – it was that simple. I kept repeating this to him during training sessions that week because he was lifting in front of me and the last thing I wanted was to look like a prat. We were just about to go into the game and he called me over in the dressing-room and said: 'What letter was it?' I thought: 'Oh, no.'

CHAPTER 21

THE 2007 RUGBY WORLD CUP AND MY DREAM IS SHATTERED

Meeting for the first time pre-World Cup was a very exciting time for me. The chance to really take part in another World Cup was genuinely something I felt might have escaped my grasp! Each preliminary squad member received news that the World Cup training camp would take place in Portugal and that we would be setting off from Bournemouth Airport. This strange departure venue immediately brought about suspicion. It was not long after our arrival at the airport that we would be informed that our flight was cancelled due to severe weather warnings! This again was a little strange given the almost perfect cricket weather we were experiencing that particular weekend. The whole thing was a rouse and the real location for our first few days of camp was to be in Poole Harbour spent in the company of more of Her Majesties finest, not corgies', but Royal Marines!

This brought back some not so fun-filled memories, but buoyed with a new found confidence borne out of my re-selection I entered into the daily tasks with real enthusiasm. I very quickly took on the role of a father figure within our group despite being a couple of years younger than our group leader Mike Catt. I think the guys saw him more as Mum! This experience took on a very different feel to previous outings with the military and despite Paul Sackey moaning about just about everything, it was pretty good fun. Paul's moans were partly justified given his inability to swim and the amount of time he ended up spending in the Solent, being scooped out of the water by yours truly!

Lawrence who was injured at this stage, spent most of the camp in a Land Rover being driven from pillar to post by the chief-of-staff, but would still sleep in the tents that the boys had erected once darkness fell. Lawrence's team went onto win the majority of the tasks and walked away with a trophy. At the awards ceremony, 'Lol' was the last to make his way up to collect his medal and in doing so lifted the trophy. This was greeted with a few jeers from the rest of the boys, to which he responded 'Well it's another medal to add to the collection!'

Sitting in the Twickenham dressing-room at one of the early squad get-togethers in the build-up to the 2007 World Cup, I looked around at the other guys and realised we had a bloody good team. There were 2003 World Cup winners, Heineken Cup and Guinness Premiership champions with vast amounts of experience allied to a collection of young talent that was eager to impress. I said to Reg, the England kit man: 'We have got a bloody good chance here.' He said: 'Yeah, I think so, too.' Typically, things went wrong for me even before we set off for France as defending World Cup champions and it was all due to my ridiculous decision to change a habit of my rugby lifetime and shave before a game. I didn't have my clippers and I thought that, as it would be very hot, I couldn't play with all this hair on my chin and managed to cut myself. I helped defeat Wales 62–5 at Twickenham, but my chin became ludicrously swollen and I was still in real trouble as we completed the warm-up games with home-and-away defeats to France – not the best way to prepare for the tournament. The team doctor, Simon Kemp, had started me on some antibiotics but the infection continued to spread, and I developed a throbbing headache. Four days before we were due to leave for France, he arranged for me to be admitted to a hospital in London for scans and blood tests and I was put on stronger antibiotics through a drip. It all left me thinking: 'This is fucking ridiculous. I have missed all these World Cups and I can't believe this is going to put me out of another one.'

Wellsy had told me I was going to start the opening World Cup game against the USA and certainly the first three games of the tournament. These words were weighing heavily on my mind as I lay in this terrible hospital with no television and, but by the end of the third day, I was discharged. But the enxt morning, the swelling had worsened again and just before we headed to Heathrow, I stormed in to see the England doctor and said: 'Doc, seriously, you have to sort this out; it is beyond a joke. I'm getting really depressed, I have got to be on that plane.' It was clear that he wasn't sure what to do next, but he said he understood my concern. I replied: 'I don't think you appreciate where I'm at right now. I've missed out all this time and I feel this could make up for a lot of it.' He could see I was pretty riled up. 'I'll try and get you a second opinion,' he said. 'Go on then, get on the phone,' I replied. 'Shawsy, please can you give me five minutes,' was his answer. I said: 'Why can't you get on the phone now and ring someone?' He said: 'I appreciate what you want, can you give me five minutes?' I said: 'Right, okay, I'll calm down a bit. I'll be waiting outside, you can come and tell me who I need to see.' Just as I was leaving the room, he turned back to his computer and started tapping away. I want a second opinion. You're a sports medicine doctor, you're not a chin infection specialist or whatever.'

He couldn't get anyone because time was so short, but he spoke to the specialist that had been treating me in the room, and the specialist suggested that we should give the antibiotics a little longer to work and arrange a review when we got to France. I got on the flight in agony and despite the pain, I was determined to take part in our first training session to ensure I played in the opening match. Sure enough, at the first lineout, the ball hit me straight on the chin. I felt like passing out, it was so painful and I knew there was no way I could play feeling like that. Next minute, Jonny Wilkinson rolls his ankle falling over one of the other players and, 20 minutes later, there are blue flashing lights at the training ground to take Jonny to a Paris hospital for scans. The doctor had spoken to the hospital and they said that they would have both Ear, Nose and Throat (ENT) and a skin specialist to see me and suggested I may as well jump in. Jonny and I were then sat in a police car speeding through Paris, cutting across lanes at 90 mph and I was absolutely shitting myself. When we got to the hospital, Jonny was taken away for everything to be scanned and the doctor came with me to meet the specialists. The ENT doctor repeated the umtrasound scan and they took an X-ray of my jaw to make sure I didn't have an infection in my teeth. These tests weren't helpful other than again showing some swollen glands, but the skin specialist took one look at me, pulled my chin up and said: 'Yep, yep, I think I know, it's a skin infection, I'll write you a prescription.' he gave me a prescription for some more antibiotics, an antibiotic cream and an alcohol spray.

Jonny came out and we were bundled back into the car, which proceeded to race off at the same ridiculously high speed and only stopped to allow me to get my prescription sorted out at a chemist in Versailles where we were based. While I was in the chemist, a crowd built up wondering who needed a police car and out-riders. I had forgotten to pack my toothbrush and bought a new one, which I then waved to the crowd as I walked to the police car announcing: 'All right, I've got my toothbrush, emergency over.' I jumped back into the car and off we went. I applied the cream and the next morning it completely disappeared, proving that instead of being treated for a blood infection, I should have been given something to solve a skin problem. The rest of the build-up to the USA game was also unusual because we had very, very tight security assigned to us by the French, as the terrorist threat for a game between the two countries was high.

We travelled to Lens by coach and stopped off three or four times at famous World War One war memorials, ending up at the huge one at Thiepval cemetery. We had Will Greenwood's history teacher on board giving us a run-down of each battle, but I couldn't understand why we were doing this kind of tour on the way to the opening game of the World Cup, which should have been our only focus. Yes, it was right to visit these very moving memorials, but the timing was all wrong and, while it wasn't the main reason why we played so poorly and only defeated the USA 28–10, it certainly wasn't the best preparation for the match. We also had to deal with the loss of Phil Vickery, our captain, who was cited for a trip and banned. I wasn't that happy with my own performance, but then again nobody was and we immediately turned our attentions to the game against South Africa, which we all knew would decide who finished top of the group.

With rugby you fall into three categories: you either come out and feel as though you are floating on air with your feet barely touching the ground; you are very, very sluggish; or, finally, you fall somewhere in between both physical states. Against South Africa at the Stade de France, I felt fantastic and, up front, we were pushing them back in the scrum and were very aggressive. I was enjoying the physical battle with the Springboks and felt as though we were giving them real problems. Then I looked at the scoreboard and saw we were losing 36–0. There were a couple of turn-overs that resulted in tries, which meant it was all over before we knew it. Mike Catt was at number 10 because Jonny was still out injured and, despite the result, a worrying injury to Jason Robinson and the negative publicity that followed the loss, it still didn't shake my belief that we could do something in this tournament. Bar a couple of mistakes, I felt we had been on top of them, certainly up front. In the aftermath of this defeat we were in the team room when Matt Stevens, who has a good voice and who likes to strum a guitar starting singing 'The Gambler'. I didn't mind Matt's singing but the timing of this particular offering really got to me and I felt like smashing that bloody guitar over his very large head. However, I held back and the song became something we adopted and was played after every match. The media got hold of it and, before we knew it, Kenny Rogers, who wrote the piece, was sending us good luck messages. There was even a rumour he was going to turn up for the final but, in the end, only a look-a-like, who had been paid by a newspaper to come to France, arrived at our hotel.

Now, in our role as defending champions who had just been heavily thumped by South Africa, we had to adopt the attitude that every match was a knock-out situation and it is a situation I like the most. However, it was evident that the coaches were all working to their own agendas, and although they might have been getting their particular areas spot on, we weren't then turning it into a coherent strategy that we all bought into. Wellsy was doing his thing and that didn't necessarily marry up with the way Brian wanted his forwards to play with the back line plans he had in mind. Equally, from a defensive point of view, the backs weren't marrying up with the forwards to implement what Mike Ford was trying to achieve. We were getting one message from one coach and another message from another and, while these messages may not necessarily have been wrong, it was a mixed bag. It was all still pretty new under Brian and the players took the view that if they were forwards then it was sensible not to piss off Wellsy; the same attitude existed for the backs under Brian and so everyone looked after themselves.

The Springbok defeat brought everything to a head and, suddenly, we were in danger of being the worst defending champions in the history of the competition. We had a meeting with the coaches and, although it has been portrayed as a dramatic sea change, it wasn't really like that. Brian simply said: 'What do you want to do?' The thing I liked about him was his openness as head coach. I admit to being one of the many players who was trying to fit in. Having been out of the squad for a year, I was just happy to be playing. We had the meeting, lots of opinions were expressed for the first time, the coaches listened to what was emerging and then, as a squad, we did a two-hour walk-through. We went through every area of the pitch, discussing what we wanted to do, how things would be set up and then everyone assembled in a local bar and we had a massive piss-up. The coaches put a tab behind the bar and we all talked about how we could create a club atmosphere. It was something I had talked to Wellsy about after Andy Robinson's period in charge. I'd told him: 'First of all, you can't say let's go out for a drink unless you mean it and unless you expect some people to completely go off the rails, because otherwise it's not a drink, it's just like we are pretending to drink. We'll have a couple of drinks and watch what everyone is drinking, so you have to expect that to happen.' The coaches had obviously agreed to follow 'Simon Shaw's Guide to Getting Pissed', because they set the tab up and let people do whatever they wanted, knowing that training would be delayed until the following afternoon.

People got completely plastered, guys got up on the bar semi-naked and were dancing and, miraculously, nothing about it ever appeared in the media, despite the fact we had lost so badly to South Africa.

After we had all taken part in that long walk-through, everything became clear; everyone was now on the same page in terms of how we were going to play for the rest of the World Cup. As the senior guy, Mike Catt was taking more control of the back line and we looked more fluid in training. The consensus in the squad was: 'Well, let's just give it a go.'

A lot of things we did in training came off in the Samoa game played at Nantes. We had been based in a golf-course resort at La Boulez and against Samoa the team just clicked. Jonny was back at number 10 and rattled up 24 points, with Martin Corry and a fit-again Sackey grabbing two tries each in a 44–22 win. Having boosted our confidence, we then had to beat Tonga to progress to the knock-out stages.

We travelled back to Paris to take on a Tonga side who were determined to hit us with big tackles and attempt to disrupt our game, but with Sackey running in two more tries and Jonny on target once again with the boot, we won 36–20 to reach the last eight. One of our tries against Tonga had been scored by Andy

Farrell, the former Great Britain rugby league captain, whose inclusion in the squad had attracted plenty of media comment and placed huge pressure on his shoulders. I felt sorry for Andy because he was new to the union game, but I felt he had a lot to offer us in terms of leadership. Certainly when he came onto the pitch there was a directness about his play that we needed. The only problem was that he lacked the pace we had seen him produce in league. A lot of people were critical, thinking he had got into the squad at someone else's expense but, from a leadership point of view, he gave us an extra dimension. The guy had been through a lot and he could bring that to our party. You have to accept that he was a class act in rugby league and, therefore, might have had something to offer in rugby union. Jason Robinson was a quality player and worked fantastically hard at his game once he came over from rugby league and no one could ever say the move, or the RFU's financial input to make it happen, wasn't justified, because he brought so much to the game. Perhaps, if Andy Farrell had converted a lot earlier, that might have been the case as well. Jason is a very quiet guy and will very rarely say anything but, when he does, the words are delivered clearly and are always worth taking in. Some people talk for the sake of talking and that doesn't necessarily mean an awful lot. Jason was a guy who had been there and done it all in both codes and when he was talking you shut up and listened. What I liked about Jason was his ability to spot an opportunity in support, turning up alongside you and bursting through the gap with his blistering speed. He had a real feel for that moment in a game, instinctively knew what was going to open up in front of him and, as a forward, it was great to know that if you needed to offload the ball, he would make himself available.

The win against Tonga came as a considerable and understandable relief. We had made the quarter-finals, where we would face Australia, a repeat of the final from four years ago. This time, however, I would be playing against the Wallabies and not sitting in the stand drinking a vodka-laced sports drink alongside Ronnie. Even he was in the team now!

We had been given a lot of praise for our tenacious work in getting to the last eight and, although we may not have been producing anything remarkable, the effectiveness of our play, particularly up front, meant we didn't fear the Wallabies. We had pace in the backs and a reasonably expansive gameplan based on the solid work of the forwards. Whenever I have played Australia, I have always felt they are the team we have the best chance against from the big three in the southern hemisphere. It was the same leading up to this game and my confidence came from the fact that we had an immense front five, a hugely experienced pack throughout that could really put it to the Wallabies. Plus we had Jonny there to kick the points.

On the eve of the match, I thought: 'Just two games and we could be in the final here.' Everyone had drawn confidence from the wins over Samoa and Tonga, particularly as the doom-mongers had been so downbeat about our chances. We were a very confident team going into the Australia match and had fully embraced the view that, at this stage, we had nothing to lose as no one had really given us a chance in the first place. The media were focusing on loose-head prop Andrew Sheridan and what he might do to the Wallaby front row. Sherry takes the plaudits when the scrum goes well and the flak when it doesn't perform or if he hasn't completely destroyed the opposition tight-head. The scrum is very rarely about an individual, however. It is a collective eight-man unit that needs everyone operating at their best to become a really effective weapon. People just single him out and sometimes it is unfair, but he seems happy enough to deal with the flak, as well as the praise, when it comes his way. We had a very strong front five in that tournament and, even in the first South Africa game, I felt we had the edge in the scrum. The key thing when you are dealing with Sherry is to make the scrum as comfortable as possible for him, because he can then make a real impact when he has the ball in hand. If he is struggling in the scrum, the huge muscles he possesses become fatigued and his ability to punch holes in the defence as a ball carrier is diminished.

The Australia quarter-final turned out to be a big game not only for Sherry but for the whole team. Despite the heat in Marseilles, I felt as if I could keep running all day. We had cut back the training sessions to ensure everyone was fresh-legged and I remember the first fifteen minutes going by as though it was only two minutes. The crowd was fantastic and there were loads of English fans who helped make the whole weekend amazing. Andy Farrell was injured late in the week, Mike Catt took over and he had a great game alongside Jonny. We absolutely blasted Australia up front, with Sherry bullying his opposite number all day. However, it was the opposition who scored the only try of the game through Lote Tuqiri, but Jonny kicked four penalties and we went into the final minutes leading 12–10. Then, Joe Worsley was penalised and Stirling Mortlock, their captain, lined up a long-range kick with the chance to give us a very public payback for that 2003 final defeat. Thankfully, his kick missed and the final whistle led to great onfield celebrations, particularly from Ronnie, who had been wound up all week by claims from the Wallabies that much of his play was illegal. It is always good to hear the Aussies whingeing!

Our win was only the start of an amazing city-wide party, particularly as the French upset the All Blacks 20–18 in Cardiff on the same day. We weren't staying in a particularly nice hotel and didn't want to go back there – Lawrence's room still had sick on the floor from the previous occupant – and so we went down to the port where everyone was partying. It was incredibly difficult to get a few beers or to watch the France–New Zealand game because of the number of people in the area, and we tried to get on board one of the multimillion-pound yachts in the harbour. We caught up with Austin Healey, who was involved with a company who had a large boat moored in the harbour and invited ourselves on board. There were about six or seven of us and we got a frosty reception, until the people on board recognised us and started cracking open the wine and beers. The problem was that, as word got around, more and more people started turning up on the boat, including one chap who tried to impersonate one of the South African players. I think he ended up in the water.

The whole city went bonkers when France won, with French and English supporters dancing together, it was mad. I remember trying to get a taxi, because a few of the guys had left and gone on to a nightclub. I managed to flag down an off-duty French policeman, who was absolutely delighted to take me to the club, although I still couldn't find the lads. As a result, I spent the rest of the night trying to get home, was struggling to get a taxi and so I decided to walk. I asked a passer-by how far it was and he said: 'It's miles and you'll be walking for a long time.' I decided to look for any stray, unchained bike, but there aren't many of those in Marseilles because they prefer a moped. Eventually, I managed to find a moped that had been abandoned by a tree. I pushed it for around 5 miles, without being able to start it. I kept trying to fire it up and, eventually, it sparked into life – by this stage, however, I was 50 yards from the hotel! I did about five laps of the hotel, then parked it up and went in for a much-needed sleep.

The next day we opted to go on a boat trip to a village on the other side of the bay and stopped there for lunch. We were inundated with people congratulating us and were offered a trip back on a sailboat, which they said would only take about an hour but which ended up taking about five. We got back into Marseilles late at night and pulled up next to where the Fijians were staying, which, incidentally, was a far nicer hotel than ours. Having enjoyed our time in Marseilles, it was now time to return to Paris and the semi-final against France, the team we had beaten at the same stage of the 2003 tournament, but this time they were the host country.

Despite having an entire nation supporting their cause, the England players were not bothered about playing France at all, because we were all convinced the French victory over New Zealand in Cardiff had been their best performance. We felt there was no way they were going to be able to play as well as that again. Everyone was hugely confident and we all believed that if our backs could get their 'A game' into play we could win, because up front we had no fears about taking on the French. There is a comfort-blanket feeling when Jonny is in the side. It's not that he will do anything terribly flash, it's just the bits and pieces he can produce that keep everything ticking over. For example, in the Australia game there was an occasion where we had a kick-off and I spotted that they didn't have numbers straight in front of me. I signalled to Jonny to kick it there and he put it absolutely on the button where I could catch it – he does things like that. He is so accurate with his passes and is always capable of clearing our lines deep into an opponent's territory. Such consistency is fantastic for the forwards.

As we reached the quarter-finals, Lawrence was starting matches on the bench, as he had done against Tonga, and was making an impact when he joined the fray, with Nick Easter starting at number 8. Earlier in the competition he had joined us for a celebration of Tom Rees's birthday, with the guests mainly the Wasps lads. We all sang 'Happy Birthday' and had a bit of cake.

After training the next day, on returning to the hotel, I went to the medical room for some physiotherapy and the doctor said: 'We need to quarantine Lawrence. He's very ill and has got a hell of a temperature, I think he's got some flu symptoms.' I said to the guys: 'It would be a good idea if we wrote him a get-well card.' So we made a card out of physio tape and a piece of card and managed to bash a rose on the front of a piece of paper with tape. I wrote in it: 'Roses are red, violets are blue, while we were all training where the fuck were you?' and shoved it under his door. I got a text about five minutes later saying: 'Cheers mate, you've really cheered me up.' These types of things always kept the morale up and the group tight, which is what you need at a drawn-out tournament.

By this stage of the tournament, Catty was taking the reins in the back line and was operating as Jonny's second pair of eyes. Catty always took some of the pressure off Jonny and, as a forward, it helps you enormously to know your number 10 has an extra voice telling him how things are opening up or where the kick should be going. From a forward's perspective we were just getting on with our job of providing Jonny with the ball to run the game and with Ben Kay, one of the best lineout callers in the country, we were operating very efficiently in this area while the scrum had already proved its worth against the Wallabies.

Ever since I have known him, Ronnie tends to find someone on tour to link up with and never leaves their side. He did it to me early in my career and has done it to several other players along the way and when you get bored with his chat he will move on and find someone else. He found Nick Easter during the World Cup in France and they had a lot in common, although Nick would argue that he is far more intelligent than Ronnie. They got on enormously well and constantly took the mickey out of each other. It was Nick's mistake to tell Ronnie that to psyche himself up before matches he looked in the mirror and talked to himself as 'The Dominator'. Despite discovering that Ronnie was spreading this about, Nick continued to link up with our veteran hooker, because he was a constant source of amusement for the Harlequins number 8 who is known to everyone as 'Minty', after the character in *Eastenders* who has a very thick Cockney accent. Nick is a hugely underrated player who gets a lot of flak from both the press and the public because he doesn't fit the normal criteria you expect from a modern-day back-row forward. He is big and strong and great in the tackle, but what people tend to expect from a modern number 8 is incredible pace, the one thing Nick probably lacks. What he does have, however, are very good ball skills, great awareness and a hugely punishing tackle. I think he's a fantastic player and he definitely fitted in to what we wanted to achieve at the World Cup. Rugby is clearly a physical game and, although I don't want to use the word 'bullying', that is essentially what you have to do to the opposition if you want to get the edge on them physically. That is what we did to the Australians and we wanted to repeat that against France.

Brian was able to name the same team that had lined up against Australia for the semi-final clash – the first time in 28 matches an England coach had been able to do that. Phil Vickery gave us a short speech before we left the team hotel and it set the tone, emphasising the need for aggression and passion. We were ready to deliver again. Having Jason Robinson back from the injury he suffered against South Africa for the Australia and French matches was also crucial, because he had that wonderful ability to cut through even the tightest defence. We knew it was going to be a tough battle up front and we got a huge boost from Josh Lewsey's early try – particularly from the way he patted Damien Traille on the head after scoring.

When you are in a game of that intensity and pace, you don't have time to think of the ups and downs, and not being bothered about the scoreboard is a sign of great confidence. When someone gives a penalty away on your side, you don't worry about it because your immediate thought is we are just going to score more points than the opposition. You're not following the game, you're in the game, you're doing your job and if you do your job you will win. It is born out of confidence. Of course, little incidents do stick in your mind and for me it is the tackle Joe Worsley made on Vincent Clerc and as my Wasps mate said, he just 'got on his bike'. Like Joe, the whole team was cycling around the Stade de France ensuring the French didn't win and there was a deep sense of personal satisfaction as I savoured a 14–9 victory over a French side that included my Wasps team-mate Rafael Ibanez. There wasn't an enormous amount of self-gratification as I enjoyed the fact I was going to play in a World Cup final on merit. I had proved everything I needed to prove in an England shirt before the tournament had started, and proving selectors wrong is something I have repeatedly had to do, but I have never thought I had anything to prove to myself. In the wonderful moments after the final whistle at the Stade de France, all I knew is that I had done it: I had earned the right to go for a World Cup-winners' medal I would really deserve.

My motivation going into the World Cup final was: 'We've been knocked an awful amount along the way and we've proved them wrong; if we go this one step further, we can put two fingers up to everyone who has criticised us.' It wasn't about any personal achievements: as a group we had become very, very tight-knit because of what we had been through. We all had a desperate desire to show everyone what we were capable of in the final. There was a bit more fear going into the South African game than had been the case prior to the Australian or French matches, simply because of the nature of our previous defeat. At the same time, though, we looked back at the video and realised there wasn't an enormous amount wrong with that performance that couldn't be put right. The Springboks always have this arrogance, which I consider to be part of their South African make-up, but I believed they were quietly concerned about just how effectively we had been able to turn it around. Certainly, they would have come out of our pool game – despite the scoreline – thinking the English were a pretty tough pack. In the World Cup, especially in the latter stages, it's not necessarily about what the rugby looks like, it's about all hands on deck and never taking a backward step and working until you're absolutely spent, because you have only got one chance. That was the case with the French in their quarter-final with the All Blacks: every single one of them came off the pitch completely spent. The 2003 World Cup-winning England side didn't play particularly good rugby – if you look at the Samoa and Wales games all the exciting stuff was played by the opposition – but those players absolutely toughed it out. With key members of that Cup-winning side in our squad, it was inevitable we would draw on that experience to drag us through the early problems and become a real force.

How you spend your build-up time for something as huge as a World Cup final – especially when it is an evening kick-off – is quite tricky. You end up going backwards and forwards to your bedroom a hundred times and are constantly wondering what you can do to kill the time but not use up valuable energy. You end up mulling over things like: 'Shall I go for a walk? No, that's probably not a good idea. I'll have something to eat, but if I eat too much I am going to be bloated.' So, you go back to your room and have a drink of water and then feel hungry – the end result is a lot of pacing around hotel corridors looking like a lost soul.

Jane arrived in Paris on the day of the final and as she knows I'm not great at dealing with outside issues, said she would stay away. She dropped all her stuff off in my room and then had lunch with my parents and the main talking point was Beau, our youngest child, who was ill. I managed, on a couple of occasions, to say 'hello' to my parents, sister and mother-in-law and then went back up to the room. My dad didn't offer me any special advice, although he did trot out his usual line of: 'Don't try and do everything in the first five minutes.' As the departure time arrived, the coaches started giving last-minute advice, with Wellsy having a quiet word here and there and Brian saying something short and to the point because, sometimes, there's not an awful lot you can say. If you are in the World Cup final you don't need any extra motivation. It is an incredibly difficult thing to raise your game every week and you can become a bit stale week after week trying to peak and I think Lawrence is a good example of someone who can get 'up' very easily for the big occasions. He almost needed the big stage to perform at the end of his career because, while Premiership matches are not meaningless, they don't have the same circus act of a really big final. Emotionally, he struggled towards the end when it came to the run-of-the-mill game, but he was still able to do it on the big occasions.

Josh had damaged his hamstring in the semi-final and had to sit out the big one and was obviously gutted, so he kept himself to himself and was fairly quiet on the day. It is understandable: when you are injured or when you are not involved it is not a very comfortable place to be and you feel a million miles away from the squad and what is going on.

What I remember most about the start of the game was how incredibly powerful the South Africans were when they came out.

They were determined to prove a physical point: they were the big boys, despite what had been written about the English pack in the days leading into the final. They were the real schoolyard bullies and were determined to prove a point. For the first ten or fifteen minutes it was probably the most physical and intense contest I have ever experienced and they were thumping into your body from every angle. You didn't know where the next hit was going to come from. It took us almost the first quarter of the final to get ourselves through that maelstrom and it was like enduring the early part of a heavyweight fight with Mike Tyson and managing to weather it and still be in the fight.

Then we were all convinced we had scored a great try on the left wing through Mark Cueto, who got the ball down in the tackle after a brilliant run by Mathew Tait had cut the Springbok defence to pieces. We endured a ridiculously long wait while Stuart Dickinson – my old mate – looked at the tapes in his capacity as the video referee. He ruled that Mark had put a bit of his foot in touch. We all thought Mark had scored and I still believe that today. He scored and it is not an issue. It was a fantastic phase of rugby to create the try and, despite the incredulity of not being awarded the score, we weren't deflated. Our attitude remained: 'It was just one thing in a game, let's get on with it, let's get back to the job.'

As the minutes ticked down, I wasn't thinking about scorelines or anything. I had the same thought processes as the French game: to keep doing what we were doing and we would win. Joe came on and immediately injured his groin and was unable to contribute anything and still we didn't believe the World Cup was lost. All of those setbacks didn't really play into our minds, certainly not mine, until the final whistle came and you realised it was all over and that your chance had gone. I have been on the winning side on loads of occasions in finals and have often spared a thought for the opposition, because it is a horrible place to be. The ceremony seemed to go on for ever and I wanted the ground to open up. For myself, Ronnie and Gommars – the guys who hadn't had the opportunity in 2003 – it was even tougher to take. We probably felt it more than anyone else, because we knew we weren't going to get another opportunity. For us, there was no chance of going back for another final, whereas a lot of the younger guys could get that chance. We hadn't been on the pitch in 2003, so this had been our one and only chance and it had gone. For Vicks and Catty plus the other guys who had been part of the 2003 side and played in the final, it was also very upsetting, and I will always remember the feeling of desperate disappointment as I tried to complete a lap around the stadium to thank our fantastic supporters. I just fell to bits. It was all over and we all trooped back to the hotel.

While everyone at the hotel came down for a consolation beer, as one of my kids was ill, I just sloped off quietly to my bedroom, looked after Beau and spent the evening with Jane, although there wasn't much left of the night. Any time you finish a tournament or anything that requires as much effort and hard work as a World Cup, you want to have a blowout and I had that the following day in Paris with Joe, Gommars, Josh and Tom Rees. However, having a beer with anyone in the early hours as I dealt with the fact I had ended up with a losers' medal from the final, was well down my list of priorities. I couldn't sleep and ended up heading to our team room in the basement of the hotel where a couple of people – friends of other players – were lounging around sleeping on the couches. It was a bit painful not being able to find a place to be alone. I remember wandering around, not being able to sleep, and desperately I didn't want to bump into anyone, because you would get the 'never mind, you tried your best' – all that kind of crap that you really don't want to hear, no matter how well meant it might be. All I cared about was that we had lost the World Cup final 15–6 to South Africa and that I would never be able to call myself a genuine World Cup winner.

I went to Dubai with Jane and the children for a week and that was very pleasant because you didn't bump into anyone who wanted to talk you through the World Cup and that Cueto try. I have my losers' medal in a drawer somewhere in the house and, looking back now, the worst moment was hearing Rob Andrew, the RFU's elite rugby director who lost in the 1991 final, telling us: 'Unfortunately, it will never leave you and you'll never get over the disappointment.' That really cheered us up. I don't think that is the case for me and I would have been more upset if I hadn't been involved at all. Clearly it was a World Cup final and so the disappointment of losing is hard to take, but I was so grateful for the chance to get back to where I never thought I would be again.

CHAPTER 22

WARREN AND SHAUN GRAB A SLAM AS BRIAN IS DUMPED FOR JOHNNO

Under Brian, I had real hopes for the post-World Cup period and thought that, if we remained as a unit, we could take our form into the 2008 Six Nations Championship. Leading into the Wales match, I was keenly aware they had taken on Warren and Shaun and a few other former members of the Wasps backroom staff and that as a coaching unit, they would pose a real threat. I had always felt that Wales had a very strong team, but they just never seemed to have the right man in charge to produce their magic on a consistent basis. They had shown some amazing attacking rugby in previous games, but had never done it on a regular basis. However, thanks to our own failings, the Welsh got off to a winning start under Warren and Shaun. As a result, Jonny came in for the kind of criticism he didn't normally receive from the critics.

Throughout his career, Jonny has been forced to deal with an enormous amount of pressure and expectation. If he misses three kicks, but nails the two that win the game, Jonny is a hero, so I guess he knows the flip side that comes with the territory of a kicker. However, the expectation is much more in his case because he is supposedly this absolute, sure-fire bet to kick the goals and win the match. I felt a little bit sorry for him, because I think he was struggling to find his form at Newcastle after the latest in a seemingly endless list of injury problems that included the ankle problem in the World Cup. Newcastle weren't doing particularly well either and club form can have a huge impact on your own performance. I know from personal experience that, no matter how hard you try to turn things around, it can lead to even more mistakes and, as a consequence, your confidence level drops. At Newcastle, Jonny has always been cast in the role of club saviour and he hasn't had enough quality players around him to take some of the burden off his shoulders. I remember seeing him very early in his England career and wondering how we could base so much of our game on this young lad. How would he cope? Yet, there he was, addressing team meetings saying: 'This is what we are going to do in this part of the pitch.' In my view, Jonny has always played at his best when he has had someone like Catty or Will Greenwood at inside-centre to take some of that pressure off his shoulders, playing the role of that extra pair of eyes. Because of his early success, various coaches have looked to him for inspiration and to provide that get-out-of-jail card with his boot. From what I saw, the only people who have really assisted Jonny with coaching advice and help were Dave Alred and his close friend Steve Black at Newcastle. Jonny is a lovely guy who keeps himself to himself and who is quite guarded about how much he reveals about his life away from rugby. The interesting thing I have discovered over the years from our conversations is that he is hugely fascinated by celebrity and what goes on in the celebrity scene. He always wanted to know what the gossip was in London and who was doing what with whom, which I found quite strange given his reticence and desire for privacy. He is, after all, the man who had a cinema built in his home so that he wouldn't have to go out to watch his favourite movie.

WARREN AND SHAUN GRAB A SLAM . . .

The ramifications of the 26–19 home defeat to Wales would not be felt immediately for either Jonny or Brian, but things had been set in motion behind the scenes. As happened at the start of the World Cup, the coaches appeared to revert to looking after their own areas of control and the important points we had raised in France were not being given enough prominence in terms of how we were trying to play to ensure we were all singing from the same hymn sheet. Because of individual errors against Wales, we threw away a 16–6 half-time lead and only managed to score three points in the second half while the Welsh rattled up 20, including tries by Mike Phillips and Lee Byrne. It was Wales's first win at Twickenham for 20 years and gave Warren and Shaun the perfect start. I was moderately happy with my own form, but believed we could get better very quickly. However, there was a general feeling that Brian might be going at the end of the tournament. I thought this was unfair on him because I don't think the Welsh defeat and the later loss to Scotland were his fault. The Welsh defeat was entirely the players' fault; there was nothing the head coach could have done up in the stands.

We bounced back to defeat Italy 23–19 in Rome and people always underestimate the difficulty of taking on the *Azzurri* in their own backyard. Jonny passed 1,000 points for England during the game, but there was little else to write home about. However, that all changed in Paris. We returned to the scene of our semi-final win over France – also the stage of our World Cup final loss – and felt confident. I don't believe we had any ghosts to exorcise, the team just wanted to recapture our best form and I was confident the Stade de France would bring the best out of the players. We triumphed 24–13 with the help of a late Richard Wrigglesworth try and up front we did the business against the French and registered our first Six Nations away win in Paris for eight years, which set up the clash with Scotland at Murrayfield. The build-up featured the loss of Danny Cipriani, who was left out of the squad after being photographed leaving a London club in the early hours and, to be honest, the incident didn't really affect our preparations, as Danny was due to be on the bench and not in the team. Once again, Murrayfield was to be a dreadful day for England and it almost felt like a re-run of that Grand Slam debacle in 2000. Everything was hauntingly reminiscent of that day and, as the game unfolded, I remember thinking: 'No, no it can't be, it can't happen the exact same way.' But it did. We lost 15–9 and not even Jonny's kick, which made him the highest points scorer in rugby history, was able to save him from the axe. He dropped down to the replacements' bench for the match against Ireland with Danny handed the number 10 jersey in a match that proved to be Brian's final one in charge of England. The England players had anticipated Danny's inclusion, but at full-back and not in place of Jonny. It came as a huge surprise. I don't think Jonny was playing particularly badly; he was just suffering from the fact that England did not have rock-solid centre partnership. It hadn't been in place since the 2003 World Cup, when Greenwood was the number 12, and it doesn't help the outside-half when the inside-centre changes on a regular basis, because it is a key communication area.

Brian was under pressure and it cannot be easy to be the coach that drops Jonny, but after the Scotland game it was an easier decision to make. Danny is the kind of character who tends to flourish when there is the least amount of expectation on his shoulders. I have seen it with his kicking and I don't know whether it is a matter of concentration or if he feels the additional pressure with kicks in front of the posts, but if he gets them over they tend not to be absolutely dead centre. However, from wide out, with a wider margin of error, he seems to nail them with confidence. In the Ireland game, Danny was given licence to run the show and he thrived on that responsibility, producing a fantastic performance as we won 33–10. It was a hugely enjoyable game to play in and, while Danny collected 18 points, it was a clear example of what England could achieve when given the licence to play with real freedom and pace.

We finished second in the Six Nations, but it wasn't enough to save Brian. I really enjoyed playing under him, because he gave the players freedom rather than scrutinising every single decision on the pitch. There is currently a huge emphasis on stats and looking at an individual's continuous contribution to a game, which fails to acknowledge that a couple of phases can decide an entire match. Brian didn't ignore the fact that players needed to work hard and put in a huge effort, but at the same time he emphasised the skill factor. Playing under Brian, players seemed to have a lot less fear of making mistakes, which more often than not produces better looking rugby. Clive had started with this kind of ethos when Brian had been part of his coaching set-up and the theory of heads-up rugby, playing what you see, was embraced. However, once Clive started to see those Grand Slam opportunities slip away after suffering the defeats in Scotland, he felt the need to pull back on the reins and only play winning rugby, which might also be termed 'ugly rugby'. Funnily enough, that is what we did in the early stages of the 2007 World Cup to get things back on track.

I don't think Brian enjoyed all the added requirements of being a team manager compared to the more hands-on role of a head coach. It meant he had to deal with the pre- and post-match press conferences, along with the logistics of being in a tournament like the World Cup, and he could have done with someone experienced to take some of that off his plate. To add to his worries, Brian had various people constantly looking over his shoulder and that appeared, to me, to undermine him.

I never discussed the England team manager's job in any great depth with Johnno while all the speculation was swirling around immediately after the Six Nations had finished. He attended a private dining evening for my testimonial year and I asked him how he was getting on as patron of Sparks sporting charity. I asked him if he was going to get back into rugby and he said he wanted to take a bit of a break and that he had no immediate plans to return to the game. Following that conversation, I didn't expect anything to happen imminently, but clearly something was fuelling all the media speculation about Brian's moving out of the job and being offered something to do with the National Academy in Bath, which he had previously run.

Brian was never given the chance to say goodbye to the players: his change of job was announced in the media and then he was gone. I felt Brian, who had taken us to the World Cup final and to second place in the Six Nations, was arguably dealt with poorly. I feel sure that if Brian had been offered anything meaningful in English rugby he would have stayed. However, that option, it appeared, wasn't made very attractive to him. His departure meant England had yet another chance to instigate a complete clear-out which, yet again, they didn't take.

When we had come into the 2007–08 season, Lawrence still had a year to run on his contract, so it was a question of will he, won't he? I think he began to see the writing on the wall when he started to share the number 8 shirt with James Haskell. I felt that pride was eventually going to get the better of him. While Lawrence was still hugely influential in the changing-room, Haskell would more often than not come on and really change the game. It was quite a good tactic for a period to have Lawrence start the game and be the motivational voice, get everyone riled up and then do his bit, walk off and let Haskell do his stuff.

Wasps have never had the resources of the other top clubs, but we have made up for this thanks to the presence of real characters throughout the squad. Even guys who are not so well known or talked about – like Richard Birkett, George Skivington and John Hart – are real gutsy, hardworking guys with a lot of experience and pride. They will never admit that whoever is keeping them out of the team is better than them and relish every chance they get to come out and prove it. They have never chucked the towel in and said, 'I've had enough of playing second fiddle to him,' which is a great asset to have at a club, because these guys really hold the fort when others are away on test duty.

Kingy left after the 2007 Heineken Cup victory and went to France to finish his career and his number 10 jersey was grabbed by Danny Cipriani, who had Dave Walder putting real pressure on him. While we didn't have Kingy, we had this young upstart who was full of confidence and who appeared to be taking us all the way to the Premiership final. However, Danny badly broke his ankle in the semi-final win over Bath and it was an injury that would bring his career to a halt. I wasn't too far away from the incident, heard Danny's yelp of pain and knew immediately it was bad because I had done virtually the same thing at Bristol. Because of that fact, I think it affected a lot of the guys more than it affected me. It's strange, but I think I have become a bit numb to these things on a rugby pitch over the years, not because I have lost my sentiment, but because I know the game will restart in a few minutes and I have to remain focused. Saying that, I appreciate that, while the game is important, someone's health has to remain the main concern. Fortunately, medical care at the club is brilliant – it has to be: nowadays they are having to deal with a lot more head injuries and collisions in which people have been knocked out, something that seems to happen on a far too regular basis these days.

Having lost Danny, the number 10 position became a real problem for us and Riki Flutey moved from centre, where he had formed a fantastic partnership with Fraser, into the outside-half role. He did brilliantly in the final against Leicester, which we won 26–16 with tries from Josh and Tom Rees. Being Lawrence's farewell match, it was inevitable that we would be the champions. For some reason whatever Lawrence does, it's good to be alongside him as good luck falls his way. I just didn't see the result going any other way and no one was going to ruin his big day. There is no doubt that, whoever he was playing under and whatever team he was involved with, Lawrence would have been successful. Whether he would have been quite as successful had he not played for Wasps, we'll never know, of course. All I will say, though, is the fact that he worked with so many great directors of rugby and head coaches only increased the number of winners' medals he collected. It wasn't only Lawrence who was waving goodbye to our fans that day, because Fraser had decided to play in Italy at the end of a marvellous career that should have brought him more England recognition. After the disappointment of the World Cup, it was great to win another trophy and, although the medal didn't say 2007 World Cup winner, it was still hugely important to me, because it was achieved with my mates at Wasps, including Raf, who finally stopped crying every time we lifted a trophy.

When Johnno took over it was the first time in my entire career that an England manager actually rang me up. We spoke on three or four occasions and, after so many years of not knowing what the man in charge really thought, it came as a breath of fresh air. Johnno asked if I still wanted to be involved and whether I was still passionate about playing for England. He wanted to know how was I feeling in terms of injuries. I made it clear to him I was still keen to be involved. Johnno wanted to know if anything in particular had gone wrong or what I felt could be changed, including the location of training and the times of the sessions. Together with a number of experienced players, I didn't take part in the two-test summer tour to New Zealand and only learnt about the off-the-field problems – involving a serious sexual allegation made by a local woman – from the media. The allegation became the subject of an RFU investigation and the whole incident did not reflect well on the England squad. It seemed to be an absolute nightmare start for Johnno, even though he hadn't been out there and it was one of those things that could have happened in the amateur era without the same kind of publicity, but the game now is very different and players have to accept they are under the spotlight, even if they are 12,000 miles away from home.

As we prepared for the autumn test-match series you couldn't help looking at the fixtures – Pacific Islanders, Australia, South Africa and New Zealand – and think: 'Christ, who agreed to this?' I knew Johnno was very keen for me to remain involved and even rang me to check on this on his way to Heathrow to meet/bollock the players on their return from New Zealand. I said, 'Yeah, absolutely,' although I realised I wouldn't be picked unless I was performing well for London Wasps. It was nice to get Johnno's vote of confidence, but at the same time I realised that only one second-row place was up for grabs, because Steve Borthwick had been appointed the captain and had the number 5 jersey.

We had a pre-season camp with England in Twickenham and it all added up to a shorter-than-normal build-up for me in terms of what I like to undertake. If you are going from the Wasps pre-season squad to the England sessions you can get mixed messages and don't know quite which role to fit into because you are juggling both. This was the first England squad to be nominated under the new agreement between the clubs and the RFU that guaranteed release periods before internationals and time away for training camps like the one in Twickenham. Satisfying what the England coaches want you to do doesn't necessarily marry up with what your club coaches are looking for in the build-up to the Premiership season.

Despite feeling in pretty good physical shape, things didn't go particularly well for Wasps as the new season got underway and we were involved in yet another 'poor start' as champions. Lawrence's decision to retire from rugby meant that guys like myself, Josh and Rafael Ibanez took our poor start to the season more personally because we were now perceived to be the leaders and felt more pressure to do things on our own when that probably wasn't the obvious fix. I found myself saying one thing to the group and then doing something very different. I was trying to force the game, attempting silly offloads, because I felt the pressure to try and make something happen. It just wasn't coming off for me and every time it didn't come off my confidence took a bit of a hit. And then I didn't get selected for the opening England matches. I could see why Johnno had gone for Nick Kennedy, because I still needed to back up my cause with club performances, and it was the first time I have ever said, 'Well, they [England] have got a point,' by not picking me. During this early part of the season, I was playing one week for Wasps, getting injured, training through the injury, playing another week with an injury and stupidly trying to claw back lost ground. I probably put the club ahead of my own personal well-being and form because I was trying too hard. After all these years I should have realised it was a ridiculous and self-defeating strategy.

I noted that Johnno didn't do much talking at the England training camp in Portugal and again during the autumn internationals. He did speak about what had happened in New Zealand, discussed team conduct, established a set of rules for our behaviour and what we needed to do to rectify any wrongdoings. We talked about all the peripheral things to do with being an England player and Johnno left it up to the coaches to lead the team. For the first time that involved Brian Smith, the attack coach, who had arrived from London Irish. I didn't know anything about Brian and was quite excited to have a new coach and a different attacking philosophy, and had quite big expectations of how things might change. From the outset, the plans they revealed may not have been revolutionary, but they were different from what we had previously been used to and were a big change for everyone. Having banged on about the need for change, it probably sounds a bit daft to say that I now felt it was just too much too soon. With the autumn fixture list being so demanding, I felt it would have been better to opt for a more conservative attitude and to see where we were as a squad. Johnno had spoken about winning three out of the four games and, given the opposition, I found that quite surprising. In effect, he was saying we were going to beat at least two of the top three teams in the world from a standing start with a completely new attacking philosophy. Because Johnno didn't necessarily step forward and talk as much or be involved as strongly in the rugby side of things, many of the young players probably wondered what all the fuss was about. They were no doubt thinking: 'We have heard about Martin Johnson the player and what an incredible leader he was, but he is not showing us anything.'

Significantly, the difference I noticed between Johnno in the autumn and the two games I was involved with in the Six Nations was the way he had started to be more involved in every aspect of the England team. He was lot more direct with the players, spent time on the pitch and got involved in training, not just verbally, but he was out there holding a tackle pad while wearing body armour. Clearly, he had spent the autumn evaluating not only the players, but the coaches as well – seeing what their strengths were and what they brought to a week of international preparation. After gathering that evidence, he decided how his role needed to change for the Six Nations campaign.

To be honest, I didn't think I deserved to be a replacement during the autumn tests and appeared near the end of the defeats by Australia and South Africa. The Springbok game constituted my 50th cap for England and I was presented with what looked like a silver mushroom at the after-match function. In fact, it was a rather nice silver version of the England cap and it is proof that if you hang in there long enough and survive various coaches and managers you'll eventually join the select group of English players who have been privileged enough to play for their country 50 times. I joined my parents in the Twickenham car park after the Springbok defeat and my father – in time-honoured fashion – greeted my arrival by referring to me as Geoff Boycott, on the basis that it had taken me so long to get to a half-century! I wasn't needed for the New Zealand game, which brought our recurring disciplinary problems to a head with four players yellow-carded. The 39–13 win over the Islanders had been followed by heavy losses to Australia (28–14), South Africa (42–6) and the All Blacks (39–13) and the critics were climbing into us, highlighting the disciplinary problem in particular.

I had a debrief with Johnno after the autumn series and said I pretty much agreed with all his comments about my form and accepted that when I came off the bench for England I didn't really show what I was capable of producing. I told Johnno I would much rather go away and get some good rugby time with Wasps rather than constantly juggling the club/England sessions. I made the point that I had always played my best rugby when I was performing week in, week out and fully fit. That is why I had been playing poorly at club level and the same when I had come off the bench for England. During that period I probably managed half an hour's live play in five weeks. We agreed that if there was an opportunity to let me stay with the club then we would do that during the Six Nations period, and that's how it panned out.

The yellow-card issue wasn't a case of players being penalised for acts of violence and it could be put down to frustration and a real need to get a win – any kind of win. You could just see the whole team was desperate for some positive press and a victory, but when you get beaten as heavily as we did in the autumn, it appears as if you are caught in a vicious circle – one that only a victory can break. It's a fact that when you are winning, those close penalty calls and yellow cards don't seem to go against you. It is a very fine line. You could argue that the All Blacks play the referee better than any other test team and, because they win so often, things just seem to go their way. England were at their best when they had the best 'cheaters' in the world and very few of those guys collected yellow cards. Lawrence, Neil Back and Johnno himself were brilliant at pushing things to the absolute limit and getting away with it. The ironic thing was that here we were in team meetings listening to Johnno telling everyone not to give away penalties when he had given away quite a few in his own career.

The 2009 Six Nations again featured yellow cards for various England players and, by the time we had lost 14–13 in Ireland, the total had reached a staggering ten in the previous four tests. We had opened with a 36–11 win over Italy, a game in which we benefited hugely from their decision to ask flanker Mauro Bergamasco to turn himself into a world-class scrum-half. It was a bonkers idea that lasted until half-time and everyone felt for Bergamasco, who had a shocker at number 9. Although we lost 23–15 to Wales in Cardiff the negativity that followed was more to do with the yellow cards than our play and we had pushed the reigning Grand Slam champions hard. However, the storm of criticism over the yellow cards reached its peak after Dublin when cameras caught Johnno's angry response to Danny Care's yellow card. I was recalled for the home game with France, having been able to prove my form in Wasps colours, and felt ready to show what I could still offer at the highest level. There was also the Lions tour to South Africa looming and, if I wanted to have a shot at selection, then playing well in the remaining two Six Nations games was absolutely vital. However, my main focus was on trying to help England break out of that vicious circle.

Despite our losses, I remained convinced we had a fantastic crop of young players coming through and all we needed was a little bit of good fortune. Our first-half performance against France was hugely impressive as we raced into a 29–0 lead with Toby Flood running the show from outside-half. I was happy with my own contribution, winning some key turn-overs, which went some way to atoning for the penalties I gave away. We may have lost the second half in terms of points scored in that 40 minutes, but we put in a huge defensive action and were very worthy winners on the day. Sitting in the dressing-room after the match, you could almost touch the relief that was sweeping over everyone, particularly the guys who had played in the majority of those defeats in the autumn and who had suffered the losses to Wales and Ireland. Now we had broken the cycle it was a case of bring on the Scots and we were raring to get stuck into them. The final match of the championship saw us register a 26–12 win, which helped England finish second in the table – not bad for a side that was described by critics as a disciplinary basket case earlier in the campaign – and even Johnno was cracking a smile at the end of the game. Phil Vickery got concussed early in a match that confirmed Delon Armitage as a real find at full-back for England, while in those last two games Riki Flutey produced the kind of form that we had seen in Wasps colours and that rightly, after his try-scoring heroics, earned a call-up to the Lions tour of South Africa. Having been unhappy with my form in a misfiring Wasps team at the start of the season, I was pleased to have got myself into the kind of physical state to make a positive contribution both in the tight and with the ball in hand for England during those final two championship matches, and felt I had lived up to what I had promised Johnno during those earlier chats. Now it was a case of getting back to the day job with Wasps and hoping the Lions selectors had seen enough to take me back to South Africa.

Continuity in selection is something any team requires and while I may have questioned Clive for not playing me as many times as I thought I deserved, he picked a side and pretty much stuck with those players throughout his time with England. That enabled Clive to mould the team into, effectively, a club side and the guys knew one another inside out. So, you have to give him credit for this. If you look at Munster, most of those players have been together for a hell of a long time and the same was true of Wasps three or four years ago when the majority of the squad had been alongside one another for nearly a decade. England have definitely got the talent and sometimes we need to accept that, although people are going to go in and out of form, we have to show faith if we want to create a consistent side. I think that is partly the reason why Wasps went for Geech to replace Warren, because they knew he wasn't going to change a huge amount in terms of structure and the way we went about things on a day-to-day basis.

While things picked up for me on the test front, the club season tailed off with no trophies and we missed out on qualifying for the Premiership playoffs. Looking back on the season at Wasps, I would argue that the loss of Fraser had just as much impact on our playing fortunes as Lawrence's retirement. The main problems during the 2008–09 season were our defensive frailties in the back line and not scoring enough tries. Fraser would have made a huge difference. From a forward's perspective, I think we more than held our own on most occasions in the league and in the Heineken Cup. Without Fraser, it meant that Josh was our most experienced back and he played the majority of the games on the wing, which put him some way away from Danny in terms of being a mentor and having a constant word in his ear. In the past we have always had the confidence that, no matter how far a team may be out in front, we are capable of scoring tries. However, last season, our top try scorers only managed three and, in a very tight Premiership, it just wasn't good enough. Hopefully, the decision to bin the ludicrous experimental law that made mauling redundant – as the opposition could just pull you down – has been scrapped. Funnily enough, Wellsy told me there was no room in the international game for a mauling, brawling forward any more and I took great exception to that – hopefully, he has now changed his view, or will do by next year. At Wasps, we have had several reviews and audits during the season to establish what went wrong and how we need to put things right and I think the change of owner, with Steve Hayes now taking charge, has been a massive step forward. As long as we can carry on with the same ethos and spirit, then I don't see there being a problem.

CHAPTER 23

SEX, DRUGS AND RUGBY

It started on a Sunday morning when texts kept appearing on my mobile urging me to buy a certain tabloid newspaper. I have to admit I was intending to buy that paper anyway following the previous Sunday's story about Danny Cipriani and a 'liaison' he was reported to have had with Miss Larissa Summers, while he was going out with Monica Irimia, one of the Cheeky Girls. As a result of the latest revelations, Danny was responsible for the biggest turnout ever for a Wasps recovery session after a match. Danny took considerable stick from the guys over the story, but to give him credit, he handled himself really well. I must admit to having kept a low profile over the whole saga, because I know that if you rip into a team-mate, it's not very long before the tables are turned – although the particulars of the case were rather unique. Danny has found himself in the tabloids more than Lawrence managed in his entire career and I do have concerns about the kind of publicity surrounding a young player of outstanding talent. His relationship with Kelly Brook ensured that, while Danny was coming back from that horrendous ankle injury, he was still very much in the public eye. For Danny to have come back so soon after his injury and to expect him to be at the same level was a tall order. In that situation, I would have probably shied away from any extra publicity until I was back and on form – not that I have ever sought that kind of exposure. To be in the spotlight before you have actually done anything is ill-advised for anyone. He is still young and, to a degree, he is very naïve and needs guidance: I don't think that is necessarily what he is getting at the moment. He needs to get his profile up for the right reasons and that comes from playing rugby, and while I don't know who is telling him what to do, it appears to be more media- led than rugby led. Danny needs to get the balance right.

Wasps are no strangers to finding their players in the tabloids. Lawrence was at the centre of a *News of the World* sting in 1999 that ended up with his fined by the RFU and losing the England captaincy. In many ways, what happened to Lawrence was a very loud warning to every high-profile rugby player that the sport was now considered big enough to warrant this kind of attention from certain sections of the press. Nigel Melville had always joked that something would happen over one weekend and that he would have to bail someone out of trouble. He would be ringing up golf clubs and apologising for Paul Sampson and Martyn Wood's reckless driving, which had put a golf cart into a green-side bunker, or he would be required to sort any issues with Trevor Leota. The Lawrence incident, however, was very much out of the ordinary because he was the England captain and it was big news. When I heard the news, I have to admit I fully expected Lawrence to land on his feet, because he always did. We have joked about it endlessly since. We had this kind of comedy interlude every week and the lads couldn't wait to see who would be the next target. Lawrence ended up suing another Sunday paper that tried to make allegations about his off-the-field lifestyle and this time other members of the squad got involved in the court case. Kingy had to identify some of the photos taken on the evening in question, which included a shot of four or five of the lads pulling a moonie. He had to identify the bums in the picture. It was easy to identify Gareth Rees's – it was bigger than anyone else's!

SEX, DRUGS AND RUGBY

The recent banning of my England team-mate Matt Stevens, who admitted using cocaine, was hugely disappointing for everyone involved in rugby. I am pretty naïve when it comes to things like cocaine and, although I'm told it is taken in nightclubs, I have never actually witnessed that happening. I assumed some people took it but, because it wasn't performance enhancing, I didn't think anyone would take it, particularly so close to a match that it could appear in a test sample. Surely, it can only be detrimental to your performance, just as having a lot of alcohol in the run-up to a game is also a pretty stupid idea. Matt's a great guy and I was really surprised he was caught by a match-day test. He is young enough to come back into test rugby: he is a guy with an enormous amount of talent who hasn't had to try particularly hard to get to the top. Consequently, I don't know if, mentally, he has it within himself to get back up to the required level. It's purely down to Matt's desire and the mental strength to put himself through the mill to get into the right shape for test rugby. I don't think what happened to Matt has harmed the sport; the damage would have been far greater if he had been caught taking steroids. I heard lots of comments along the lines of 'Why is Matt being banned if it wasn't a performance-enhancing drug?' The bottom line is he broke the rules and did something that was wrong. If alcohol was a banned substance then, as a professional rugby player, you wouldn't take the risk. Thankfully, it's not so that's all right then!

CHAPTER 24

HOW KENNY AND I FOUND OUR OTHER HALVES

I met my wife Jane on a blind date thanks to Chad Eagle, my old flatmate from my Bristol days, whose girlfriend lived in London. She was my only point of contact when I first moved to the capital and set me up on various different dates with horrifically foul-mouthed women. Despite those nightmare evenings, I agreed to turn up at a pub in Fulham after she announced: 'I'm meeting up with a few girlfriends, do you want to meet up as well?' 'Is it another one of these set-ups?' I asked. 'No, no, there are a couple of gorgeous blondes I'd like you to meet,' came the reply. Being a true romantic I answered: 'Okay, whatever.'

I had already met Jane on a previous occasion when she was with her then boyfriend and when I saw her in the pub I assumed the ladies in question were yet to arrive. 'Where are these fit blondes?' I asked, at which point Kim, Chad's girlfriend, stared at me with a look that said: 'This is one of them.' I suddenly died of embarrassment but, fortunately, Jane didn't actually hear me. Still, I spent the rest of the evening avoiding her, thinking I had just put my foot in it. Jane got chatted up by everyone else in the bar, which made me jealous, so at the end of the evening I put her in a taxi and kissed her goodnight. She rang me up again, which was an enormous surprise and we started dating from there, eventually getting married in Tuscany in 2004. Jane's family are Australian or else from New Zealand and as her parents were planning to come over to Europe, everything seemed to drop into place to make that the right time to get married. We decided to invite only our immediate family and friends that we both knew and the rugby guys included Will Green, Kenny Logan, Peter Scrivener, Johnny Ufton and Chad Eagle.

When I first met Jane she was a primary school teacher and, despite having lived in Auckland for 25 years, she knew relatively little about rugby. It was quite refreshing. The school she was teaching at was near Paddington and, because they barely had any outdoor space, they didn't have rugby on their sports programme. I used to go to the school to pick her up and the pupils thought I was a WWF wrestler and friends with the Rock, because I could do the same eyebrow movement as him. When we first met, Jane used to get the kids to sing down the phone to me before games. They made up various songs and good-luck messages, which I'm not too sure were part of the curriculum, but she did it anyway and they all found it fun. Jane used to get me to turn up for the sports day held in Hyde Park, which involved rounders and relay races. I would end up carrying almost her entire class on my back, running around the park. This was usually about the same time as Wasps would get to a final and the children would write good-luck cards and hand them over at the sports day. Most of the cards either featured a wrestler – in honour of my supposed sporting career – or a Manchester United goalkeeper. Significantly, after the 2003 World Cup, I went to the sports day and by then kids were allowed to dress up in whatever they wanted and most had swapped from Tottenham, Arsenal or Chelsea shirts to wearing replicas of the England rugby kit. By the time Jane finished at the school, they had worked out I wasn't actually a WWF wrestler and that I played rugby.

Jane is convinced I am going to be playing the sport for ever and is hugely supportive, despite having to look after our three children – Samantha, Tyler and Beau – while I am away, putting myself in harm's way all over the rugby world. Finding myself the father of three wonderful children and still playing rugby is rather perplexing given I was adamant that, due to the commitment needed to be a professional player, starting a family was going to be a post-rugby challenge. My big mistake was revealing this promise to myself to Kenny, who promptly told Jane that I didn't want to have children very early in our relationship and leaving me having to work bloody hard to convince her it was all a big mistake. I told her that something had been lost in translation – not difficult when you are dealing with a Scot. Until I met Jane I never thought of getting married or having children and now I have three!

There are downsides to being married to a rugby player and Jane has regularly been left to attend weddings, celebration parties and other social events on her own because I have been away on tours or preparing for a game. People, quite naturally, do things at the weekend when I am playing, which has an impact on your partner, because they want you with them at these occasions. With our first child arriving just before the 2003 World Cup, I travelled to Australia not really thinking I would be deeply affected because Samantha was so little and 'just a baby'. I had no concept of the emotional ties that quickly exist. I soon realised the error of my ways when I was walking around, would suddenly see a pram and start to well up. While at the World Cup, there was a Father's Day and Jane sent me a special video. It took me ages to find a player with whom I could watch this message, as I didn't want the rest of the lads to see me bawling my eyes out. I found a secluded part of the team hotel and, sure enough, there I was watching this video crying my eyes out. I kept telling myself I had to pull myself together, but it had absolutely no effect. Jane has been incredibly supportive throughout our time together and although there have been periods when I thought it should be my last season at international level and that I should only play for Wasps, Jane has constantly told me to 'get back out there', which probably has something to do with the financial benefits of being involved! She has never wanted me to give up and this kind of unbending support from your partner/wife is so important. Rafael Ibanez's wife highlighted this for me. When he was considering retiring, a year before he was forced to do just that by injury, she had gone back to Dax to run a pharmacy and told him that if he wanted to play for another year she would totally back him. Raf's wife was happy to let him play, even though they would be apart for long periods because, in five years' time, she didn't want to hear him say that he really wished there had been another season. It takes someone pretty special to say that and Raf and his wife only saw each other once a month. I'm sure Jane would say exactly the same thing to me. Jane insists she is 5 ft 6 in. while I am 6 ft 9in. and height is something of a factor with all my side of the family. Jane keeps on saying I have gigantism and is fearful that the children have the same. At the moment, however, they are showing no signs of taking after Dad.

Clearly, the day when I do retire is fast approaching and then it will be a question of deciding what comes next. Given the way former rugby players have embraced some of our more popular television shows, anything appears to be possible – if you are prepared to wear a skin-tight sequined outfit or wear a chef's hat. The list of those ex-players willing to stand in front of a camera and look ridiculous is growing every year and now includes Kenny, Matt Dawson, Kyran Bracken and Austin Healey – what is it about scrum-halves that makes them crave attention? Watching Kenny and Gabby Logan on *Strictly Come Dancing* was fascinating as Jane and I were able to go to the studios for the filming. I still cannot work out how Kenny lasted longer than Gabby and all I can think is that he played the village idiot card with the public and they bought it!

One of my claims to fame is that I played a part in bringing Kenny and Gabby together – well, me and a concrete bollard. Kenny had come down from Scotland with his then girlfriend

HOW KENNY AND I FOUND OUR OTHER HALVES

Kirsty Young and the Wasps players had started going to the Pitcher and Piano in Fulham. Kenny said, because I lived in Chiswick, I should leave my car at home and sleep at his house. We got heavily drunk and Kenny returned home before me, so I arrived at his front door at about one in the morning to no answer. I knocked several times and it was freezing, which made me particularly angry. I tried ringing him and he wasn't answering his phone. In my drunken state, I went back to the P&P where there was a concrete bollard and, for some unknown reason, I spent 45 minutes to an hour trying to uproot the bollard from the ground. I pushed it back and forth until I managed to uproot it by snapping the metal rod that kept it upright. I then put it on my shoulder – it weighed an absolute ton – and walked about four or five metres, stopped, put it on someone's wall, caught my breath, regathered my strength and then walked another five metres, until I got back to Kenny's front door. I parked it right in front of the door, dusted off my hands and thought: 'That will teach him.' I don't know what I was thinking, but anyway, I realised I had enough money to get a taxi home, so I departed. We always saw Kirsty as too mature and intelligent for Kenny and I don't think she took too kindly to his childish ways and late-night drinking. On this particular night, he was worse than ever, woke up in the middle of the night, couldn't find the toilet and peed over the end of the bed. She used to present the early morning news and had to get up at some ungodly hour and go to work. The thing that really nailed Kenny's fate, and led to his ending up on my doorstep, bags in hand, was that she opened the front door and walked directly, at crotch height, into the concrete bollard I had left behind. He turned up at my front door with all his bags packed and stayed for four or five months. We both pretty much met our wives at almost the exact same time. I remember him meeting Gabby in the K Bar in Fulham, because he ran up to me excitedly, as if he couldn't believe his luck, and announced he had met and snogged Gabby Roslin. I went: 'Gabby Roslin, really, from the *Big Breakfast*?' He said: 'Yeah, yeah.' I said: 'Are you sure it's Gabby Roslin, because

I haven't seen Gabby Roslin among this lot?' He said: 'Yeah, yeah, yeah, the football one.' I said: 'What, do you mean Gabby Yorath?' He said: 'Ah, yes, that's right.'

I really can't see myself following Kenny, Kyran, Austin and Matt onto a celebrity show. It seems to me that you go on those shows for three reasons: to raise your profile because you want to get into the media industry; because you are totally and utterly in it for a charitable cause – the only reason I would do it; or because there is a particular challenge that excited you, like climbing Kilimanjaro in order to boost the profile of a charity. When Kyran first started playing rugby he was the golden boy, the pretty one who did the publicity shots, but I never anticipated he would get onto TV or start ice skating, particularly with his dodgy back. I always anticipated Austin and Matt would embrace the celebrity thing and they have changed since playing rugby. I saw one interview with Austin after a dance he performed and thought: 'This isn't the Austin I know.' He was polite, very well-mannered and came across as an absolute delight on TV, something he has never been in rugby circles. When Daws was doing the chef bit I think he had a few inside tips from a friend, but hats off to them for making new careers and for having the balls to take a chance in front of the public. A public that voted Gabby off the programme and that still kept Kenny dancing – amazing.

CHAPTER 25

SO CLOSE TO GLORY: A TEST LION AT LAST

'You were crap.' Not exactly the verdict I was hoping for after my first Lions game of the South African tour against a Royal XV in Phokeng. Gats, the forwards coach, has always given it to me straight and, in truth, I knew I had been struggling. We had trained for five days in Johannesburg at the same altitude, but the physical demands of a game are very different, and my mouth was dry and I felt short of breath from the opening moments. Everyone was in the same situation and it made the whole experience very tough to deal with.

We had targeted the scrum as one area where we wanted to dominate the opposition and so you put real effort into every set piece, but then, as you moved to the next phase of play, there was this real burning sensation in your thighs and quads that was difficult to shrug off. Alun-Wyn Jones, who took over in the second row – and would win the battle to play alongside Paul O'Connell in the first test – came up to me after the match and asked how I had managed to last more than an hour in those conditions, when he felt shattered after 20 minutes! The team spirit created so early amongst the players and coaches is why we pulled things around and won 37–25, with Jamie Roberts, the Wales centre, making an early impression as a ball carrier (and he would turn out to be major force throughout the tour, along with scrum-half Mike Phillips).

Even at this stage of the trip, the mood in the squad was in stark contrast to 2005 in New Zealand, where we had, basically, two different teams operating. It had started at Pennyhill Park when a planned sailing trip on the Solent had been cancelled because a number of the players didn't fancy the trip. Geech had made it clear our views would be listened to and this was an early indication of that fact; the plans were changed and it was obvious the management cared about what we thought. Instead of bouncing about the Solent, we headed off for a few beers and meal, and that really was the start of the outstanding team spirit we created.

I had heard on the grapevine that Geech was planning to leave Wasps before the tour started, although having taken part in an audit commissioned by the club's board, where I had spoken freely about the way I saw the club's future, there had been no discussion about Geech's position. It was a little bit awkward, but I didn't feel it was right to go into any details with Geech on the tour. I suppose what happened is just part of professional sport – people move on – and his priority last season, quite naturally, was the Lions. Despite Geech's departure, I am confident Wasps can continue to be a force, and I am sure he will offer professional rugby his coaching experience at some point in the future.

As the Lions built up to the first test, there was plenty of debate in the media over the decision by the Springboks management not to let their players turn out against the Lions before the series, but one guy did feature: Heinrich Brussouw. He caused all kinds of problems, but we still managed to beat the Cheetahs 26–24, having registered a hugely impressive 74–10 win over the Lions in Ellis Park in midweek. I came off the bench for the second half as we beat the Sharks 39–3 and felt I had made a real impact; Gats made a point of telling me exactly that after the game. That was very pleasing given his verdict after that first game, and I felt my chances of making the test side had been improved. However, I didn't build on this against Western Province as we struggled in dreadful conditions to win 26–23, and I really needed to impress against the Southern Kings in Port Elizabeth, the final match before the first test in Durban. It turned out to be a game no one would forget, for all the wrong reasons.

The Kings players threw absolutely everything at us and it was obvious they wanted to get under our skins and affect our performance. We showed a lot of collective restraint because we could have let what they were doing get to us. I thought the referee could have stepped in a little earlier because many of the cheap shots that were going on off the ball continued until the end of the game. I know because I received a heavy blow to the side of my head and heard ringing in my ears for the last ten minutes! There's no real defence when you are crumpled up in a heap and there is a blow with a knee or someone throws the shoulder in. It wasn't very pleasant, but it became one of those games where you just have to tough it out. Rog (Ronan O'Gara) was pretty incensed over the cheap shots, including the hit that concussed James Hook, and the attention they were giving his Ireland team-mate Gordon D'Arcy. While I wasn't able to produce the perfect game at least I tried my very hardest, and we won 20–8.

A new feature for me on the tour was the lack of after-match meals or receptions. The Kings game was yet another 'beer and sandwich in the opposition dressing-room', but given what had gone on, it wasn't a very convivial session. The only time we had a traditional post-match dinner was after the final test, when a local politician decided to bore us all to death with a droning speech that included advice on how fans could find their seats more easily! Each time he paused, the Lions table loudly applauded in the hope he would stop. My mother, who was also at the dinner, joined in the clapping – he was that bad. That had to go down as the most laborious and boring dinner I had ever been to in rugby, and the Springboks were pretty subdued, having lost the match, and didn't even bother joining in the barracking. My father was amazingly well behaved, and that was despite our attempts to ply him with gin-and-tonics in bid to get another 'tits out for the boys' moment.

The first test saw me sitting amongst the rest of the squad who either weren't playing or were on the bench in the Kings Park stadium in Durban, and I was gutted. I believed I deserved a place on the bench, and despite being upset, I had knuckled down to helping the test side prepare to take on the Springboks. For the first time, the crowd featured thousands of Lions supporters, and while there had been support from travelling fans in all our game, this was a much bigger contingent and they helped create a great atmosphere, which made our poor start even harder to explain. We had problems in the scrums and missed three great try-scoring chances, but we fought back incredibly well, with Tom Croft and Mike Phillips scoring tries. But that early period hurt us, and we headed back to Cape Town having lost that crucial first test 26–21.Throughout the series, a lot was made of the physical play of the Springboks, but I couldn't see any difference from every other time I played them. As a squad, we had decided to concentrate on our own discipline, and this was something Geech drove home. I believe we had the physical edge, which, initially, took them aback.

It had always been planned that we would stay at sea level and head up to Pretoria at altitude on the Friday before the second test, but no one knew that one of worst storms for ages was going to hit the Cape. There were frequent squalls and heavy rain, and it made the match with a useful Emerging Springboks side difficult. They earned a 13–13 draw with the last kick of the match, and then it was a case of waiting to discover if I had done enough to get selected. Before the team was announced, my room-mate Nathan Hines, who was also hoping to get the test number 4 jersey, was cited for what was deemed to be a dangerous tackle and banned for two weeks. Of course, you don't hope something like that happens, but a little bit of luck in your favour can create a huge opportunity. When Nathan came back from the disciplinary hearing, I said 'bad luck mate,' and he just congratulated me on my selection, despite it being an awkward situation as we are both second rows. I don't think I had ever spoken to Nathan before the tour and there we were sharing a bathroom!

It just summed up what is so great and special about a Lions tour. The friendships you make last a lifetime, particularly from a tour like the 2009 Lions. Clive Woodward introduced a system with the England squad that meant that you shook the hand of the guy who got picked ahead of you, and this is actually a rule in the England Player Squad agreement. However, on this tour that evolved naturally because of the great team spirit. Every one of the other second rows came up and shook my hand after the team announcement, and it showed just how much we were backing each other.

It took me some time to settle down after being told I would be making my first appearance in a Lions test match after 12 years of wondering if it was ever going to happen. Despite having played in a World Cup final and winning Heineken Cups and Premiership finals, I found myself with knots in my stomach, not being able to sleep and feeling light-headed. I had never been affected like that, and it was bizarre to feel that way so late on in my career because I didn't experience anything like it building up to that 2007 Cup final in Paris against South Africa. It was as if my body went into overload and wanted me to play the game right away, but I did manage to get everything nice and settled and adopted my normal pre-match routine to get the best out of myself on match day. The way things turned out, I got all the preparations spot on.

After being told I was playing, I sent text messages to my wife, Jane, and also to my mother and father. I didn't hear back from my parents, who were in South Africa on safari north of Durban and must have been out of mobile-phone range, because they are usually straight back with a 'hooray', or a 'we still love you' if it hasn't been great news! Jane couldn't wait to speak to me, but I was out with the players for a squad meal and it wouldn't have been very good form to depart to speak to your wife about how excited you are about making a first test appearance when there are guys who are gutted at not being involved. I knew how they were feeling and it's total misery.

The second test side featured seven Irish players, six from Wales, and me and Tom Croft from England, and I can honestly say that until I was told those figures, I didn't even register the various contingents. The way we all gelled meant it felt like a single team under Paul O'Connell instead of a collection of players from different parts of Britain and Ireland.

The test exploded into controversy after just 34 seconds when Schalk Burger, the Springboks flanker, was yellow-carded for making contact with the eyes of wing Luke Fitzgerald. At the time I wasn't aware of exactly what had happened, but having seen the video of the incident, an eight-week ban is fairly lenient because gouging is the worst thing a player can do on the pitch to an opponent. It looked blatant on the video, but maybe at the moment it happened the officials decided there wasn't real intent and that's why he didn't get the red card. I wasn't aware of the reaction of Peter de Villiers, the Springbok coach, to the Burger incident until after the test series, when I watched a video of his press conference. I had heard rumours about his comments, but assumed this was just media spin – how wrong I was. I watched the video in utter disbelief that a national coach was coming out with excuses for Burger, about having a God-given talent and all that delusional stuff. Brian O'Driscoll's comments about this were spot on in my opinion.

After the Burger 'gouging', we played well and established a solid lead only for a series of injuries to cause serious disruption, and the Springboks staged a second-half revival to win the second test 26–23 and take the series 2–0. My own performance earned the Man of the Match medal, but I would have gladly played badly if it meant the Lions had still been in the test series. Yes, I was proud of how I had performed, having waited twelve years for the chance to pull on the famous red jersey; however, the overwhelming emotion was one of bitter disappointment that we had lost the series, despite playing some outstanding rugby. I hoped I would never have had to endure the dreadful feelings I experienced after losing the 2007 World Cup final to South Africa in Paris, but in the immediate aftermath of Saturday's loss it was eerily reminiscent of that same desolation, knowing something special had been within your grasp and it had been snatched away.

If I am truthful, there aren't any words to truly sum up the way I felt after the final whistle. It was my last Lions tour, and the realisation I wasn't going to get another chance to help contribute to the Lions winning a series was gut-wrenching and probably explains why I was unusually emotional in public after the match. I found myself welling up during a television interview when I was asked to give the viewers an insight into that very personal moment. What could I say? 'I feel like breaking down and sobbing in front of you all?' I had spoken to Jane on the eve of the match, and she told me about all the publicity my selection had generated and gave me the instructions 'don't mess it up' and 'don't give any penalties away'. Marvellous!

Knowing that family and friends are giving you so much support and backing meant it was impossible not to get emotional. No one in the Lions squad blamed Ronan O'Gara for giving away the penalty that Morne Steyn kicked to win the series for South Africa in the final act of the second test. We should not have allowed the Springboks to get into the position to win it with a single kick, and it's not about one player, it is a collective responsibility. We were in control of that match, showing the Springboks how physical we could be, refusing to take a backward step and unleashing our back line with real intensity and purpose. Then came the injuries.

We lost Adam Jones, who had done so well against the 'Beast', to a shoulder injury caused by Bakkies Botha's charge into a ruck, which earned him two weeks and initiated a protest by his team-mates in the final test that saw them wear white armbands saying 'Justice #4'. This earned the Springboks a rebuke from the International Rugby Board. Bakkies is a fantastic player but has never given me that much trouble and doesn't bother 'cheap shotting' me. He usually tries to intimidate opponents; however, that didn't work with me, and his partner Victor Matfield was very quiet in the series and looked exposed without Bakkies in the third test.

Adam's departure in the second test was a hugely significant moment because it meant uncontested scrums, and I had to head up to tight-head prop for the second time in my career. Typical, I wait 12 years to play for the Lions and end up as a prop! Gethin Jenkins had suffered a broken cheekbone and also left the pitch, and the uncontested scrums really hurt our cause as the Springboks were struggling with fatigue because we made them work so hard in this area. We got in their faces from the first minute, but then kicked away too much possession in the second half, when we had to totally reshuffle the back division, and the Springboks took full advantage. Packing down at tight-head against the Beast was not something I had planned to be doing, but due to the move to uncontested scrums I was volunteered to join the front row. It happened to me during my days with Bristol, when I really did have to play tight-head in a 'live' match for 50 minutes against Leicester, and my back took a whole week to recover.

Geech came into the dressing-room after the match and told us how proud he was of every one of us and that we didn't deserve to be 2–0 down in the test series. He was right, but the record books show we lost the series and that's what really hurts. I wanted to make an impact in that test, and despite those feelings of desperate disappointment, I felt I had done justice to the number 4 jersey and brought to the Lions test team the attributes that I had wanted to show 12 years earlier. I am sure that in the years to come, I will fully appreciate what I was able to produce under that intense pressure, but at the time it was all too raw, as that post-match television interview showed.

Injury robbed us of Brian O'Driscoll and Jamie Roberts after that test, and the injury 'Drico' suffered was an example of how even the most experienced players are prepared to go that extra yard because they are wearing a Lions jersey. The tackle that put him out of the final test with concussion is one he probably wouldn't have made wearing any other jersey. Because of the special nature of a Lions tour, players are prepared to do anything to help the cause, and that produces more injuries. It may sound daft, but it's something that happens on a Lions tour – emotion turns off your self-preservation button. Having established the 'back row of the bus' group with Drico, Martyn Williams and Stephen Jones, it was a real blow to see him head home.

My last room-mate of the tour – they were all great, although Keith Earls did scare me with stories of 'gangster' battles near his home in Ireland – was Tommy Bowe, the Ireland wing. Tommy, myself and Lee Mears were the tour entertainment committee, although it was Mearsy who did all the work. Tommy and I were watching coverage of Wimbledon while lying around our hotel room when the camera showed Andy Roddick's girlfriend – a swimsuit model – who he met by ringing up her agent. I made it my mission that night to spend three hours trawling through *FHM*'s one hundred most gorgeous women to find one for Tommy and, I have to admit, I failed. Sorry mate! Jamie Heaslip, the Ireland number 8, was never going to make any committee on tour, having been the entertainment officer for the Irish squad who turned down an offer of a free gig for the team from Snow Patrol. He told the band's manager 'some of the boys are already doing something that Sunday'!

The final test team featured four Wasps players: myself, Riki Flutey (yes, I know he was off to Brive), Phil Vickery and Joe Worsley. 'Vicks' was back in the tight-head position after the problems he experienced against the Beast in the first test and was very fired up in the dressing-room, banging heads with Andrew Sheridan and going through those strange routines front-row boys love in the final moments before we head onto the pitch. Vicks turned to me at one point before the match and said, 'Give me everything you've got, Shawsey,' which I found funny because I have always done just that when packing down behind him. I have never known Vicks to have a problem in the scrum and was totally confident he would do the business against the Beast, and that's exactly what happened.

I wanted to prove to myself that I deserved to be there again and leave my mark on a Lions test, but not by picking up a yellow card and ten minutes in the bin for my knee connecting with the back of Springbok scrum-half Fourie du Preez. It happened because I got far too close to him as I went to make the tackle, and I could either fall over him or try and stop short. I took the second option. There wasn't any malice at all. I was cited for the incident with du Preez, which meant I had to be careful about how hard I celebrated with the boys after our victory. Richard Smith QC, who was our legal guy on tour, said after the hearing on the Sunday it had been lucky the panel listening to my evidence had been on the other side of a very wide table – it meant the smell of alcohol didn't register!

When I got back to the hotel after being handed the two-week ban, some of the boys were still partying, having pushed on through from the night before, but others had given up and gone to bed. Those players still in the bar, wearing women's dresses or flat caps, had white tape around their right arms with 'Justice 4 Shaw' written in pen, which was a nice touch. Inevitably, Andy Powell – a top man – looked the most ridiculous, in a kaftan with a sweat band around his head.

We were the better side in the series and could have whitewashed the world champions in their own back yard, but the history books will show a 2–1 series loss. Paul did a great job as captain, and the speech he gave to the players on the eve of the final test was very emotional and he came close to breaking down. He was adamant we weren't going to leave South Africa without proving a point and we were all choking up. Too many captains talk for the sake of opening their mouths, but Paul got it absolutely right and we responded with a great win. The management under Geech were also hugely impressive, and while I have heard rumours from outside the camp that the coaches did not always agree on selection, there wasn't any evidence of that within the group and we remained united throughout. Given the preparation time and the injuries that affected us, we had every reason to be proud of our tour, and it was a real pleasure to have been part of the 2009 Lions. As a result of the tour, I am going to break the habit of a lifetime and create room in our new home in Twickenham to show off the medals and special jerseys I have been fortunate to receive, and pride of place will go to my first Lions test jersey.

ACKNOWLEDGEMENTS

For their love and support over the years, I would like to thank my wife Jane, my parents Charles and Rita and my sister Sarah; Jane's family for supporting me from the other side of the world; and the following families who have been great friends to me over the years: the Samuels, the Halls, the Gordons, the Futters, the Browns and the Rees-Thomases (my token Welsh supporters).

Since the first time I stepped onto a rugby pitch, I've played with and been coached and helped by some great people at fantastic clubs. In no particular order, I'd like to mention Ian McGeechan, Warren Gatland, Shaun Edwards, Jack Rowell, Cranleigh Rugby Club, everyone at Bristol and London Wasps, Ross Bell and Jeff Walker at Dunedin Pirates, John Spence, Phil Keith-Roach, Lawrence Dallaglio, Nigel Melville, Rob Smith and everyone I've ever played with along the way. Apologies if I've forgotten anyone, especially the guys who are mentioned in the book!

I have had countless injuries during my career, and if it wasn't for the brilliant work of many physios and doctors, I wouldn't have been able to play for anywhere near as long as I have. In fact, I've been looked after by so many that I would fill another book if I mentioned each one individually. So here's a big thank you to all of them.

Thanks also to Iain MacGregor and everyone at Mainstream Publishing, and to my literary agent Humfrey Hunter. Finally, very special thanks to Chris Jones, who managed to decipher what the bleeding hell I was waffling on about well enough to turn my words into a book.

Simon Shaw
August 2009